It's a
Mitzvah!

It's a Mitzvah!

STEP-BY-STEP TO JEWISH LIVING

Bradley Shavit Artson

 Behrman House
Rabbinical Assembly

The author and publisher gratefully acknowledge the following sources of photographs for this book:

Hector Acebes/Photo Researchers, 206; Jim Anderson/Woodfin Camp and Assoc., 15; Mark Antman/Image Works, 72, 128, 155, 192; Bill Aron, 20, 29, 35, 42, 81 105, 107, 109, 115, 134, 136, 162, 164, 176, 182, 219; Bachman/Image Works, 58; Fredrik Bodin/Stock Boston, 18; Brady/Monkmeyer, 11; Gary Buss/FPG, 208; Ron Chapple/FPG, 90, 187, 203; R.M. Collins/Image Works, 81; Joyce Culver, 166, 172; Crews/Image Works, 131, 144 (top); Jill Fineberg/Photo Researchers, 214; Forsyth/Monkmeyer, 92; FPG, 90, 151, 170; Harriet Gans/Image Works, 156; Mark Glass, 81(top), 154; Steve Goldberg/Monkmeyer, 67; Spencer Grant/Monkmeyer, 88; Hazel Hankin/Stock Boston, 75; Dollar Hyde/Monkmeyer; Francene Keery, 45, 51, 85, 94, 97, 101, 125, 137, 138, 140, 144, 149, 159, 168, 190, 205, 212, 229; Rick Kopstein/Monkmeyer, 23, 119; John Neubauer/Monkmeyer, 6; R. Nowitz/FPG 202; Dion Ogust/Image Works, 122; Ilene Pearlman, 112; C.J. Pickerell/FPG, 54; Reuters/Bettmann, 127; Barbara Rios/Photo Researchers, 200, 211; Ann Marie Rousseau/Image Works, 81; April Saul, 63, 69, 99, 106; Rabbi Stephen Shulman/Jewish Chaplain at Memorial Sloan-Kettering Cancer Center, and John Twiname, 70; Jack Spratt/Image Works, 53; Erika Stone, 93, 193; Sherry Suris, 25, 57, 104; Joey Tranchina/Photo Researchers, 195; Mike Valeri/FPG, 76; Carl Vella, 3; Susan Wagner/Photo Researchers, 181; David Wells, 46, 141; Ulrike Welsch/Photo Researchers, 103; Jim Whitmer/Stock Boston, 64; Harry Wilks/Stock Boston, 120; WZPS Photo, 116; Ellan Young/Photo Researchers, 197.

Special thanks to Congregation Emanu-El of the city of New York for their cooperation (photographs appear on pages 45, 137, 138, 159, 168).

Pages 233–237 reprinted with permission from *Living Torah in America*, ©1993 by Maurice Lamm, published by Behrman House, Inc.

Project Editor: Adam Siegel

Book Design: Robert J. O'Dell

Editorial Consultant: William Cutter, Ph.D.

Photo Researcher: Lynn Goldberg Biderman

Library of Congress Cataloging-in-Publication Data
Artson, Bradley Shavit.
    It's a mitzvah: step-by-step to Jewish Living /
by Bradley Shavit Artson.
      p.   cm.
Includes index.
ISBN 0-87441-585-3
1. Jewish way of life. I. Title
BM723.A73   1995   95-14058
296.3' 85—dc20   CIP

Published by Behrman House, Inc.
235 Watchung Avenue
West Orange, NJ 07052

The Rabbinical Assembly
3080 Broadway
New York, NY 10027

MANUFACTURED IN THE UNITED STATES OF AMERICA

Printed on Recycled Paper

♻

To my precious children
Shira Esther Artson
&
Jacob Dov Artson
"These are my children,
whom Adonai has given me."
(GENESIS 48:9)

and

to my beloved *ezer*,
Elana Shavit Artson,
"Many women have done well,
but you surpass them all."
(PROVERBS 31:29)

Contents

I. Introduction

II. Mitzvot to Grow With

ACKNOWLEDGMENTS

This book is for all who want to explore Jewish observance but are not willing (or able) to immerse themselves instantaneously. The book is unique in two ways: First, it explicitly advocates a gradual approach to Jewish life without abandoning the traditional goals of Judaism. Because an all-or-nothing mentality places Jewish living permanently beyond reach for all but a select few, this book actively involves each reader in risking but one step at a time. Such a method permits the time necessary to absorb a new skill, value, or priority while also taking into account an individual's life history. Some growth is better than none, and a lot is better than a little. This book provides high standards but divides the ultimate goal into several progressive steps. In this way, Judaism becomes possible for most striving Jews.

The second innovation offered here is that a community of nonprofessional Jews actively edited this work. Because this book is not directed to rabbis and scholars, I sought the advice and insight of Jewish laypeople—students, scientists, men and women in business, teachers, salespeople, and others. These congregants formed a reading group. I mailed them a chapter each month, and we all met approximately two weeks later to discuss the weaknesses in the chapter and how we could strengthen it. In a very real sense, the Mitzvah Reading Group of Congregation Eilat is the co-author and midwife of this book. In particular, I would like to thank Howard Altman, Max De Liema, Janet Fohrman, Roger Gordon, Norbert Kaufman, Jeff Leider, Neal Linson, Joseph Mendelsohn, David Okun, Eva Piotrovsky, Floris Pittler, David Plotkin, Wendy Seid, Lindi Siegel, Richard Stein, and Dan Stork. This is a much better guide because of their help.

I also benefited from the careful reading by and thoughtful discussions with friends and colleagues, primary among them my wife, Elana Shavit Artson; my mother, Barbara F. Artson, Ph.D.; my father, David T. Artson; my step-father, Kurt Schlesinger, M.D.; my in-laws Reuben and Hayah Shavit; my Talmud *ḥaver* and friend Lee Bearson; and my dear friend and colleague, Rabbi Elie Spitz. Thanks also to my brother, Matthew. I am also grateful to Rabbi Elliot N. Dorff, Rabbi Pesach Krause, Rabbi Joel Rembaum, Rabbi Yaakov Rosenberg, Ms. Alice Greenfeld, and Professor Joan Bissell. Their guidance notwithstanding, I alone am responsible for this book.

I also want to thank my sister-in-law, Dawn Amy Osterweil, who is my dear friend, counselor, and a sister in the fullest sense.

Thanks also to my favorite sister, Tracy. Throughout the years, our love and loyalty have grown. She has been, and still is, my best friend.

Three institutions deserve special note: The congregants and leadership of Congregation Eilat provide a home, a haven, and a community. I am particularly blessed that they value a rabbi who contributes beyond the confines of our own locality and that they protect and share my commitment to study and to learning. The presidents of Congregation Eilat during the time of the conception and gestation of this book, Kelly Adams, Sherry Miller, Ernie Binstock, and Ellen Guzik, have all been supportive leaders, capable partners, and caring friends. This fact remains true—and remarkable—to this day. In this regard, I want to thank and praise Fay Zeramby. No rabbi has ever been blessed with a better secretary, friend, guide, student, and confidante. I also want to thank Mary Mayo, our children's first nanny, and Margie Davis, their current nanny.

Members of the administration and faculty of the Jewish Theological Seminary (New York) and the University of Judaism (Los Angeles) were always willing to discuss issues of method and content on many of the topics presented here. Much of my perspective was nurtured, molded, and informed by these fine teachers, scholars, and rabbis. American Jewry is well enhanced by these two schools of piety and learning.

Several of the book's chapters were published previously (sometimes in edited versions) in journals and magazines, and thereby exposed to a wider audience. I am grateful to the Women's League *Outlook* (Chapters 2, 3, and 15), to the *United Synagogue Review* (Chapter 5), to *Conservative Judaism* (Chapter 18) and to the *Jewish Spectator* (Chapters 11, 12, 13, 14, and 17). The overwhelming response of their readers confirmed my conviction that today's Jews would welcome this guide to gradual growth in Jewish observance.

This book benefited from the superb editing skills and indefatigable energy of my editor at Behrman House, Adam Siegel. He is kind, capable, insightful, and a pleasure to work with. His innumerable contributions, and those of the rest of the Behrman House staff, have markedly improved the book. I am deeply grateful for their confidence, their skill, and their humor.

I also owe a great debt of gratitude to the Rabbinical Assembly; its Executive Vice-President, Rabbi Joel H. Meyers; and its Presidents, Rabbi Gerald Zelizer and Rabbi Alan Silverstein, all of whom encouraged the writing of this book and made possible the participation of the Rabbinical Assembly in its publication. I also thank the readers for the Rabbinical Assembly, Rabbi David Vorspan and Rabbi Allen Juda. The men and women of the Rabbinical Assembly are the modern heroes of Judaism, diligently sharing their love of Torah and mitzvot, their wisdom and kindness, and their devotion to God and the Jewish people. I am honored to be one of them.

This book is dedicated to my children, Shira Esther Artson and Jacob Dov Artson, and to my wife, Elana Shavit Artson. Jacob and Shira are the greatest miracle of my life. Their vitality and their promise sustain the core aspiration of this book. With each passing day, they grow more sweet, more loving. The thrill they give their Abba when they kiss the mezuzah, "ooh" and "ahh" at the Shabbat candles, sing "Dayeinu," and blow their plastic shofar toys are my connection to eternity, a richer gift than they could ever know. I pray that the Torah will always be sweet in their mouths and that the mitzvot will make sure their step and wondrous their way.

My wife, Elana, is a treasure beyond wealth. Her loyalty to the traditions and values of Judaism, her sparkling integrity, goodness, charm, humor, and intelligence well earn her comparison to the *eshet ḥayil* (the woman of valor) of Proverbs 31. Charm may be vain; and beauty, fleeting. It may even be true that the ultimate praise of a good woman is her piety and her loving deeds. I wouldn't know: with Elana, I've never had to choose between them.

Beyond words, I am thankful to the Holy Blessed One, whose mitzvot provide a path at once loving, profound, nurturing, joyous, and beautiful. Writing this book offered many opportunities to grow in the service of God, the Jewish people, humanity, and the world, and in the development of my own Jewish identity. I am overwhelmed by the privilege of bringing God's mitzvot to a new audience of seeking people.

May we all find renewal, blessing, and contentment in the sacred path of the mitzvot.

תם ונשלם שבח לאל בורא עולם

Bradley Shavit Artson

Ḥanukkah 5755/1994
Mission Viejo, California

I. Introduction

1

Why This Book?

The Jewish individual needs nothing but readiness. —FRANZ ROSENZWEIG

Several years ago, the thirteen-year-old students in my religious school class discovered that I had graduated from Harvard. They could not contain themselves: "You went to Harvard and you became a *rabbi?*" Harvard, for these children, represented the peak of power, prestige, and success. In their eyes, I had climbed to the top, to the pinnacle they hoped to reach someday. I could have been someone wealthy and respected—a lawyer, a doctor, or a businessman. But I discarded my promising future and inexplicably settled for life as a religious functionary.

When they expressed their horror and amazement at my poor judgment and strange values, I responded that each person cultivates different interests and different ways of helping the world. Some work for justice, some prefer to heal people, and some choose to provide for people's physical needs. I like to build a holy community and to help people lead more meaningful lives.

My students rejected that explanation as ridiculous, so I tried another line of reasoning. I asked them, "If your parents were given two million dollars, would they continue doing their jobs?" Most of the

Judaism doesn't have to stop with the bar or bat mitzvah. Instead, it can be a lifelong journey of growth and discovery. All it takes is a willing heart, a searching mind, and a desire to let God and Torah into our lives.

children guessed that their parents would no longer work but would buy beautiful mansions on the beach and live a life of ease. "Okay," I said, "some people work for money. But I don't. If I had a million dollars, I might buy a nicer home and many more books, but I'd still go to work each day because I love what I do." (Later I discovered I was not the only one who shared this sentiment: A visitor was touring Mother Teresa's hostel for the poor lepers of India. On seeing the severity of their illness and the strenuousness of her work, the visitor exclaimed, "I wouldn't do your work for a million dollars!" to which Mother Teresa responded, "For a million dollars, I wouldn't do it either.")

That explanation, however well intentioned, struck my class as no less foolish than the first one. In retrospect, their reaction is not surprising. To assert that there is something more meaningful, more valuable than wealth, power, and prestige goes against so much of what our society preaches every day on television, in the news, and through its bestowal of fame and fortune. To a large extent, the values of these children were molded by the priorities of Wall Street and Madison Avenue, not by the standards of the

WHAT MATTERS MOST?

A member of my synagogue confided to me that his daughter, now eleven, would surely become a bat mitzvah (a girl, age twelve years and one day, or thirteen, who is responsible for her own deeds according to Jewish law). This father insisted that his daughter learn the basics of a religious background, but after that she would choose whether or not to continue in Hebrew school. I listened and then asked whether he would also allow her to choose to discontinue her science classes after she turns thirteen. Would his daughter, I wondered, be allowed to choose never to take another writing course in school? Incredulously, the father said no, his daughter must continue with both science and writing, because no thirteen year old is in a position to make such an important choice as that.

In establishing this preference—that the acquisition of skills, facts, and possessions deserves precedence over sensitivity, values, meaning, and compassion—we divulge our adherence to the "wisdom" of the world. We convey to our children that ultimate questions—What is my place in the universe? What is the purpose of life? and How are we to treat other human beings?—need concern us only until puberty.

Torah and the Talmud. I knew the assumptions and priorities of those children, because I had been there myself.

As a child, I was a fervent atheist. Religion, for me, was synonymous with ignorance, bigotry, and superstition. While always proud of my Jewish identity (although quite ignorant of what that identity entailed), I remained nonetheless firmly secular. I continued in religious school through the last year of the Confirmation program only because I wanted to join the class trip to Israel. From that point until college, I had no formal contact with the organized Jewish community. I had little more than scorn for Judaism in particular and for religion in general.

My attitude toward religion remained relatively unchanged until my freshman year at college. As for so many others, for me college was a time of upheaval, a time when all my certainties no longer looked so sure. As I questioned many of the assumptions of my childhood, I also questioned my rejection of religion, paradoxically because of an abiding respect for my parents' values. My passion for morality (the legacy of my secular Jewish childhood) prompted me to rethink some of the insights of religion. If there were such a thing as good and evil, it had to represent more than mere social convention. Perhaps the standard for identifying good transcends humanity and is a gift from God. I recognized that I could never accept Christianity, so I decided to explore Judaism.

At the time, I knew very little about Jewish thought or history. I made an appointment to speak with the campus rabbi, Rabbi Ben-Zion Gold. Our meeting in his small, book-strewn study marked a new beginning for me. Gradually I began to incorporate the insights, teachings, and practices of Judaism into the rhythms of my soul. Rabbi Gold persuaded me to attend Shabbat services every Saturday morning for two months and to read an account of the life and philosophy of Franz Rosenzweig, a German Jewish theologian who had traveled spiritually from the periphery of

Many of us are more familiar with the buzz of Wall Street than with the rituals of the synagogue. Yet we still feel the need for something more in our lives. The goal of wisdom and spiritual fulfillment beckons even to those who have achieved wealth, power, and fame.

Judaism to its center. In my junior year of college, I took my first course in Jewish history and philosophy, and in my senior year I finally enrolled in introductory Hebrew. After graduation, I continued to study with Rabbi Saul White, the rabbi of a Conservative synagogue in San Francisco, my hometown.

Throughout this time, I was intent on becoming a politician. I worked as a legislative aide for the speaker of the California State Assembly, attended political meetings and banquets, acted as the speaker's liaison to various communities within San Francisco, and worked on special projects in his district. But Judaism exerted a growing claim on my heart. As my love for God and Judaism grew, I experimented with new aspects of Jewish living. I embodied the wise words of a more observant friend in college, who had cautioned me to "go slow, and take it one step at a time." Kate's advice still forms the backbone of my Jewish experience and the perspective of this book.

After two years in politics, I decided that the life of a candidate and elected official was not for me. My wife suggested I consider rabbinical school, and one week later I was sitting in the office of Rabbi Elliot Dorff, the Provost of the University of Judaism in Los Angeles, a completed application for the rabbinical program in my hand. A few weeks after that, an admissions committee interviewed and admitted me during that brief (and for me, fortunate) window of opportunity when the Jewish Theological Seminary (the central scholarly institution of Conservative Judaism) did not require proficiency in Jewish law, Hebrew, Bible, or Talmud for admission into its rabbinical program. Burdened by my ignorance, I began rabbinical studies in New York City. Five years and many classes later, I was ordained and returned to California to begin my life as a rabbi at Congregation Eilat in southern California.

❖   ❖   ❖   ❖   ❖

As a result of my own personal journey from the outskirts of Jewish living to its center, I can well understand the perspectives and the struggles of my congregants' lives. Time and time again, I have watched the families of my congregation awaken to the realization that being Jewish matters. Some are motivated to search because they have realized lifelong ambitions with the shocking recognition that something is still missing, that those dreams, now accomplished, are somehow not enough. But what else is there? For others, the catalyst is an inquisitive child who insists on asking childish questions like "Why are we alive?" "What happens when we die?" and "Who made God?" Still others are drawn to Judaism through a flirtation with Eastern religions and the desire for spiritual depth within their own traditions or by a growing identification with grandparents or parents no longer living. As the rabbi of a growing community, I am confronted by people in all stages of life, in a range of different situations, all of them confronting an inability to articulate their own highest ideals:

- A congregant shares his frustration when his twelve-year-old child walks into his den and announces that after becoming a bat mitzvah, she intends to quit her religious school education. My congregant is frustrated by his own inability to explain why being Jewish feels so important to him yet occupies so little of his attention and time.

- A young woman who completed Hebrew high school at our synagogue returns during spring break and pays a visit to her rabbi. She is about to graduate from college, and the thought of spending the rest of her life working from nine to five with only weekends for escape seems absurd to her. Is this what all those years of study were for? When will she get a chance to live? And what constitutes living? How can she build a meaningful life around our culture's requirements of security, status, and success?

- Each year, I teach an introduction to Judaism class. A significant percentage of the students had abandoned Jewish learning as teens but now wanted to understand their heritage on an adult level. The majority of the class, however, are non-Jews considering conversion, often because they are planning to marry a Jew. Representative of the ironic stress that converts often experience was a tearful phone call from a Jew-by-choice. She had originally consented to investigate Judaism because her Jewish-born husband insisted she do so and because Judaism seemed intrinsically appealing to her. After months of study and the formal conversion itself, she wants her conversion to add depth to the way she and her husband conduct their married life. Her husband now accuses his wife of making too big a deal of this whole "Jewish thing." Her passion for her newfound faith threatens her love for her husband. Is there a way they can grow together rather than apart?

These situations and countless more testify to a continuing need to respond to religious questions and to learn more about Jewish traditions. What typifies us are not so much our beliefs as our doubts, not so much our behavior as our aspirations. Many people are caught between the demands of modern success and an aching for meaning, identity, community, and God. Yet even though they desire something more out of life, even though they are dimly aware that they lack a dimension of depth and caring and love, they have forgotten how to look for it. Most of us are probably more familiar with Bartlett's *Familiar Quotations* than with the Talmud, more at home with a ball game than with a synagogue service.

The Talmud (an anthology of rabbinic wisdom, legend, and law compiled over hundreds of years and largely completed by the sixth century) asks whether a Jewish child who has been kidnapped by barbarians is obligated to practice Judaism. The rabbis concur that such a child cannot possibly be held to the high moral and ritual standards of Jewish religion, because he or she had never participated in the fullness of Jewish living and consequently couldn't know it firsthand. We, American Jewry, are that kidnapped infant. Like the fourth child of the Passover seder, we don't know how to ask the right questions.

❖   ❖   ❖   ❖   ❖

This book has been written for all who want to explore the wisdom and joy of Jewish observance but aren't willing or able to immerse themselves all at once.

Judaism can change our lives. But transformation is rarely quick and never simple. Acclimatizing ourselves to the ways and the wisdom of an ancient heritage can seem an overwhelming task. Patience, persistence, and humor provide the essential tools for anyone wishing to explore his or her Jewish identity and return to Judaism more fully. Above all, such growth requires vision and the ability to see the world and ourselves anew. The rewards of such a journey are not difficult to discover: connection to an ancient and wise way of life, one that has fashioned a compassionate people and caring families for thousands of years; access to God and a sense of the sacred that can infuse our busy lives with purpose and depth; and a deeper awareness of our truer self, informed by our history, our heritage, and our own experiences in life.

One of the excuses Jews use to disregard the demands of our religion is an inability to observe its totality immediately. Far too often we look upon Judaism as an all-or-nothing affair; either observe it 100 percent or don't even bother. Such an approach ends up discouraging willing Jews from exploring their own heritage and distorts the true nature of Judaism. This book advocates a gradual approach to Jewish life without abandoning the traditional goals of Judaism. Convinced that the all-or-nothing mentality places Jewish living permanently beyond the reach of all but a select few, I have sought in this book to involve the reader actively in risking but one step at a time. Such a method allows the reader to absorb a new skill, value, or priority while taking advantage of his or her life history. Some growth is better than none, and a lot is better than a little. This book provides high standards but divides the ultimate goal into several steps. In this way, Judaism becomes possible for today's striving Jews.

In learning a new language, students assimilate it a few words at a time. A class learns one new grammatical form, which its members then practice until it feels natural. The next step is another small advance, another list of vocabulary words and a new grammatical form. No one expects fluency overnight. Slow, gradual advances tempered with patience signal the mastery of a language.

Learning how to live Jewishly is not so different from learning to walk. One step at a time, one foot after another is the only way to gain sureness of foot, balance, and a sense of mastery that will lead to further journeys on life's road.

The language of Judaism is its mitzvot, מִצְוֹת ,
the commandments by which a Jew makes the world
a more sacred, sensitive, just, and compassionate
place. Some mitzvot appear to focus primarily on ritual (such as the dietary laws or Shabbat), whereas
others seem to attend more to ethical considerations
(such as caring for the elderly or visiting the sick).
But all are rooted, as is any language, in a common
syntax, grammar, and culture.

The only way to feel natural and comfortable
with the mitzvot is to become acquainted with them
gradually, over a period of time, with lenience,
patience, and encouragement so that the deeds of
Judaism become an opportunity to excel rather than
a burden or a new source of guilt. Jewish practice
must grow by degrees. It must emerge from each
individual temperament; each person must respond
individually to an inner sense of when an advance
feels right, of when a new deed may be internalized
and reflect a truer sense of self.

Each chapter of this book presents a mitzvah
(such as prayer or feeding the hungry), explains its
significance, and then divides it into several parts.
Each reader will therefore be able to try out different
practices, growing in a particular mitzvah at his or her
own rate as each new practice feels manageable.
Each chapter concludes with recommendations for
further reading for those interested in pursuing the
topic in greater depth. To help build a Jewish vocabulary, common Jewish words and phrases that appear
in this book are listed in the glossary.

There are two ways to read this book. Some
will prefer to read it all the way through, from cover
to cover, and then return to work through each chapter. The advantage of this approach is that it will provide a comprehensive overview of the body of Jewish
practice and Jewish concepts. The disadvantage is
that it may threaten to overwhelm. A second method
is to read the introductory section (Chapters 1–3) for
a glimpse of the conceptual framework of the book,
and then to select the mitzvot that appeal most strong-

ly, reading about and implementing them at the pace and in the order that seem most appealing.

Both of these approaches to Jewish growth can provide a path toward a richer life, a deeper sense of community, and a deeper sense of holiness. Choose the method that matches your own temperament and level of ability. Above all, don't lose heart. In the words of Rabbi Naḥman, "the entire world is a narrow bridge; the essence is not to fear" (LIKKUTEI MAHARAN 2:28).

For Further Reading

Abraham Joshua Heschel, *I Asked for Wonder: A Spiritual Anthology,* ed. Samuel H. Dresner. New York: Crossroad, 1986.

Simcha Kling, *Embracing Judaism*. New York: Rabbinical Assembly, 1988.

2 Our God and the God of Our Ancestors

Come, let us turn back to Adonai.

—HOSEA 6:1

God is like an icon which never changes, yet everyone who looks at it sees a different face.

—PESIKTA DE-RAV KAHANA, 176

This book is about mitzvot—the concrete actions Judaism uses to fashion lives of ethical rigor and spiritual insight. Performing mitzvot is the way Jews bring justice, compassion, and holiness to the world. Throughout this book, our focus will be on the deeds themselves, but no guide to Jewish living would be sufficiently grounded without pausing to reflect on the authority behind the mitzvot, the Commander who is met in the commandments. To understand that the performance of mitzvot is not just an empty formalism, not merely the imposition of an ancient tradition, we need to renew our relationship with God, the source of all mitzvot.

To reduce God to any philosophical strand within Judaism or to a single system of expression is

Mitzvot are the Jewish arena for knowing and experiencing God. Rather than relying on contemplation, Judaism has placed primary value on doing as the principal path for serving God. Mitzvot translate the lofty principles of the Torah into the tangible acts of caring individuals and righteous societies—feeding the hungry, freeing the captive, observing Shabbat, honoring our parents. Those sacred deeds embody the conviction that we best imitate God through sacred deeds of love.

to miss the full extent of God's majesty. Precisely because God is God, our understanding of divine will is always partial, approximate, and tentative. As the medieval Jewish theologian Rabbi Yosef Albo exclaimed, "If I knew God, I would be God!" This caveat is not intended as an excuse for sloppy thinking or indifference but is meant merely to underscore that we experience God on many levels. People are complex creatures (made, after all, in God's image), and any theology that ignores our complexity, and our limits, cannot even begin to do justice to its subject. These tentative perceptions of God are offered with the hope that we can all emerge somewhat wiser, more sophisticated, and capable of experiencing greater *kedushah* (קְדֻשָׁה ,"holiness").

❖   ❖   ❖   ❖   ❖

As an atheist, years ago, I was unable to justify even the simplest moral claims. For many years, I had no theoretical grounding for assertions as clear as "raping my sister is wrong" or "murdering the Jews in Nazi Germany was wrong." If there were no external, nonhuman source of morality, then the most I could assert was that "I think raping my sister is wrong." But if the rapist thinks it is right (or at best, has no notion of right or wrong), then the matter must rest there.

Even more upsetting, if morality were based on human or social need, the Nazis could make an irrefutable argument that Germany's national revitalization required the murder of millions of Jews—not that the Jews were really a threat, but that the German people needed a scapegoat. If consensus were the basis of morality, then surely the Germans were right because there certainly were more Germans than there were Jews.

For me, the only way to ground morality in a system that does not collapse into fads or fanaticism is to place moral authority beyond human judgment. God is the source of morality. God is the reason raping my sister is not simply wrong in my opinion but wrong by any standard; God is the reason why mur-

---

EXPERIENCING GOD
So many of the experiences and perceptions in my life, even amid tragedy or disappointment, point to God's love and involvement in the world. These experiences sustain and nurture my relationship with God: When I say the Aleinu (the concluding prayer of any Jewish service), I know that I stand before the Ruler of space and time and that we have shared a moment together. When my wife lights Shabbat candles, I know that we are enjoying a gift from the Holy One: God's comfort and love. When I spend a night in a shelter for the homeless, I know that I am God's ally, and when I speak about a Jewish response to the threat of nuclear annihilation or to the assault against the environment, I serve my Creator by caring for creation.

dering the Jews cannot be justified on grounds of social utility.

We may understand God's moral imperative imperfectly, but doing so does not make the imperative or its source less real, just as an imperfectly transmitted letter would not render its author's existence false. God has planted in each person a moral force, akin to our drive for food, sleep, and sex. Just like those other drives, it can be denied, perverted, or rationalized. But it is real nonetheless.

❖　❖　❖　❖　❖

Two fundamental observations that emerge from everyday miracles direct my gaze toward God: the first is that of life itself; the second is the continuing vitality of the Jewish people.

I have no explanation for the fact that I, a composite of carbon, hydrogen, nitrogen, oxygen, phosphate, and sulfur, can think, feel, and behave. As Einstein marveled, "The most incomprehensible thing about the universe is that it is comprehensible." I find this fact—the possibility of comprehension—staggering and silencing. Consider, for example, a human body, which one minute is alive and able to laugh or cry, and the next second is reduced to a lifeless pile of organic elements no different from any other. A God-given ability reposes in our abilities to maintain our own health (to renew creation every day), to impose our will on our environment (including our ability to reproduce—again, acting as creators), and to make moral judgments (distinguishing between good and evil). The miracle of life testifies to me of God.

I marvel, too, at the Jewish people. With rare exception history records no other people who were separated from their land for most of their history, lacking even the power to govern themselves or the stability to control their own destiny, who nonetheless retained a strong and continuous identity. There are no weekly meetings of Edomites in Brooklyn or of Hittites in Los Angeles. But every day the descendants of ancient Israel gather to participate in, and strengthen, their unbroken identity. We not only

WHAT MAKES ALL PEOPLE EQUAL?

It might be argued that the moral treatment of people derives from human equality. This assertion, however, cannot be demonstrated exclusively through reason; it is, rather, a dogma of faith. People are clearly not equal unless they are measured against something that is perfect. There must be an outside point of comparison, one whose nature is so radically superior from the nature of any person that in the face of that other, all people are essentially equivalent, despite their distinctions.

The "other" by which people become equal is the Holy Eternal One. In the words of the prayerbook, "Compared to You, all the mighty are nothing, the famous nonexistent, the wise lack wisdom, the clever lack reason." It is only when people are compared against God that the moral argument that all people are equal ("created equal," in fact) and deserve equal moral treatment gains force.

know we are Jews; we care that we are. Jewish creativity continues to flourish.

This Jewish creativity began when we understood ourselves as God's people. And this self-understanding finds expression in the *brit*, בְּרִית, the covenant linking God and the Jewish people. A covenant is an agreement between two parties that spells out the prerogatives and the responsibilities of both participants toward each other. Our *brit* with God is codified in the Torah and is expressed through the observance of God's commandments, the mitzvot. It is that

"Those who love Adonai hate evil." The Psalmist understood that justice and morality, good and evil, weren't simply products of social consensus, but reflected the judgments of God, who is passionate about justice and compassion.

brit, together with the mitzvot, that implements our covenant, that has sustained us through millennia, and that still makes the Jewish people unique.

❖ ❖ ❖ ❖ ❖

The final pillar that directs my gaze toward God is the written record and the response of the Jewish people to God throughout the ages. Our sacred writings, millennia old, and the sacred deeds that emerge from them reveal a power to bind a community around eternal values and shattering insight unequaled in world history. Biblical, rabbinic, and contemporary Jewish religious writings shine with a light that has sustained us and projected us from anonymity to the very center of world history time and time again.

Consider, for example, an unprecedented insight from the Torah: Throughout the ancient world, in every other culture, crimes against property resulted in execution, whereas crimes against people could be "repaid" simply by inflicting the same cruelty on the perpetrator or a member of the criminal's family. If I chopped off the hand of my neighbor's spouse, then he could chop off my hand. But if I stole, then I violated the very underpinnings of society, and for that the only just retribution was death.

The Torah turned that ancient consensus on its head. The Torah consistently affirms that capital punishment can apply only to crimes against people or against God. No property crime merits the loss of human life. In a world of seemingly common sense, the Torah demonstrated, and continues to advocate, an insight that is anything but common.

Consider that ancient law codes maintained different penalties based on the social caste of the victim. An injured person received a different compensation based on whether the person was male or female, free or enslaved, rich or poor, aristocratic or common. The more elevated the victim's social status, the more heinous the punishment. Not so in the Torah. Building on its insistence that all people are made *b'tzelem Elohim* (בְּצֶלֶם אֱלֹהִים, "in God's

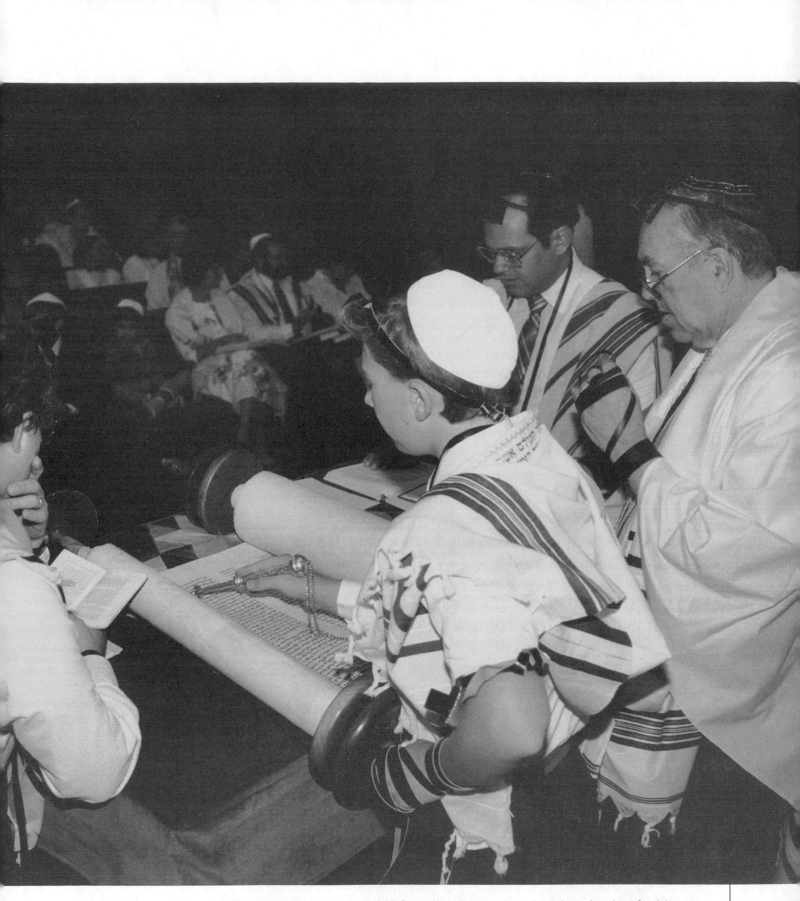

Unique among the works of antiquity (and rare to this day still), the Torah insists that ritual and ethics must remain inseparable in the transmission of sacred values and meaningful living. Thus, lighting Shabbat candles and honoring parents, caring for the sick and observing the dietary laws—as well as countless other commandments—become a means for education and renewed commitment to our Jewish heritage and to God.

image"), the laws of the Torah cut across social and economic lines, affirming the infinite worth of all human beings, whether free or enslaved, whether Jewish or gentile, regardless of their wealth or prestige. This concept is a breakthrough that the rest of humanity has been seeking to implement (or resist) ever since.

The striking insights embodied in the Torah and in subsequent Jewish writings, unprecedented in their time and still infrequent in their fulfillment, embody the infusion of a higher wisdom, a Guide who could transcend the limited perspective of consensus to reveal a sacred reordering of values.

The unparalleled depth of the Torah and of the talmudic traditions whispers the insights of God. Those insights and directions are implemented through the mitzvot, the network of sacred deeds that structure the life of the Jew and form the lifeblood of Jewish values, continuity, and belonging.

It is as a pathway to the mitzvot—the Jewish arena for knowing and experiencing God—that this book is a guide.

For Further Reading

Neil Gillman, *Sacred Fragments: Recovering Theology for the Modern Jew*. Philadelphia: Jewish Publication Society, 1990.

Harold Kushner, *Who Needs God?* New York: Summit Books, 1989.

Seymour Siegel and Elliot Gertel, eds., *God in the Teachings of Conservative Judaism*. New York: Rabbinical Assembly, 1985.

David J. Wolpe, *The Healer of Shattered Hearts: A Jewish View of God*. New York: Henry Holt, 1990.

3

What Is Jewish Law?
Why Does It Matter?

The mitzvot were only given to refine creation through them.
—GENESIS RABBAH 44

It is within our power to mirror God's unending love in deeds of kindness, like brooks that hold the sky.
—RABBI ABRAHAM JOSHUA HESCHEL

In the last two chapters, we considered Judaism as a path for spiritual growth, and we explored our age-old covenant with God. The time has now come to ask: Will growing as a Jew entail more than reading some books or quiet contemplation? Does it make any difference in the way we live our lives and spend our time? In short, does Judaism relegate spirituality, the emotional bounty of religious life, to the private recesses of our soul, or should it change the way we treat each other, ourselves, and the world?

At the conclusion of their wedding ceremony, this couple have created a sacred space in which to celebrate their love. Joyous occasions gain depth and power when linked to the age-old commandments of Jewish tradition. Precisely by expressing our private joys and sorrows through the mitzvot, we affirm our membership in the covenant between God and the Jewish people.

Human beings are ritualizing creatures—we develop routines and patterns that allow us to act without having to stop and think about every detail of every action. By establishing expected ways of behaving, we are able to create order, comfort, and meaning. My twins have a bedtime pattern: bath, bottle, say good-night to all the paintings and toys, read the same book night after night, then sing the Shema in the crib. Any deviation in the most minute detail disturbs them.

We use structure and ritual to provide security in a chaotic world, to reinforce and communicate our values, our community, and our identity. Halakhah (הֲלָכָה , Jewish law) is the source of, and the guide to, Jewish ritual and behavior. Halakhah is the tool that Judaism provides for implementing the goals of holiness and righteousness in every aspect of our daily lives: in our diet, our wardrobe, our calendar, our sexual habits, our leisure pursuits, and our acts of *tzedakah* ("righteousness") and goodness, to name just a few. Jewish law matters because it shapes and nurtures our growth as Jews.

❖　❖　❖　❖　❖

If our goal is a lofty ideal—living a moral life, integrating a renewed spirituality and community into our sense of self, responding to the will of God—then who needs all the minutiae of Jewish law? Why bother with the details of method when it is the grander objective that we seek?

Asking why Jewish law matters is really asking why people need structure and guidelines for living their lives. As a congregational rabbi, I have been surprised by the tenacity with which Jews turn to Jewish law for comfort, order, and connection regardless of the extent to which the commandments of Judaism govern their personal lives. So many Jews, even those who don't yet implement all of the requirements of their religion, continue to perceive halakhah as the foundation of Judaism. At life-cycle events and our holy days, even less traditional Jews look to their synagogues to provide the standards and norms of behavior that have guided our people through the ages. Two examples illustrate this connection to halakhah:

• It's not unusual for me to receive a call summoning me to counsel a bereaved congregant after the death of a spouse or parent. One occasion stands out as typical: As I walked into the dimly lit stillness of our local funeral home, I recognized an elderly congregant whose mother had just died. That I recognized her is noteworthy because I see her only on Rosh Hashanah, Yom Kippur, and occasionally for a bar mitzvah celebration of a friend's grandchild. Otherwise, she and her hus-

Often during a crucial life-cycle event—a birth, marriage, or death—Jews return to the comfort and wisdom provided by the mitzvot. Even those who don't normally integrate the mitzvot into their lives often want their loved one's wedding or funeral "done right."

band don't participate much in the programs of the synagogue. I assume that they, like many Jews, are not observant in their personal lives. As I entered the room, she stood and took my hand. We exchanged hushed greetings, and the first thing she said to me was, "Rabbi, it's important to me that this be a traditional funeral. I want to do it right." Struck by the dichotomy between her personal life and her insistence that we go by the book, I couldn't help noting that even a minimally observant woman would find comfort and security in falling back on practices she had discarded long ago. Jewish law, for her, was home base—a secure haven to rely on in difficult times.

GOD IS IN THE DETAILS

We've all experienced the need to attend to the details in order to accomplish something far-reaching—I can't even remember what my wife wants me to buy at the store without going to the trouble of making a list. The discipline of making the list, remembering to bring it with me, and consulting it in the store makes it possible to shop successfully. That blend of foresight, preparation, and persistence accompanies all human attainments, whether trivial or lofty.

How much more is it needed to construct a richer spirit and to establish a sacred community!

The shopping list that makes Judaism meaningful is its mitzvot: feeding the hungry, observing Shabbat, visiting the sick, caring for the earth, loving and supporting the State of Israel, to name a few. These are the precious details that enable us to achieve our larger objectives—the creation of a holy, caring, and sacred community.

• Two months before a child celebrates his or her bar or bat mitzvah, I routinely ask the celebrating family to schedule a preliminary meeting with me. At that discussion, we read the haftarah and explore its meaning. When I ask these twelve-year-olds why they are willing to go to all this trouble, the almost universal answer from both children and their parents is, "Because that's what

Jews do." When I comment that Jews do lots of things that they don't do and that they wouldn't become murderers just because other Jews killed people, they clarify their answer with, "This is the Jewish way to become an adult." Most of these children are no more personally observant than the woman who was concerned about her mother's burial, yet for them, becoming a responsible Jew means following the ancestral practices as they have been transmitted through time.

The apparent unwillingness of Jews to abandon halakhah completely shows their appreciation that Judaism is more than just abstract concepts or lofty morality. Judaism is the indispensable framework that translates ideas, emotions, and values into the organization of home, family, and community. That framework is embodied in halakhah. Halakhah touches every aspect of Jewish living, transforms mundane habits into opportunities to renew our commitment to Jewish values, links us to Jewish history and the Jewish people around the world, and opens pathways to God and to a sense of the sacred in the everyday. Halakhah is Judaism's method of identifying mitzvot—commanded deeds.

❖   ❖   ❖   ❖   ❖

Those who constantly create new interpretations
of Torah are harvesting her.
—*OR HA-ḤAMMAH* ON THE ZOHAR

Knowing that we need structures through which we can cultivate our spirit and our community, and knowing that halakhah is the vehicle to accomplish these goals within Judaism, we still must discuss what, precisely, characterizes Jewish law.

Jewish law is a dynamic process, rooted in the love between God and the Jewish people. The earliest expression of that love and commitment is the Torah (תּוֹרָה, literally, "instruction" or "teaching"), the first five books of the Hebrew Bible. All later Jewish traditions grew out of this first encounter with the ineffable. And it is in the Torah that the Jewish insistence on expressing through our actions our sense of community, values, and love of God first becomes manifest.

Jews have always understood the laws of the Torah as an expression of God's love for the Jewish people. While many non-Jewish propagandists have claimed to see a conflict between law and love, the Torah insists that true love must have behavioral implications—as love is implemented in practice. Two lovers who didn't care how one another behaved (who didn't care whether the partner ate or slept or was healthy) would practice a narcissistic love indeed. As the Mishnah recognizes, the sheer number of mitzvot in the Torah (traditionally understood to be 613, of which 297 are still capable of fulfillment today) is evidence of just how much God cares for, and about, the Jews. Law, from the perspective of the Torah, does not oppose love; it implements it.

Just as love must breathe and grow if it is to live, so must law. Consequently, the Torah establishes a judicial system for resolving disputed cases. Absolute authority is placed not in any body of writing but in the hands of living sages, flesh-and-blood people who can integrate the priorities of ancient traditions with the contemporary needs of the community. The Torah itself (DEUTERONOMY 17:8-13) authorizes the living representatives of Judaism—the religious leaders of each generation, priests in one period, rabbis subsequently—to apply and amend halakhah to meet the continuing needs of the Jewish people, in order for halakhah to continue to reflect God's loving role in human life. The sages of each generation translate the timeless language of the Torah into the words and framework of each succeeding age. In the light of the relationship between the written traditions and the rabbis, a fit definition for Judaism would be the Jewish people's continuing interpretation and application of the Torah, through its sages, with the intention of cultivating and enhancing its

Torah is the name we give to the first five books of the Bible (shown here in the scroll), and is also the name of the process through which Jews discern God's will. That process continues in our own age, applying ancient wisdom and divine priorities to issues such as the role of men and women, medical ethics, and many other contemporary concerns.

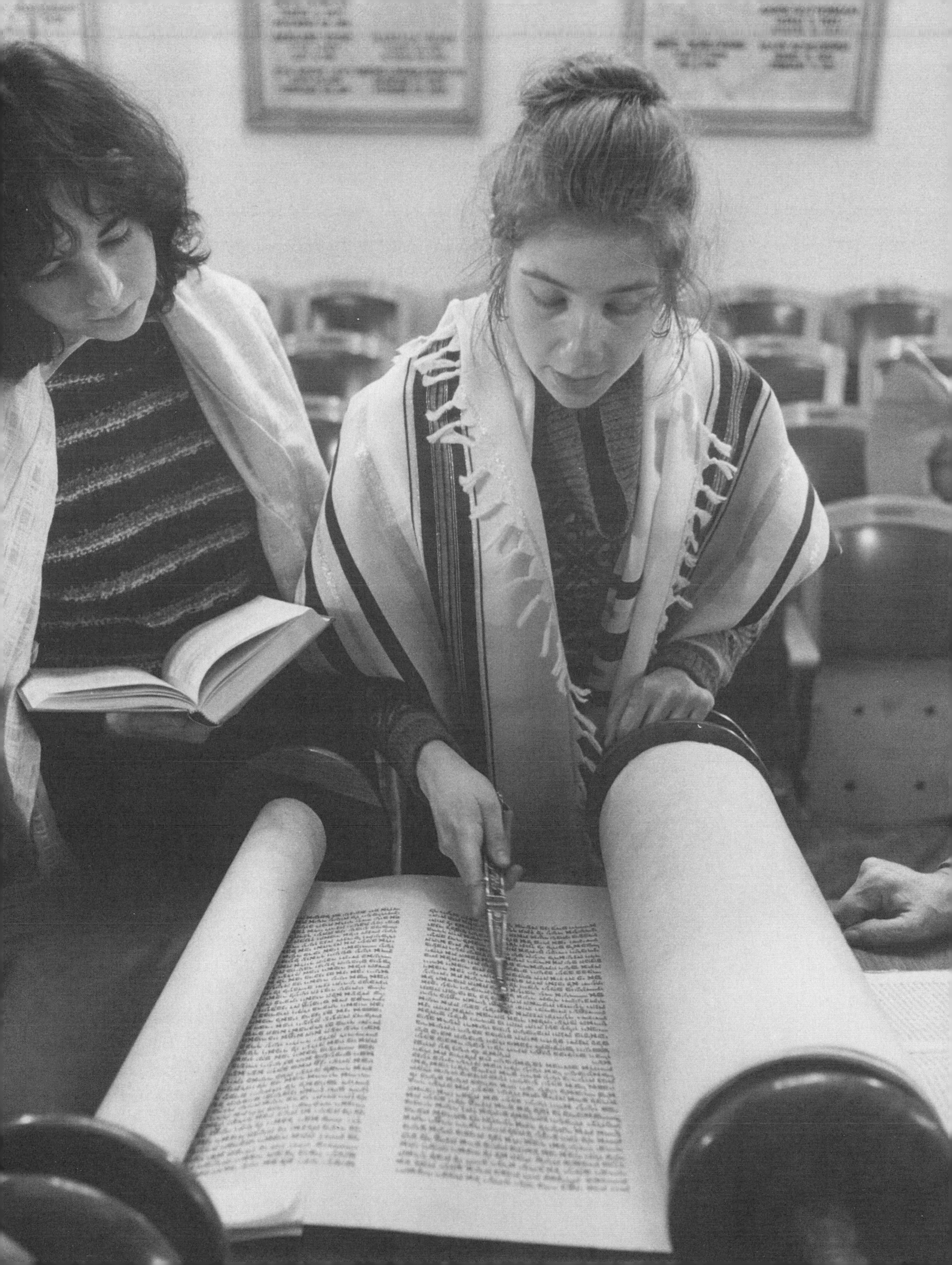

covenant with God. (For a detailed discussion of halakhah, see the Appendix: Jewish Law: Its Roots and Development.)

❖　❖　❖　❖　❖

Choose life . . . by loving Adonai your God, heeding God's commandments, and holding fast to God. For thereby you shall have life.
—DEUTERONOMY 30:19-20

We have embarked on a journey together. Where it will lead is still unknown. The remainder of this book will focus on halakhah and the practice of mitzvot. This book is rooted in the age-old Jewish conviction that precisely those ideas that lead to action are the most real and transforming. Through deeds of love, we teach ourselves compassion; through deeds of holiness, we respond to the awe of being alive. These sacred deeds—these mitzvot—create an environment in which Jews and Judaism can flourish, in which our covenant with God is renewed, and in which our souls and our families are nurtured by a deeper level of existence.

For us as individuals, Jewish law plays an additional role. We are not all scholars. Few of us can afford to immerse ourselves in our Judaism even if we wanted to do so. Our Hebrew may be rusty or inadequate, our familiarity with Jewish history and Jewish thought may be minimal. Amid the pressure of raising a family, sustaining a marriage, developing friendships, building community, and providing an income, we often struggle to find the time or energy to fulfill all our ideals. Halakhah provides us with a path of holiness and meaning that has been tested through the ages wherever Jews have lived.

All of us, regardless of our learning, regardless of our commitments, have the time to begin the path of mitzvot. All of us can take the time to visit someone ill, to abstain from eating pork, or to comfort a mourner. It requires but a moment to light Shabbat candles on Friday night or to curb our participation in gossip.

All of us can incorporate halakhah into our lives. By growing in observance, we renew our connection to a sacred past, thereby allowing the holy into the present as well. Through the mitzvot, we permit God into our homes and into our hearts.

For Further Reading

Elliot N. Dorff and Arthur Rosett, *A Living Tree: The Roots and Growth of Jewish Law.* New York: SUNY Press and the Jewish Theological Seminary, 1988.

Seymour Siegel, ed., *Conservative Judaism and Jewish Law.* New York: Rabbinical Assembly, 1977.

II. Mitzvot to Grow With

4 *Ahavat Tziyon:*
Zionism and Israel

The Jewish People … forced to leave their ancient country, has never abandoned, never forsaken, the Holy Land; the Jewish People has never ceased to be passionate about Zion. It has always lived in a dialogue with the Holy Land.

—*RABBI ABRAHAM JOSHUA HESCHEL*

A good land, a land with streams and springs and fountains issuing from plain and hill; a land of wheat and barley, of vines, figs, and pomegranates, a land of olive trees and honey; a land where you may eat food without stint, where you will lack nothing; a land whose rocks are iron and from whose hills you can mine copper. When you have eaten your fill, give thanks to Adonai your God for the good land which God has given you.—DEUTERONOMY 8:7-10

Israel's existence is a miracle. After having wandered in exile for almost twenty centuries, the Jewish people have returned to their homeland, where they govern a Jewish state, speak the ancient language of the Torah and the Mishnah, and conduct their daily routine in the neighborhoods of King David and Isaiah. It is easy to take this collective resurrection for granted. Even after visiting Israel three times, I still forget how astonishing the establishment of Israel really is. Occasionally, however, a simple event can abruptly focus my amazement on that little state.

One March a few years ago, I received a small airmail package from my former college roommate, who had moved to the Negev (the desert region of southern Israel) shortly after graduation and now lives on a kibbutz. It was a few weeks before Passover, and he had mailed me a copy of the newly printed kibbutz Haggadah. It was beautiful. Although it was similar to many others I've seen, there were two striking differences: the text was entirely in Hebrew, and the Haggadah emphasized agriculture and land over the traditional rabbinic concentration on liberation and the giving of the Torah.

In the half century of its existence, Israel has become a vital part of Jewish identity throughout the world. Israeli food, music, fiction, and scholarship enliven Jewish life. Israeli pride contributes to Jewish pride the world over, as this Israel Day celebration in Los Angeles demonstrates.

Only in Israel, I thought, would such a Haggadah seem perfectly natural. Where else would a translation be superfluous, since even the youngest child at a kibbutz Seder understands the Hebrew of the Bible and the Mishnah? And where else would the emphasis on agriculture and the cycle of the seasons seem so natural? Restored to their own land, with farming a significant part of the national consciousness, Israeli Jews experience a heightened sensitivity to the seasons and natural rhythms of growth and harvest. Within the confines of this little package, I was once again reminded of how unique Israel truly is.

❖ ❖ ❖ ❖ ❖

One of the most remarkable achievements of the Jewish people has been our virtual unanimity in our love of Eretz Yisrael (אֶרֶץ יִשְׂרָאֵל, "Land of Israel") for close to three thousand years. That love is not only a shared passion; it is a mitzvah, the mitzvah of *ahavat Tziyon* (אַהֲבַת צִיוֹן, "love of Zion"). The prophet Isaiah records the command: "Rejoice with Jerusalem and be glad for her" (66:10), and the psalmist (PSALM 137:5-6) speaks for the Jewish people when pledging,

> If I forget you, O Jerusalem,
> let my right hand wither;
> Let my tongue stick to my palate
> if I cease to think of you,
> if I do not keep Jerusalem in memory even
> in my happiest hour.

Our continuity as a people is due in some measure to our ability to unite around the memory of a common home and to our determination to restore that home to a physical reality. Since the first Exile from Israel, in the year 586 B.C.E., we have incorporated a longing for the Holy Land into our daily lives. We face Jerusalem (יְרוּשָׁלַיִם, Yerushalayim) in prayer, observe a day of fasting in memory of the destruction of Jerusalem and of the First and Second Temples (the fast of Tisha b'Av, the Ninth of Av), recall the Temple service on Yom Kippur, and cultivate the centrality of the Land of Israel in Jewish dietary laws, Shabbat observance, and virtually every aspect of Jewish life.

This passion for the land, however, was never limited to the realm of ritual and religion. Throughout history, small groups of Jews sporadically left their homes and villages to live in Eretz Yisrael, where there was a continuous Jewish presence. Funds collected in the Golah (גּוֹלָה, countries outside of Eretz Yisrael, also referred to as the Diaspora) supported Jewish settlements in Yerushalayim and other cities in Israel. Several medieval Jewish movements that supported the return to Israel were significant enough to receive attention from European and Middle Eastern monarchs.

Despite the historical attachment of our people to Israel, it is still worthwhile to ask a fundamental question: Why should the Land of Israel matter to us today?

• *Israel has been the central focus and symbol of Jewish unity and peoplehood throughout the generations.*

A visitor to Israel cannot but be moved by the archaeological testimony of our ancient roots—David's city, Masada (the site of the Jewish resistance to Rome), the tomb of Maimonides, the synagogues of the fourth and fifth centuries, the synagogues of the medieval mystics in the city of Tsfat (also known in English as Safed). Each age of Jewish civilization has left its mark in Eretz Yisrael.

The great treasures that have come to light because of the careful studies and explorations of Israel's archaeologists—the most notable of which are the Dead Sea Scrolls—enrich our sense of belonging and of peoplehood wherever we live. The last time I was in Jerusalem, I went to the Israel Museum near the Knesset (the Israeli parliament) building and viewed an exhibition of pottery, jewelry, and glass from an unearthed tomb of the seventh century B.C.E. I passed each case fairly quickly until I was stopped by a spotlight illuminating a metal strip no larger than my thumb. Scratched onto this thin silver band were the ancient Hebrew words of the Birkat Kohanim (בִּרְכַּת כֹּהֲנִים), the priestly blessing. That little scroll, unearthed in Jerusalem, is the oldest existing fragment of biblical text. I stood staring at this prayer, one I recite every morning as part of the Shaḥarit (morn-

Israel's diversity often surprises those who know how small the country is. From the natural beauty of mountain, field, forest, and desert, to the ancient remains of the biblical and rabbinic past, to the modern metropolis of Tel Aviv, Israel is a marvel on many levels.

ing) service, and I began to weep. I wept at the mystery and majesty of finding my own spiritual expression rooted in almost three thousand years of Jewish living. Across the ages, a distant soul mate had found purpose, comfort, and identity in the same prayer that Jews today use at the start of their day.

• *Israel has restored pride and creativity to the entire Jewish people.*

For too long, Jews were reputed to be weak, passive, and incapable of productive work. Hidden inside dimly lit houses of study, Jewish pedants would supposedly mull over obscure and archaic books as the rest of the Jews lived in fear, poverty, and ignorance. Although that characterization is not an accurate reflection of Jewish history, it was shared by many Jews and non-Jews alike.

In the late nineteenth century, as nationalist movements planted the idea of independence in the minds of peoples around the world, a group of Jews recognized the need for a Jewish state to ensure Jewish liberty. Led by Theodor Herzl (1860–1904), these Jews created a political movement dedicated to establishing a Jewish government on Jewish soil. Herzl's stirring slogan was, "If you will it, it is no dream." They called themselves Zionists, reflecting their *ahavat Tziyon* (Zion being the hill in Jerusalem on which the Temple stood; Zion later became a name for all of Eretz Yisrael). A Zionist, then, is one who affirms the right of the Jewish people to exist as a free and sovereign people on their own soil.

The Zionist movement, and later the State of Israel, deliberately encouraged a new self-image for the Jew. Zionist women and men were pioneers. No longer figures of weakness or passivity, they transformed the desert into bounteous farmland, restoring ruined cities to prosperous settlements. Israel's ability to defend itself against a sea of hostile and implacable neighbors, Israel's vibrant (and occasionally chaotic) democratic system, and Israel's first-rate schools, research laboratories, and universities have restored

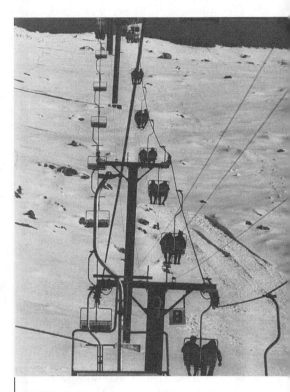

For those who want to ski, Israel's Mount Hermon offers snow-capped mountains and an opportunity to practice Hebrew at the same time.

an image of Jewish self-worth that had been denied for too long.

- *Israel is a center of Jewish cultural life.*

While it is certainly true that many Jewish artists, writers, and thinkers adorn Jewish communities of the Diaspora, it is no less true that Israel has had a tremendous impact on Jewish culture and thought throughout the world.

Think about how many synagogues and Jewish centers offer classes in modern Hebrew. Now recall that until this century, Hebrew was not a spoken language. Like classical Greek or Latin, Hebrew was a language that scholars and worshipers used for reading ancient literature and for prayers, but it hadn't been a living language for two thousand years. Zionism restored Hebrew to life.

Israel is a living laboratory for Jewish expression in the modern world. In Israel, Jews must resolve questions of power, violence, government, and the responsibility of being a ruling majority in ways that Jews elsewhere only think about. Israel's writers and thinkers exert an influence out of proportion to their numbers. Writers such as Amos Oz and A. B. Yehoshua, poets like Yehudah Amichai and Lea Goldberg, and philosophers such as David Hartman, Emil Fackenheim, and Eliezer Schweid have profoundly shaped Jewish thinking and Jewish culture through their insight and their talent.

- *Israel is a haven for Jewish refugees and an advocate for Jewish concerns on the international level.*

During the Shoah (שׁוֹאָה, "Holocaust"), practically every nation in the world closed its borders to the Jews. Countless millions would have survived if the Western democracies had taken them in. During World War II, Jews had nowhere to go. With the establishment of the State of Israel, all Jews acquired a second home. Israel has welcomed hundreds of thousands of refugees from Egypt, Yemen, Syria, Iraq, Iran, Eastern Europe, the former Soviet Union, Ethiopia, and elsewhere. By taking in tens of thousands of Ethiopian Jews, Israel became the only white

A SOURCE OF PRIDE
One morning, after I had just finished shopping in my neighborhood supermarket and was waiting to pay for my purchases, a group of nine-year-old boys walked in, absorbed in their conversation. I recognized one of them from our religious school. He saw me, smiled, and shouted across the entire store, "Hello, Rabbi!" Then he returned to his conversation with his friends.

He didn't notice what he had done. His friends thought nothing of it either—after all, they would just as easily have greeted their minister or priest the same way. But I was amazed. This child was so comfortable with his Jewishness that he didn't even consider whether or not to reveal it to the entire world. Being Jewish, for him, did not mean weakness or passivity. Instead, it was a source of pride. That lack of self-consciousness is, in no small measure, an outgrowth of the State of Israel.

country in the history of the world to voluntarily welcome and integrate as equals a large population of African people. Oppressed Jews are no longer abandoned—they now have a haven in Israel.

That concern for abandoned people extends beyond a concern for Jews alone. When the boat people of Southeast Asia were drowning at sea, Israel opened its arms to them. In fact, Israel took in more Indochinese refugees than any other country except the United States. When Arabs in Jordan or Lebanon need advanced medical help, they utilize the free medical expertise of Israeli hospitals. And following the catastrophic nuclear accident at Chernobyl, Israeli experts flew to the Soviet Union to help save hundreds of lives.

For all of these reasons—biblical memory, rabbinic longing and love, unity of the Jewish people, renewed Jewish culture, pride, and character, and a haven for oppressed Jews—we can benefit from a deepened link to the land and the citizens of Israel. What follows are steps toward renewing that relationship and demonstrating our love of Israel—*ahavat Tziyon*.

Israel is a nation of refugees from all over the world, an assurance that persecuted Jews will never again fear that they will be without a home. This group of Holocaust refugees found a haven in Israel, as have refugees from Asia, Africa, Europe, and elsewhere.

At times a source of tension, Israel is also a source of great joy. These people celebrate their love of Israel with their whole bodies, by joining in Israeli folk dancing.

1 **Reach out for news of Israeli current events.** Begin by reading any article in a newspaper or weekly magazine pertaining to Israel or the Middle East. Gradually, the welter of names, political parties, and geographic locations will start to make more sense. It is a common Jewish practice to scan the morning paper for any Israeli or Jewish news and only afterward to start over again for everything else. Get into the habit of reading the paper this way.

2 **Try reading one or two books about the State of Israel and its history.** The books listed in For Further Reading at the end of this chapter convey the emotional bond between Jews and Israel. For help in grasping the concrete reality of everyday events, the following are unsurpassed:

Howard Sachar, *A History of Israel* (2 vols.: Vol. 1, Philadelphia: Jewish Publication Society; Vol. 2, New York: Oxford University Press). There is

no better history of the modern State of Israel than this one. It provides an in-depth analysis of the country, and the writing is vivid and gripping. For the feel of Israeli history as well as for its facts, this book is highly recommended.

Abba Eban, *My Country: The Story of Modern Israel*. New York: Random House, 1972. A loving reflection by one of the founders of the State of Israel.

3 **Attend an annual Israel festival.** Reading about Israel is indispensable for those of us who don't live there, but capturing the vitality and humanity of Israel and its people also requires contact with other human beings. A good introduction to Israel is therefore the annual Israel festival, sponsored by all urban centers and many smaller towns as well. These fairs feature Israeli music, food, and dancing and often provide Jewish organizations with the opportunity to distribute information about programs in the local community and in Israel itself. Make a point of finding out where and when the local Israel festival is held, and enjoy it.

4 **Participate in Israeli folk dancing.** Israeli folk dances capture the excitement and idealism of the Israeli pioneers who returned to the land and established the state. They are also a way to cultivate a love of Israel while meeting people who share a common interest. Almost every community offers Israeli folk dance lessons. Often one evening a week is reserved for Israeli dancing, with instruction in the first hour and dancing the rest of the evening. The music is wonderful (and provides a chance to learn some Hebrew, too!), the participants are friendly, and the exercise is aerobic. Explore the local options for Israeli dancing, and try it out. Don't hesitate to show up alone—most Israeli dances are circle dances, so you don't need a partner.

5 **Begin a collection of Israeli and other Jewish music.** Collecting music is an easy way to learn synagogue melodies and Shabbat songs, and you can use time spent in the office, kitchen, or car to enjoy an Israeli experience. A growing knowledge of Israeli dances will naturally feed a desire to hear more Israeli music. There are many talented Israeli singers and instrumentalists who perform a wide range of music—cantorial, Israeli folk, jazz, rock, and even classical. Many cities have shops that carry Jewish religious items and recordings of Israeli music; some recordings are even available in popular record stores.

6 **Hang a *mizraḥ* on the eastern wall of any room of your home.** A *mizraḥ* (מִזְרָח, literally, "east") is a specially hand-lettered Hebrew hanging that can have any design, although it generally bears some representation of Jerusalem. A *mizraḥ* hangs on the eastern wall of a room because the east has

come to symbolize the direction of the Holy City. These hangings are a simple way to remember Israel inside your home. They are available at most Jewish gift shops and can be made with relative ease. It is also possible to hire an artist to design one that includes biblical and rabbinic verses that are personally meaningful.

7 **Use Israeli products.** A Friday night Shabbat dinner can feature Israeli wine, and many salads will improve with the addition of Israeli tomatoes. Using Israeli products helps Israel's economy and also strengthens a personal connection to the Jewish homeland.

This *mizraḥ*, in the style of Eastern European Jewish folk art, shows the classical symbols of the dove (symbol of peace and of the Jewish people), the fish (symbol of fertility), and a flowering of plants, symbolic of God's bounty in general and of the Land of Israel in particular.

8 Read Israeli fiction and display Israeli art.

The use of Israeli products can extend beyond food and clothing. Israeli writers are producing first-rate creations that are readily available in English. Fiction by writers such as Amos Oz and A. B. Yehoshua and poetry by Yehuda Amichai and others are sold in popular bookstores nationwide. Artwork by Israeli painters and sculptors is displayed in galleries everywhere. Familiarize yourself with Israeli writers and decorate your home or office with works by Israeli artists.

9 Help rebuild Israel's land by planting trees.

By planting millions of trees and carefully tending the soil, Israel has revitalized land that was once fertile but became desert. The driving force behind this reclamation has been the Jewish National Fund. The JNF organizes massive tree plantings and provides equipment and machinery to maintain and cultivate Israeli land. Parks, settlements, homes, and nature preserves all emerge from the work of the JNF. There are two simple ways to help improve Israel's land:

• *Get a JNF* pushka *(a coin box), and make a daily practice of dropping a quarter in the box.* Other members of the household should be encouraged to do the same. Not only will they learn the value of *tzedakah* (צְדָקָה, literally, "righteousness"; a monetary contribution), but they will also feel a growing connection to the soil and the plants of Israel.

• *Celebrate special events (birthdays, anniversaries, graduations) by planting a tree in Israel.* The JNF will send a beautiful certificate in honor of the occasion.

The address and phone number of the national office are
Jewish National Fund
42 East 69th Street
New York, NY 10021
212-879-9300

Planting a tree in one of the JNF's forests is a wonderful way to celebrate a *simḥah*, console a mourner, and strengthen the Land of Israel.

Children's Forest in Israel יער הילדים

A TREE HAS BEEN PLANTED

In honor of
MR. and MRS.
STEPHEN KLINGHOFFER &
DAUGHTERS

In celebration of

MELANIE KAYE'S
BAT MITZVAH

JEWISH NATIONAL FUND   קרן קימת לישראל

Local offices exist in many larger communities. Check your phone book, or call a nearby synagogue to find out where there is a local office in your community.

10 The inevitable next step—and it's a big one—is to visit Israel.

Israel is a beautiful country. Its climate ranges from snow-capped Mount Hermon in the north to the sunny beaches of Eilat in the far south. There are archaeological remains of biblical Israel, the Jewish revolt against Rome, Crusader castles, and Moslem shrines. But Israel is more than a tour. It is the Jewish country. Those who have never been to Israel are in for a surprise. Jews do everything—they drive the buses, they walk the beat as police officers, they are construction laborers, professors, and politicians. In Israel, banks and schools close on Saturday, because that is Shabbat, and Jewish holy days are the national holidays, in contrast to Christmas and Easter in Europe and North America.

A first trip to Israel should probably be with an organized group. That way, you will be sure to see all the main sights and receive a good overall picture of the country and its people. Many organizations sponsor these kinds of trips. The American Jewish Congress is known for its wonderful travel plans (they organize vacations of Jewish interest worldwide, not just in Israel), and synagogues regularly sponsor trips to Israel with their rabbi. The advantage of such trips is that they allow you not only to explore Israel but also to build community and friendships at home.

A visit to Israel is in many ways a homecoming. There are no words to describe adequately the feelings of being there. For the treat of a lifetime, go already!

---

11 **Begin to learn Hebrew.** An essential aspect of modern Israel is the revitalization of *Ivrit* (עִבְרִית, the Hebrew language). Although *Ivrit* was the language of the Bible and of the earliest rabbinic writing, by the time of the destruction of Jerusalem's Second Temple (in 70 C.E.) many Jews no longer used Hebrew as a living language. For two thousand years, Hebrew was a language for scholarship, writing, prayer, and reading. The early Zionists made a conscious decision to revive a "dead" language, and the father of that effort, Eliezer ben Yehudah, created thousands of words to describe modern experiences and inventions (there was no word for *electricity* in the Bible, so ben Yehudah borrowed the name of a fiery angel last heard of in the tenth century!).

There are many ways to study Hebrew. The most effective way is to spend a summer in Israel studying at an Ulpan (אֻלְפָּן, an intensive language program for learning spoken Hebrew). Class conversation is conducted exclusively in Hebrew, and learning becomes a game of conversation and dramatizations, using a variety of approaches, such as advertisements and pictures from Israeli newspapers and magazines. A variety of settings in Israel—universities, kibbutzim, and yeshivot—offer excellent programs. If it is at all possible to spend a summer learning Hebrew, don't think twice about it.

Many of us, however, can't take so much time off. Fortunately, Hebrew is a hot item even in North America. The language is taught in most colleges, and synagogues and Jewish community centers also offer a range of Hebrew classes (although synagogue Hebrew classes tend to focus more on prayerbook Hebrew and less on conversational skills). In any case, the essential first step is to find a Hebrew class and begin to learn the language.

For many adults, learning Hebrew conjures up memories of after-school memorization. But how many of us still remember what we learned? It's never too late to learn again our language, the language of the Torah and prophets, the language of Israel.

12 **Become active in an Israeli advocacy organization.** A growing awareness of the political realities of Israel will doubtless compel advocacy of Israel. As a passionate lover of Israel, it's important to remember that it is possible to love Israel without supporting every action of the government and every action of every Israeli politician.

Focus your advocacy on certain basic facts: Jews have a right to a national homeland, just as all other peoples do. Israel's millions of Jews have a right to live and work in peace and security. Israel is the only democracy in the

Middle East, the only state in the Middle East in which women have the right to vote, and its Arab citizens vote freely in all elections. Israel, a country equal to the size of New Jersey, has been surrounded by twenty-two hostile Arab states. It has taken almost fifty years for Arab states to begin recognizing the Jewish state, and that recognition resulted in Israel's ceding almost one third of the territory under its control to Egypt as part of a peace negotiation. Israel has absorbed millions of Jewish refugees from Arab states, Africa, Europe, the former Soviet Union, and elsewhere and has defended itself against the attacks of the combined Arab armies in four wars.

Many recent events have been extremely encouraging: The PLO, an organization once devoted explicitly to the destruction of the Jewish state, has publicly recognized Israel's right to exist and now deplores acts of violence against civilians and soldiers alike. Several Arab governments have begun to make overtures to Israel, and negotiations with many of them are under way. Still, formidable challenges remain: the status of Jerusalem as Israel's undivided capital, the Arab boycott against any corporations that do business with Israel, and the question of how to allocate the rare resources of the Middle East, especially water. These challenges, as well as the continuing issue of Israel's security, will require the vigilance of concerned people everywhere.

There is a wide range of organizations and groups speaking on behalf of Israel and mobilizing American resources to further several different points of view. You might want to explore the different emphases of such groups as the American Israel Public Affairs Committee, the American Jewish Congress, the American Jewish Committee, the Zionist Organization of America, and a host of other groups. Their commitments range from activism promoting relations between Israel's Jews and its Arab populations, specific peace initiatives, and support from the United States government. Some of these organizations represent the social mainstream of America while others are more aggressively on the "right" or the "left" of the political spectrum. Research into the work of these organizations is a good way to learn about Israel's needs and America's Jewish pluralism.

13 **Open savings and checking accounts in Israeli banks.** Israeli banks have branch offices in American cities with large Jewish populations. In North America, those banks are Bank Leumi, Bank Hapoalim, and the Mizrachi Bank. Your accounts will help support Israel in a concrete way, and each check you write will remind you that a part of your heart is in Jerusalem.

14 **Subscribe to an Israeli English-language newspaper or magazine.** For many American Jews, Israel means military conflict, Jewish political parties, and rabbis arguing about legislation. Our focus on Israeli politics, especially foreign affairs, is understandable but ignores the real drama of Israeli life. Israeli culture, education, and art produce vibrant expressions of what it means to live as a Jew in the modern world. Our understanding of ourselves and our heritage can blossom if it includes contemporary Israeli culture. There is no better way to keep informed of Israel's breadth and depth than by subscribing to an Israeli English-language paper. *The Jerusalem Post, International Edition,* is an excellent weekly. To subscribe, contact

Jerusalem Post, International Edition
P.O. Box 1181
Danbury, CT 06813
203-792-1450

A weekly magazine, *The Jerusalem Report,* offers a broader coverage of Israeli politics and culture as well as reporting on Jewish news from around the world. Subscribe by calling 1-800-827-1119. *The Jerusalem Report* is by far the best available coverage of Israel in English.

15 **Work on a kibbutz, study at one of Israel's excellent universities, or enroll in a yeshivah course on traditional Jewish writings.** A growing awareness of Israel reflects an expanding definition of community that includes the Jewish people worldwide. That loving bond, a sense of responsibility and belonging, will enrich life and alter the way the world looks. It is a link well worth cultivating. After a first trip to Israel, you can return with the benefit of having had a good overall introduction to the country. Now a different kind of trip is possible. Rather than repeating the basic tour, look for a program that will focus on one aspect of Israel: living on a kibbutz, studying at an Israeli university, or enrolling in a yeshivah course on traditional Jewish writings. Noteworthy among the latter is Pardes:

Pardes Institute
P.O. Box 926
Avon, CT 06001

Pardes enables men and women to study together as equals rather than separately, as is the custom at most yeshivot, and offers excellent programs for those who have no previous exposure to Talmud study.

16 **Strengthen your family's connection to Israel by enrolling your children in an Israeli summer program.** Programs affiliated with the Conservative movement include

Camp Ramah in Israel
3080 Broadway
New York, NY 10027

United Synagogue Youth Israel
    Pilgrimage
155 Fifth Avenue
New York, NY 10010-6802

Programs affiliated with the Reform movement are organized through

Department of Israel Programs
Union of American Hebrew
    Congregations
838 Fifth Avenue
New York, NY 10021-7064

Programs affiliated with the Orthodox movement are organized through

Orthodox Union
333 Seventh Avenue
New York, NY 10001

All of these programs allow children to establish friendships and learn about Judaism and Israel to the rhythms of Jewish living. At the same time, their parents are free to spend time in Israel pursuing their own interests.

17 **For those in a position to give money, Israel is a worthy cause.** Jews have always shown a sense of collective responsibility, with one Jew providing for others in times of need. Helping Jews live in freedom and security in their own land and as productive members of the international community is a lofty ideal that can be realized in part with our help.

The preeminent means of getting donations from here to there is the Jewish Federation/United Jewish Appeal, which exists in almost every community in North America. A way of lending money to the Israeli government is through the purchase of Israeli bonds. If you prefer a less establishment-oriented organization for your charity, consider the New Israel Fund, which channels money to foster Jewish–Arab relations, religious pluralism, and improved status of women in Israel.

New Israel Fund
111 West 40th Street, Suite 2300
New York, NY 10018

Another fine organization that channels American contributions to a wonderful array of deserving Israeli institutions is Danny Siegel's ZIV Tzedakah Fund. For more information write

Danny Siegel
Danny Siegel's ZIV Tzedakah Fund
263 Congressional Lane, Suite 708
Rockville, MD 20852

By joining MERCAZ, the Zionist organization of Conservative Judaism, you can show your support for Zionism, Israel, and Conservative Jews in Israel.

MERCAZ
155 Fifth Avenue
New York, NY 10010-6802

Additionally, each religious stream of Judaism has a fund-raising organization to help establish synagogues and religious schools in Israel:

The Foundation for Conservative/
    Masorti Judaism in Israel
Presidential Building
6525 Belcrest Road, Suite 305
Hyattsville, MD 20782

Association of Reform Zionists
    of America (ARZA)
838 Fifth Avenue
New York, NY 10021-7064

Orthodox Union
333 Seventh Avenue
New York, NY 10001

By donating to these organizations, you make possible the flowering of the kind of religious pluralism which characterizes American Judaism at its best.

---

18 **The ultimate demonstration of the mitzvah *ahavat Tziyon* is to live in Israel.** More than money or visitors, Israel desperately needs Jews to commit their future, their career, and their family to building a home in Eretz Yisrael. Making aliyah (settling in Israel) provides for your growth as a Jew in a way not possible elsewhere. Only in Israel can a Jew live in a society in which a majority of the citizens are Jewish, where the spoken language is Hebrew, where the holidays are Jewish holidays, where the schools teach children the literature of Torah, Talmud, midrash, and the Hebrew poets. Only in Israel do Jews wrestle with questions of integrating their Judaism with sovereignty and power. And only in Israel is there a total rootedness in Jewish history and destiny.

Many Jews will choose not to live in Israel, but every Jew should consider the possibility. Like every other mitzvah, aliyah does not have to be an all-or-nothing venture. Spending a month each year or acquiring a second home in Israel instead of elsewhere is a way of embarking on a partial aliyah, one that creates a permanent connection to the land and the people of Israel.

❖   ❖   ❖   ❖   ❖

Rabbi Abba used to kiss the stones of Akko, while Rabbi Ḥanina would mend the roads, and Rabbi Ḥiyya ben Gamda would lie down in the dust of the Holy Land. All this to fulfill the passage, "Your servants take delight in its stones and cherish its dust." —TALMUD, KETUBBOT 112A

For Further Reading

Saul Bellow, *To Jerusalem and Back: A Personal Account.* New York: Viking Press, 1976.

Abraham Joshua Heschel, *Israel: An Echo of Eternity.* New York: Farrar, Straus and Giroux, 1969.

5 Bal Tash'ḥit:
Preserving the Earth

How varied Your works, Adonai; in wisdom have You made them all. The Earth is filled with Your creatures.

—PSALM 104:24

The Holy Blessed One took the first human and, passing before all the trees of the Garden of Eden, said, "See My works, how fine and excellent they are! All that I created, I created for you. Consider that, and do not corrupt or desolate My world; for if you corrupt it, there will be no one to set it right after you." —KOHELET RABBAH 1, ON 7:13

The Torah begins with both a challenge and a responsibility. After creating the world, God instructs the first humans to "replenish the earth and master it." As the appointed caretakers of the Garden of Eden, they are to "till it and tend it." The beginning of the Torah thus reminds us that we live in a world we did not create, a world we do not own; we are the tenants and residents of God's world. As such, it is our role to live responsibly as a part of the world God created. We demonstrate our mastery of the earth not by despoiling it, nor by endangering habitation, but by fashioning a way of living that nurtures human potential and sustains all life.

There are so many ways that the earth gives us pleasure: the warmth of the sun, the crash of the waves, the comfort of the rain, and the tranquility of a fresh snowfall. All of those gifts nurture our lives and add beauty to our days. They also summon us to respond by taking responsibility for the well-being of the earth and its ability to sustain life.

This chapter is a summons to address consciously the way we live in the world, the way in which we can curtail our extravagance and wastefulness, and the way in which we can restore a sense of balance between our need to live off the earth and our need to preserve it. The cardinal mitzvah in this regard is *bal tash'ḥit* (בַּל תַּשְׁחִית , "do not destroy"). In essence, it is a prohibition against being wasteful, a recognition that the objects we fashion and own are not so much created by our will as borrowed from nature. According to one medieval rabbi, those who are mindful of this mitzvah "will not destroy even a mustard seed in the world, and they are distressed at every ruination and spoilage that they see; and if they are able to do any rescuing, they will save anything from destruction, with all their power."

In previous ages, concern for the well-being of our surroundings reflected a basic philosophy of living in harmony with God's creation. Now, however, human ingenuity and the need for new sources of energy have affected that outlook. Too often we treat the earth as an instrument for our manipulation rather than as a system in which we live and of which we are a part. The effects of our overproduction together with our constant need for convenience have global implications that have already caused permanent and destructive changes to the natural order:

• Humanity has increased the level of carbon dioxide by 25 percent in the last century, and that level will double in the next. The release of this and other gases has produced the greenhouse effect: the trapping of gas emissions under the atmosphere's blanket. The greenhouse effect is expected to produce global warming of three to eight degrees by the year 2050. United Nations reports suggest that an increase of as little as three degrees could cause the sea level to rise by two meters, a phenomenon that would cause widespread flooding of coastal cities.

• Chlorofluorocarbons (CFCs) used in airconditioners, refrigeration, plastic foam, and other products are burning a hole through the ozone layer, which blocks harmful ultraviolet radiation from reaching the earth's surface.

• Air pollution has created yet another disaster—acid rain. This downpour has impaired twenty thousand Canadian lakes and has damaged more than 14 percent of Europe's forests as well as historic buildings and monuments.

• Ten percent of the world's rivers are heavily polluted, and the Environmental Protection Agency notes the presence of more than 700 chemicals— more than 129 of them termed "dangerous"—in American drinking water.

• Twenty billion tons of waste end up in the ocean each year, and over 180 million gallons of motor oil, the equivalent of sixteen Exxon *Valdez* oil

If we handle waste recklessly, the Talmud (*Bava Kama* 50b) reminds us, we will only harm ourselves.

The annual celebration of Earth Day reminds us to cherish our connection to the earth and to care for its well-being. It also reminds us that it takes effort, cooperation, and spirit to keep our planet vibrant.

spills, are either sent to landfills or poured down the drain. The EPA estimates that 80 percent of the landfills now in operation will reach capacity within twenty years.

We already possess the knowledge to prevent this destruction, but we may not have the vision and the will to alter the way we live. What we require is not only behavior modification but a different framework for understanding the world and our place in it.

EVERY DAY IS EARTH DAY

There is a little-known ritual that is performed every twenty-eight years: *Birkat ha-Ḥammah* (בְּרְכַּת הַחַמָּה , "Blessing the Sun"). According to the Talmud, the vernal equinox cycle takes twenty-eight years, so Jews thank God for the sun and its life-giving rays at the commencement of each new solar cycle. This is one of many Jewish rituals designed to sensitize us to the wonder of nature. As the year of the *Birkat ha-Ḥammah* approaches, a flurry of articles, classes, and books are published to educate the Jewish people about this ritual. Once the date has passed, the excitement wears off and most of us forget that such an event ever happened.

In the West, we have begun a practice that occurs once a year, known as Earth Day. Like the *Birkat ha-Ḥammah* , it seeks to direct our attention to the importance of the natural world. As with the *Birkat ha-Ḥammah* , the hoopla and commitment that surround Earth Day reach a crescendo and it is soon forgotten. Earth Day may pass, but the earth does not go away. This planet, our home, is in need of our attention not once a year but every day.

As a result, today's environmental concerns reflect another mitzvah, *va-ḥai bahem* (וְחַי בָּהֶם , "and you shall live by them"). Our very survival depends on adopting a more balanced approach to the way we live our lives and the way we measure our wealth and well-being.

Traditional Judaism is not a proselytizing religion. We do not seek to convert through missionary activity or religious argument. Instead, we try to demonstrate the benefits of sacred living by making ourselves role models. This approach is no less appropriate in transforming our way of living in the world. How we use resources in our homes and personal lives can have a significant impact on the health of our planet. The following are suggestions on how to begin this process. Our future, our children, and our planet hang in the balance.

❖   ❖   ❖   ❖   ❖

1 **Become a member of an environmental group.** At its core, the environmental movement is about expanding our ability to empathize and revere. We need to transcend the borders of states, nations, even species. As *shomrei adamah* (שׁוֹמְרֵי אֲדָמָה, "guardians of the earth"), we can cultivate our identification with the earth and its cycles.

A first step is to join an environmental organization that will educate, provide a sense of common purpose, and effectively guide practical involvement. Countless groups exist to cultivate an appreciation of nature and to produce effective advocacy on its behalf. There are organizations that quietly raise funds and use them to purchase wild lands, organizations that sponsor camping and hiking expeditions, and groups that lobby politicians in behalf of environmental issues. (The books listed in For Further Reading at the end of this chapter contain comprehensive lists of such groups.)

A Jewish environmental group, Shomrei Adamah ("Guardians of the Earth"), has launched programs for religious school curricula, lecture series, and social action and has produced many publications. Shomrei Adamah is a valuable addition to the array of Jewish organizations functioning in the public arena. Contact them at

> Shomrei Adamah
> 5500 Wissahickon Avenue, Suite 804C
> Philadelphia, PA 19144
> 215-844-8150

2 **Practice traditional Jewish rituals that reflect our connection to the natural world.** A step toward cultivating an awareness of the natural world involves using the tools of traditional Jewish practice. Judaism is permeated with environmental consciousness: Shabbat (see Chapter 12) and the holy days can sensitize us to the cycles of the seasons and remind us not to intervene in nature. They repre-

sent a call to fulfill our sense of self-worth by reflecting God's image, not by amassing more possessions. Kashrut (see Chapter 8) encourages us to be more conscious of animal life and its sanctity. Over and over, the Jewish way of life encourages an awareness of the wonder and connection to all creation. The following are three opportunities for developing this awareness.

• *Begin reciting the* birkhot ha-nehenin (בִּרְכוֹת הַנֶּהֱנִין, "blessings of enjoyment"). These blessings can be found in most traditional prayerbooks.[1] As a way of becoming sensitive to the wonders of nature, practice reciting the *birkhot ha-nehenin* at the appropriate occasions. There are blessings to say when smelling fragrant spices; when smelling trees, shrubs, fruit, or fragrant oils; when witnessing wonders of nature, hearing thunder, and seeing a rainbow, the ocean, or trees in blossom.

• *Buy a Jewish calendar, and make a point of following it throughout the seasons.* The Jewish calendar corresponds to natural phenomena: the length of the year is determined by the cycle of the sun, and the months are determined by the cycle of the moon. By living according to the Jewish calendar, we become connected to the rhythms of nature. Notice when Rosh Ḥodesh (רֹאשׁ חֹדֶשׁ, the "new month") begins, and correlate that date with the phase of the moon. When the moon is not visible or when it is just a sliver, then it is Rosh Ḥodesh. When the full moon is visible, around the fifteenth day of the Jewish month, then the month is half over.

• *Between the third and fifteenth days of the Jewish month, it is traditional to bless the new moon.* This blessing, *Kiddush L'vanah* (קִדּוּשׁ לְבָנָה, "Sanctification of the Moon"), is a collection of Psalms and talmudic wisdom and a *berakhah* (בְּרָכָה, "blessing") thanking God for the possibility of renewal. It is customarily recited outdoors, under the light of the moon itself.[2]

"The Creator of heaven, who alone is God, Who formed the earth and made it, did not establish it as waste, but formed it for habitation."
(Isaiah 45:18)

These and other blessings focus our attention on the marvel of being alive and on the joy of being able to perceive natural wonders. By our cultivating an awareness of how wonderful the world is, our motivation to care for it will also increase.

3 **Celebrate Tu b'Shevat.** While almost every Jewish holy day and festival reflects some aspect of how we should live in harmony with the earth, one day is unique in its attention to the celebration of trees, and that is Tu b'Shevat (ט"וּ בִּשְׁבָט, the fifteenth day of the month of Shevat).

According to the Mishnah, Tu b'Shevat is the day that marks the new year for trees. (In biblical times, it was important to establish the age of a tree in order to observe the laws of tithing fruit.) Today, this day is often marked by a seder—a short celebration which includes drinking four cups of wine, ranging from lightest white wine to darkest red, and eating four different types of fruit. The themes of the meal include appreciating the beauty of the world, the cycle of the seasons, and our special love for the Land of Israel. Often the evening concludes with the planting of a tree.

If you've never attended a Tu b'Shevat seder, you're in for a treat. Contact a local synagogue sometime in late January to find out when and where the seder will be.

4 **Conserve water.** Because there is a limited amount of usable water (only 3 percent of all the water available on the earth is fresh water, and less than 1 percent of it is surface water, the only kind available for human use), we must make conservation and restraint a way of life, not simply responses to an emergency. A variety of simple actions can reduce the amount of water we use—and often waste:

• *Purchase sink-faucet aerators, low-flow shower head aerators, and a water-displacement device for your toilet. These inexpensive gadgets* are available at hardware stores. They will significantly reduce the amount of water consumed without compromising your aesthetic or practical sense of how much water you need.

• *Water plants in the early morning or at night, and plant regionally appropriate gardens.* When plants are watered in the middle of the day, most of the water is lost to evaporation. Water your plants at the coolest times of the day, therefore, to limit the amount of water you waste. Even more important, plant regionally appropriate gardens—don't grow a water-hungry Connecticut lawn if you live in the desert.

• *Shave with an electric razor.* By not using a disposable razor, you will avoid wasting the water necessary to clean it. You will also save the energy and material it takes to make a razor that you will probably throw away after a few uses. An additional benefit: Jewish law prohibits shaving with a razor that comes in contact with the skin (because this was an idolatrous practice of Canaanite priests throughout the biblical period). Using a triple-headed razor, in which the razor never touches the face, will save water, raw materials, and energy, and it will enable you to observe yet another mitzvah. Even shaving can become sacred!

• *Use a phosphate-free detergent.* The tons of phosphate we release into our water supply choke our rivers, lakes, and streams. Liquid detergents are usually free of phosphate. Also, use a little less detergent than is recommended—the people who manufacture the detergent often suggest using more of it than is necessary so that you will buy more of their product.

5 **Conserve Resources.** The way we use our water, handle our garbage, drive our cars, generate and use energy, and preserve life can reflect a wisdom and a concern that will preserve the environment for future generations. The key to wasting fewer resources and producing less garbage is a combination of recycling and restraint.

• *Whenever possible, recycle.* The United States recycles only 10 percent of its garbage (in contrast to Japan, which recycles 50 percent). Paper, glass and plastic bottles, and metal products can often be recycled. If your community doesn't already have a recycling program in effect, call your state or local government for information about initiating one, and then get involved. As a way to improve the world, recycling is an excellent project for a religious school, a synagogue social-justice committee, or a youth group.

• *Avoid using disposable diapers.* Plastic diapers make up 4 percent of our disposable waste and take an estimated five hundred years to decompose. According to Environmental Action, three million tons of untreated feces and urine, known to contain over one hundred different intestinal viruses, end up in landfills rather

Taking the time to recycle is a mitzvah: "Whoever destroys something useful is violating the principle, 'You shall not be destructive.'" Midrash Aggadah to Judges 20.

than sewage systems (where they could be purified and cleaned to preclude any health hazards or long-term danger). In addition, the disposable-diaper industry uses more than a billion trees each year for the inner lining of the diapers. If giving up disposable diapers doesn't seem possible, compromise—use cloth diapers at home and disposable diapers when you're out. Or alternate, using disposables only every other time.

• *Limit the amount of packaging you bring home.* Eight percent of American steel is used for packaging, as is 40 percent of American aluminum, 70 percent of American glass, and 50 percent of American paper. All of these resources are used once, briefly, and then thrown out. One third of the average American's garbage is packaging. Buy the most simply packaged products, and buy in bulk so that less packaging is required.

• *After shopping at the grocery store, keep the shopping bags in your car and reuse them the next time you go grocery shopping.* Better still, purchase some cloth bags, which can be reused indefinitely.

• *Don't use plastic.* Styrofoam and other plastic foams are made with CFCs, which destroy the ozone layer and don't decompose. At restaurants that use foam or plastic, ask for paper instead. At home, use mugs instead of paper cups, and always use paper cups instead of plastic if a disposable cup is the only option.

• *Store food in containers rather than in plastic or aluminum wrap.* In general, it is a good idea to use something that can be reused rather than something that must be thrown out after one use.

• *Avoid disposables.* Lighters, pens, plastic utensils, paper napkins—the list of disposables is endless, but our resources are not. Whenever possible, use a nondisposable version—a refillable lighter, a refillable pen, stainless steel utensils, cloth napkins.

• *Avoid toxic and other hazardous products.* The number of dangerous products we bring into our home is astounding—nail-polish remover, flea collars, the fluid used to unclog drains, oven cleaners, motor oil, paint, mothballs, and air fresheners. These products, and many more, not only cause harm to our lungs, but cause long-term damage to our air, water, and ground. In general, substitute natural products for artificial ones, and limit your use of artificial products whenever possible. For substitutes, consult the books listed in For Further Reading at the end of this chapter.

• *Stop junk mail.* Obscene amounts of paper and energy are wasted on mail that most of us never read or only glance at briefly on the way to a trash can. To stop this uninvited intrusion, write to

Mail Preference Service
Direct Marketing Association
P.O. Box 9008
Farmingdale, NY 11735-9008

In the meantime, mark all unsolicited junk mail RETURN TO SENDER and let the sender pay the postage in both directions!

---

6 **Care for your car**. The automobile is a necessity for most people, but it is also one of the principal causes of the air pollution in most areas of the industrial world. By modifying our driving practices, we can make a real reduction in air pollution.

• *Keep your car in good repair.* A well-tuned car is more energy efficient than one that is run-down. Similarly, adequately filled tires—and radial tires if possible—add to a car's efficiency.

• *Don't use a car as a substitute for an attic or a garage.* Each extra pound in your car requires that much more fuel to transport it. Take with you what you need, and leave the rest in storage.

• *Drive a fuel-efficient car.* Try to drive a car that gets at least forty miles to a gallon of gas.

• *Use your car as little as possible.* Whenever you can, walk, bike, car-pool, or take public transportation. Many environmental groups recommend not using a car one day a week. For a Jewish slant on this, consider not driving on Shabbat. Refraining from driving will help make the day distinctive, allow you to feel restful, and give the day an atmosphere of a twenty-four-hour respite. (For more on this, mitzvah, see Chapter 12, step 7.)

• *Whenever possible, avoid using the air-conditioner.* Roll down the window instead. Each time we use air-conditioning, we decrease the fuel efficiency of our cars and consume more energy. This is true in our homes and offices as well.

---

7 **Conserve energy at home.**

• *Substitute compact fluorescent lights for conventional bulbs.* These bulbs use significantly less electricity. They will save money and allow that energy to go to other uses.

• *Set your water heater to 120 degrees.*

• *Set your refrigerator to between 38 and 42 degrees and your freezer to between 0 and 5 degrees.*

• *Insulate your home.* A tremendous amount of heat and air-conditioning are lost simply because of poor insulation. Insulate your home with storm windows or double-paned windows, caulk, and weather-strip. Close off and block the air vents in unused rooms.

• *Wash only a full load of laundry at a time.*

The degree to which these simple steps will save energy—and money—may surprise you.

---

8 **Preserve life.** In addition to recycling and paying more attention to our consumption of limited resources, we can take many other steps to affirm life. Among them are the following:

• *Plant trees.* Trees are the lungs of the earth. They absorb carbon dioxide and minimize the greenhouse effect. We have already discussed the importance of planting trees in Israel, but trees are important in every part of the world, including our neighborhoods. So get out there and plant some trees.

• *Stop smoking.* Cigarette smoking is the leading avoidable cause of cancer in adults. No one is too old to derive health benefits from quitting. In addition, think of all the packaging that won't be used, all the lighters that won't be needed, and all the hospital expenses so easily avoided. Not only does smoking violate the mitzvah of *bal tash'ḥit,* but it also runs counter to the injunction *va-ḥai bahem,* to live. So quit — it's an easy way to please the people you love.

• *Get political.* Not every problem can be addressed on a purely individual basis, and cleaning up the earth is one that cannot be. The polluters are well organized and wealthy; they spend a great deal of energy, time, and resources influencing the government to encourage their profitable ways. We need to outorganize and outmobilize them on behalf of life, and on behalf of God's creation.

We need to align ourselves with environmental groups that can effectively influence our elected representatives, and we need to organize

❖   ❖   ❖   ❖   ❖

A contemporary sage, Rabbi Simon Greenberg of the Jewish Theological Seminary, taught a succinct way of understanding a Jew's overarching obligation. At the end of the Creation story, God looked at all that had been created and declared that it was *tov m'od* (טוב מְאֹד, "very good"). Rabbi Greenberg asserted that our role in life is to live our lives and organize our communities so that we vindicate God's judgment, fashioning a world that is truly *tov m'od*.

When we learn to live in such a way that life on earth is able to replenish itself and sustain the planet's inhabitants, when we replace our carelessness and wastefulness with responsibility and consciousness, when we labor as caretakers of a world that is neither our plaything nor our property, then we will have taken a large step toward bringing God's judgment to fruition.

Creation can be *tov m'od*, and it is up to us, as God's partners in Creation, to restore the world's goodness to its original splendor. The wonder and beauty of the world are an inheritance worthy of the God who made them; that we may transmit them to our descendants is a privilege and a credit to our ability to care for the world and for all living things.

Every day is Earth Day.

a neighborhood committee or a synagogue group devoted to environmental action.

Time is short, the rewards are great, and the cause is waiting.

"The earth is Adonai's, with all it contains; the world and all its inhabitants." Psalm 24:1

For Further Reading

Ruth Caplan, et al., *Our Earth, Ourselves: The Action-Oriented Guide to Help You Protect and Preserve Our Planet.* New York: Bantam Books, 1990.

The Earthworks Group, *50 Simple Things You Can Do to Save the Earth.* Berkeley, CA: Earthworks Press, 1989.

Jeremy Rifkin, ed., *The Green Lifestyle Handbook: 1001 Ways You Can Heal the Earth.* New York: Henry Holt, 1990.

WHERE TO FIND IT IN THE PRAYERBOOK

1. Birkhot Ha-Nehenin

Siddur Sim Shalom. New York: Rabbinical Assembly, 1985, pages 708-13.

Gates of the House. New York: Central Conference of American Rabbis, 1977, pages 19-23.

The Complete Artscroll Siddur. Brooklyn, NY: Mesorah Publications Ltd, 1984, page 224.

2. Kiddush L'vanah

Siddur Sim Shalom, page 704.

The Complete Artscroll Siddur, pages 612-17.

Gates of the House, pages 25–26

6 Bikkur Ḥolim:
Visiting the Sick

The Holy Blessed One visited the sick, as it is written, "Adonai appeared to him by the terebinths of Mamre," and so you must also visit the sick.

—TALMUD, SOTAH

One who visits the sick causes them to live.

—TALMUD, NEDARIM 40A

Hope is the gift we bring when we visit the sick. By sitting with a bedridden friend, we let that person know that he or she is not forgotten, that the outside world still cares. We offer hope by discussing plans for the future, by sharing the latest news from work, the latest adventures of a mutual friend, or the most recent cultural event. By bringing information from beyond the four walls of the sick room, we expand the horizons of the sick person, allowing him or her to enjoy a renewed fullness of vision and a sense of belonging. Of course, the most precious gift we can offer is our concerned attention: We can listen to the individual who is suffering from an illness.

Anyone who has ever been sick remembers how important such visits were. Each of us carries memories of the time someone touched us, of a gift that brought a sense of expectancy and a promise for

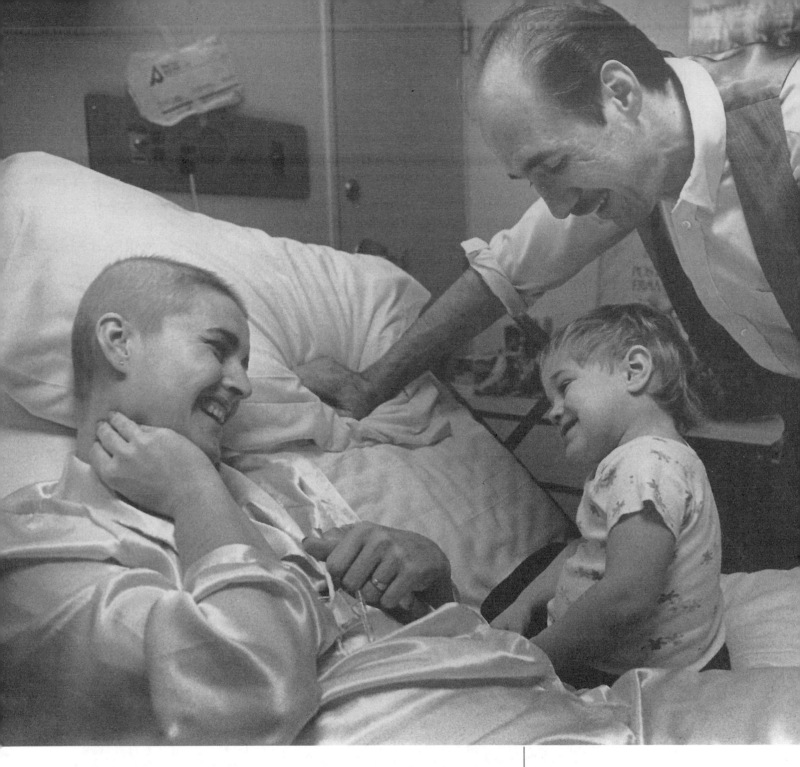

the future, of a phone call at precisely that moment when we were feeling lowest. To be able to lift someone's spirits by such a simple gesture as sending a card or visiting for a few minutes is to make ourselves truly *shutafei ha-Kadosh Barukh Hu* (שֻׁתָּפֵי הַקָּדוֹשׁ בָּרוּךְ הוּא, "partners with God").

Yet even as we recognize the importance of *bikkur ḥolim* (בִּקּוּר חוֹלִים, "visiting the sick"), even as we feel grateful to those brave and loving people who came to visit us in our sickness, we still feel hesitant,

Even in moments of illness, the love we share for each other remains a source of strength, comfort, and healing. Jewish traditions for visiting the sick give expression to our love, ensuring that illness and pain cannot separate us from the people we cherish.

awkward, and fearful when it comes to visiting the sick ourselves. Resistance to visiting the sick is quite common and emerges from several different concerns, among them the following.

    • *We are afraid of illness and death.* Watching someone wrestle with a serious illness is terrifying. It conjures the thought, "that will be me some day." Most of us apportion our time as though we will live forever. Visiting someone who is sick or dying forces us to confront our own mortality and the recognition that our time is finite, a limitation most of us would rather ignore.

While we may fear illness and death, its inevitability can also spur us to reach out to those who need our care. The gap separating the generations fades into insignificance in the face of our common humanity, and the greatest blessings are often bestowed by a hug.

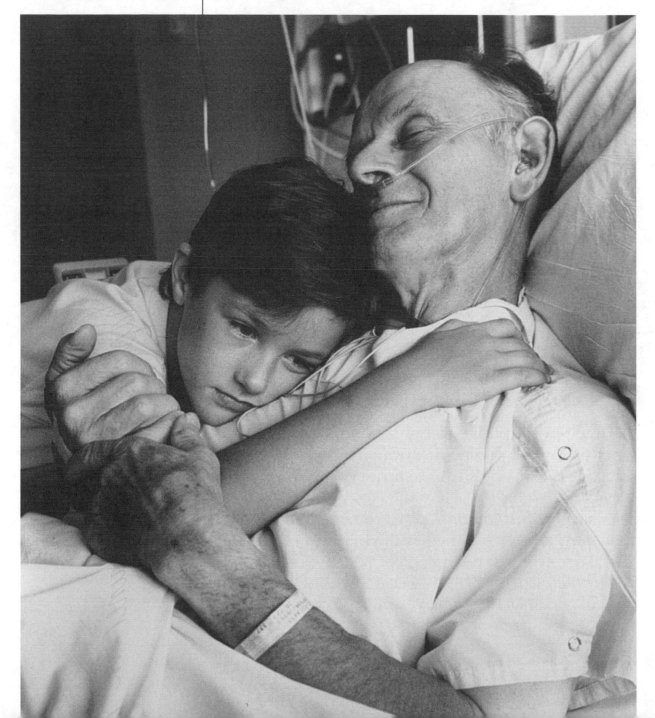

• *We fear a loss of control.* When visiting the sick, we are forced to confront the terrifying reality that life does not tailor itself to our desires or our demands. We are forced to acknowledge that many aspects of life are beyond human control, that health, fitness, and life itself are gifts. We may be able to affect them positively, but ultimately they remain beyond our manipulation.

• *We are uncomfortable in one another's presence.* We rarely reveal our personal concerns, hopes, and fears to other people. Rarely do we share the issues and goals that motivate one another's lives. Instead, we seek ways to be distracted together. We watch movies, television shows, or plays in silence. We find activities that fill our moments with other people—in sports or culture or eating. Visiting someone who is sick precludes all of these escapes from direct, personal interaction. At a sickbed, there is no alternative but to speak with one another, and doing this often forces one to delve into fundamental concerns and questions. At a hospital, the distraction of activities cannot provide an escape from the discomfort we feel in the presence of another human being.

For all of these reasons, and for countless personal ones, a chasm separates the discomfort we feel in the presence of illness from our recognition of the importance of *bikkur holim*. This chapter is a bridge across that chasm. Confronting our fears and our frailty can bring us an acceptance of reality. It can help us appreciate every day of life as a gift and a blessing, and it can bring about a deeper involvement with our families and communities. The sense of concern and hope that a sick person receives from *bikkur holim* is impossible to provide in any other way. Only the visit and attention of a friend, relative, or member of the community can inspire the sick with the knowledge that they are not alone, that they are not abandoned. The steps that follow are a means to begin providing that care.

❖   ❖   ❖   ❖   ❖

LENDING A HAND

The Talmud recounts an occasion when Rabbi Yoḥanan was ill. Rabbi Ḥanina visited him and, after conversing for a while, said "Give me your hand." Rabbi Yoḥanan gave him his hand, and Rabbi Ḥanina raised his student and friend from his bed.

What makes this story remarkable is that Rabbi Yoḥanan was himself well known as a holy man who could heal others. If he could heal the sick, then why couldn't he heal himself? The Talmud responds that "the prisoner cannot free himself."

1 **Upon discovering that someone is sick, send a brief card or a note.** It may be impossible to phone or visit the person for a few days. Rather than allowing a silence to isolate the sick, send a note to provide a sense of contact. Don't provide false cheer or lie about the sick person's prognosis. A note as brief as "I'm thinking of you" or "We want you to know that we love you" can be a great boost to someone who is ill. In addition to ensuring that the sick person hears from you (in case the phone is busy or it's impossible to visit right away), the card also provides a tangible symbol of love. Almost every hospital room I've visited has the cards taped proudly to a wall, in a place where the sick person can easily see them; they are a constant reminder that people do care.

2 **Alert the sick person's rabbi.** Call the synagogue to say that there is someone who might benefit from a rabbi's visit. A rabbi is able to represent the Jewish community in ways that no one else can. Although a visit from a rabbi is often of great comfort, many people forget to notify the synagogue when someone is ill. As a result, the synagogue or local rabbi doesn't reach out and the sick person often feels neglected. It is certainly preferable that a synagogue office get too many notices of someone's illness than that it not find out until the sick person is offended. Before notifying the synagogue, be sure to consider whether the patient will be upset by having his or her illness made public. If the patient is not Jewish (and the Talmud affirms that it is a mitzvah to visit the sick whether or not they are Jews), try to notify his or her church, mosque, or temple.

3 **Plan to visit the sick.** There is no substitute for the physical presence of caring people. They can banish loneliness and provide tangible evidence of a concerned community. A close friend or family member should visit immediately. If the hospitalization will be protracted, acquaintances and business associates should wait a day or two (the Talmud suggests waiting three days) before actually visiting. Many hospitalizations are for less than three days. For such short stays, it is certainly appropriate to visit sooner.

4 **Don't plan on a long visit.** Hospital patients have a busy schedule, and sick people often tire easily. It is better to visit briefly but repeatedly than to visit once for a long time. Be sensitive to the condition of the person and his or her stamina. When the patient tires, leave courteously with a promise to return another time.

I remember one visit early in my rabbinate. We were in the middle of a stimulating conversation, or so I thought, when the patient blurted out, "Thank you for coming, rabbi." Unaware of her exhaustion and insensitive to her need for rest, I had put this sick woman in the position of having first to tolerate, and finally to dismiss, her rabbi.

5 **Schedule your visit appropriately.** The Talmud counsels not to visit the sick early in the morning or late at night. Most hospitals have visiting hours in order to enable doctors and nurses to perform their tasks unencumbered. Be sure to respect such restrictions. Early in the morning is often the only time a patient is able to sleep, and late at night may be a time of fatigue. Similarly, don't plan to visit on the day of an operation unless the patient or the patient's family specifically requests your presence.

6 **Before visiting the patient, phone ahead to let him or her know you are coming.** This simple gesture creates the anticipation of a visit, giving the sick person that much more pleasure. Calling in advance provides a second advantage as well: it puts the patient in control. Being sick, at home or in a hospital, often results in a forced passivity. Doctors, nurses, and family members make and impose a range of decisions that a person normally would be able to make for himself or herself. When you phone and ask if it is all right to visit, the patient is able to exercise some control. If the patient declines the visit, don't insist or argue. Express the hope for a speedy recovery, invite the patient to call you in the future, and politely end the call. Never visit someone who doesn't want to be visited.

---

7 Prepare for a visit carefully and thoughtfully. You can take certain steps that will lessen the sick person's discomfort and demonstrate your concern.

• *Don't wear perfume or after-shave lotion.* Illness often makes people more sensitive to smell, and artificial odors can be disturbing to the person who is sick.

• *Don't bring bad news.* No patient need hear of an additional tragedy. Disasters in the news, a personal crisis, even the illness of a mutual friend or relative are all inappropriate topics to initiate. A significant part of *bikkur*

holim involves just listening—letting the sick person discuss whatever he or she desires. Try to restrict topics to those that will make the patient feel good. Focus on interests, loved ones, or hobbies.

• *Select one or two topics for discussion: perhaps an issue from the day's newspaper, a sports event, the weekly Torah portion, a movie or book that people are talking about.* The choice of topic should reflect the interests of the person who is ill. Preparing yourself with a few possible subjects for discussion can help you feel ready to sit and talk.

• *Bring the patient a small, practical gift.* A newspaper or magazine can reinforce a sense of connection to the outside world and leaves tangible evidence of the visit. Consider bringing a picture or poster and hanging it on the wall to enliven the room. One of the gifts I cher-

The illnesses that bring us to hospitals may be tragic, but people remain more than merely patients. By bringing cheer and activity, a visitor can remind the sick of their connection to the world and to their community, making their world larger than the space of a single bed.

ished most as a hospital patient was a bonsai tree. That little tree linked me to the outdoors and allowed me to feel less trapped by my hospital room.

8 **Before entering the patient's room, be sure to knock and ask for permission to enter.** This is another way to allow the patient to feel in control. Many people (doctors, nurses, therapists, and social workers) walk into sickrooms, often from necessity, without announcing themselves or asking permission. By simply knocking and asking if you may come in, you will help restore to the patient some sense of control.

9 **If there are already many visitors, wait outside until a few people leave.** Trying to juggle a room full of friends can be exhausting, and another visitor may simply be a strain. If there is time, wait. If not, then say, "I see that you are well cared for now. I wanted you to know I'll be thinking of you, and I'll come back when there are fewer people."

It's important, when making this or any other promise, to fulfill the commitment. A promise creates an expectation where none had existed previously; to fail to visit again will transform that expectation into disappointment and heighten the patient's sense of isolation. Let the patient know when to expect the next visit, and then be sure to visit again.

10 **When visiting, help with concrete tasks.** One of the crucial aspects of *bikkur ḥolim* is the kind of caring that can be demonstrated only in person. Help by making the bed, watering plants, straightening up the room, or any other chore that helps the sick person and makes the surroundings look well attended. Of course, it is important to get the consent of the sick person before tampering with the room. Anything that can increase his or her sense of control and dignity is an added gift.

11 **Try to be with the patient during a meal.** Eating is a social act, and the presence of company during a meal can communicate additional closeness and caring because it suggests forethought. Be sure to ask whether the patient would like you to stay during the meal—many people are embarrassed to eat in another's presence.

12 **Don't feel you have nothing to talk about.** At the heart of our discomfort with visiting the sick is a sense that we won't have anything to say. The following specific guidelines might help.

• *Be alert to objects in the room that might prompt a pleasant discussion.* Photographs of people can lead you to ask who they are and to a discussion of their activities, interests, and relationships. A book lying by the bed can lead to a discussion about the book, its author, or the topic.

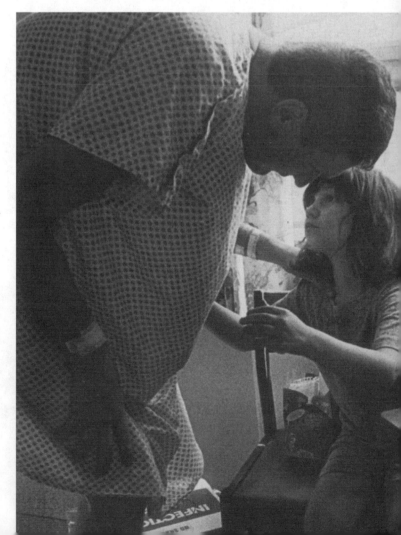

- *Don't criticize the hospital, the doctors, the food, or the medical procedures.* Criticizing a patient's medical care may diminish his or her confidence in it. If the patient is frustrated, then listen sympathetically without committing yourself to agreeing. If the complaint is specific and reasonable, consider sharing it with a close relative of the sick person. If the patient is a member of your immediate family, then find out whether there is a possible solution to the particular problem.

- *Don't evaluate a procedure or the veracity of a medical prognosis.* A visitor's purpose is not to provide medical opinions. Disagreeing with the procedures selected by the sick person's professional caretakers undermines his or her confidence in the doctor's ability to provide the best possible care. Again, if there are reasonable doubts about the medical staff's performance, then inform a close relative of the patient. If the patient is a family member, then it

might be worthwhile to call another doctor for a second opinion. At the same time, don't deny a poor prognosis. The patient may want someone who will listen openly, and not brush aside the patient's feelings of hopelessness or despair.

- *Don't defend God, religion, or nature.* None of those needs defense. Being sick is a legitimate cause for anger, and expressing that anger or rage is the quickest way to be able to move beyond it. We can best help by listening sympathetically and by saying, "It must be very difficult to go through what you are going through. It really isn't fair. I'd be angry too if I were you."

- *Don't talk about someone who died of the same disease.* The last thing someone sick needs to deal with is the inexorable conclusion of a terminal illness.

13 **Don't be afraid to sit in silence.** As with any situation where we are trying to bring comfort and friendship to someone who is suffering (whether from emotional or financial loss, or physical disability), the primary statement we can make is not through any words we speak but through our presence. Simply being with someone in a time of need is an articulate assertion of love and caring.

14 **Listen.** Besides demonstrating our involvement by offering our physical presence, we can do so by allowing the sick to speak of their concerns. In fact, this is the main service we can offer. If people who are sick want to speak about their illness, then listen. If they want to talk about their families, then listen. All of us have a need to be heard, most of all when we feel strained or ill. By providing a receptive ear, we allow the sick person to validate his or her inner feelings, fears, and needs.

15 **Offer your hand.** As a corollary to providing a loving presence and a listening ear, don't hesitate to touch the person. There

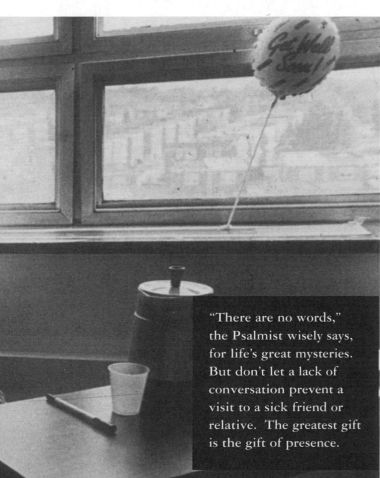

"There are no words," the Psalmist wisely says, for life's great mysteries. But don't let a lack of conversation prevent a visit to a sick friend or relative. The greatest gift is the gift of presence.

is no more immediate way to demonstrate that you will not abandon a person to illness than by reaching out and placing your hand on the patient's shoulder or by taking the person's hand in your own. The calm, love, and stability that touch provides is without equal.

Touching may be especially difficult between men, with whom the social taboos are still strong. Yet illness is a time of particular vulnerability, a time when the need for connection is most intense. Actions not ordinarily performed can affirm a link that transcends words. Every time I have held a man who was suffering, he has burst into tears, even though we both hesitated before I reached out to him. I know that being a rabbi makes me an exception to the societal prohibition preventing men from holding one another, but the comfort and warmth transmitted are so real that this prohibition is worth being ignored by everyone.

16 Offer to pray with the patient.

Bikkur ḥolim is more than just visiting the sick. It is also the performance of a mitzvah. Of all the events in a person's life, illness is one that calls for the assurance of holiness and connectedness that Jewish tradition can provide so well. A willingness to observe Shabbat or other holiday and, more especially, a willingness to pray together can establish a living link to the Jewish community and to God. The rabbis of the Talmud often made a point of praying in the

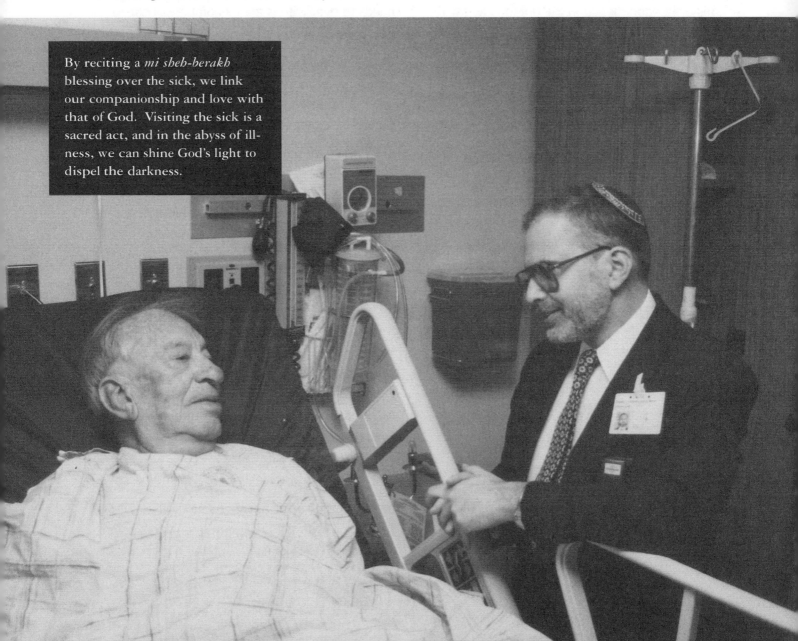

By reciting a *mi sheh-berakh* blessing over the sick, we link our companionship and love with that of God. Visiting the sick is a sacred act, and in the abyss of illness, we can shine God's light to dispel the darkness.

presence of the sick, some even claiming that a visit that did not include a prayer did not constitute *bikkur ḥolim.*

• *Prayer can be informal.* A simple wish of *rcfu'ah sh'leimah* (רְפוּאָה שְׁלֵמָה , "complete healing") or "God be with you" can bring a level of comfort that ordinary conversation cannot. Jewish tradition offers a brief prayer linking the experience of the individual to the broader community: "May God show compassion to you, together with all the other sick of the people Israel."

• *If possible, visit before Shabbat or a holiday, and bring some item that will allow the patient to celebrate that holiday.* On a Friday, consider bringing two small ḥallah rolls and a little wine or grape juice (depending on what the patient is allowed to drink). Before Purim, bring some hamentashen; provide honey and apples before Rosh Hashanah; or matzah and a Haggadah for Passover. Linking your visits to the Jewish holidays is an effective way to combat the disorienting quality of being sick and reconnect the suffering individual to what other Jews are experiencing beyond the walls of the sickroom.

• *Read a psalm together.* This simple gesture can add tremendous depth to your visit. Psalm 23 ("Adonai is my shepherd") can be a source of great comfort. Another possibility is Psalm 121 ("I lift my eyes to the hills") or Psalm 130 ("Out of the depths I call to You"). These readings link the present moment and the individual's pain to a continuity that stretches back in time to include the great figures of our biblical and rabbinic heritage. By using their words, we affirm a community of belonging that transcends illness, sorrow, and pain.

---

17 **Offer to make two specifically Jewish gestures.**

• *Offer to attend a synagogue worship service and to have a* mi sheh-berakh

(מִי שֶׁבֵּרַךְ , literally, "may the One who blessed") *recited after the Torah reading.* The *mi sheh-berakh* is a prayer for the sick. Be sure to find out the patient's Jewish name as well as the Jewish names of his or her parents, because in the Jewish tradition a person is known as So-and-so, son or daughter of So-and-so and So-and-so. By asking the rabbi to recite a *mi sheh-berakh,* you ensure that the community is informed of the illness, that more people will pray for that individual, and that the sick person has the comfort of knowing that a congregation of Jews cares.

• *Make a contribution to a synagogue or a charitable cause in honor of the sick person.* In Jewish tradition, *tzedakah* (literally, "righteousness"; a monetary contribution) is a highly cherished form of demonstrating respect and concern. Giving money in someone's name gives the person credit for an additional good deed and further links him or her to the values and activities of the larger community.

---

18 **Reestablish the ancient Jewish tradition of *va-ad bikkur ḥolim.*** The mitzvah of *bikkur ḥolim* is an obligation that falls on all members of a caring community. Rather than relying on our own personal network of people who will "take care of their own," it is time to reestablish the ancient Jewish tradition of *va-ad bikkur ḥolim* (וַעַד בִּקּוּר חוֹלִים , "committee to visit the sick"). Contact a nearby synagogue, and offer to work with the rabbi or executive director to organize such a project. All you need is a few volunteers and a willingness to put in some time. The visits of a *va-ad bikkur ḥolim* do not replace the efforts of the rabbi or the cantor. By providing regular hospital and sickbed visits by congregants, however, the *va-ad bikkur ḥolim* demonstrates that Judaism is not just for paid professionals and that the community, as a community, takes care of its members. Several

One of my most powerful memories is of the nurse who simply stood by my shoulder and kept her hand on my arm during a biopsy. That touch communicated her concern and gave me a connection to another human being. She will never know the difference she made simply by holding me. Her grasp reminded me that I am a person to be nurtured, not simply a case to be solved.

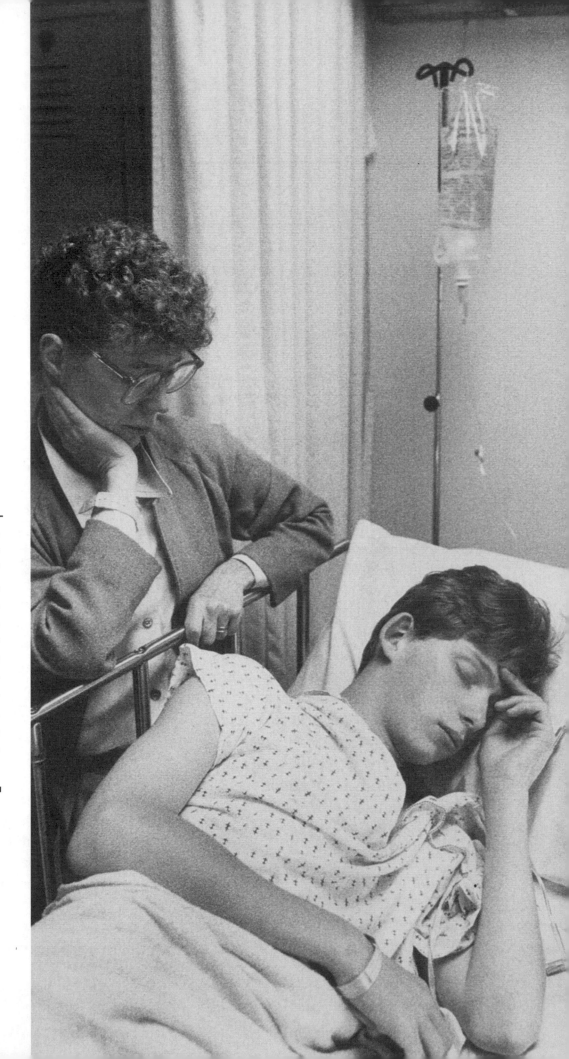

of the books listed in For Further Reading at the end of this chapter will assist you in forming this important committee.

| 19 | **Visit nursing home residents, long-time hospital patients, and** |

elderly shut-ins. Many people suffer from chronic illnesses, suffering for such a long time that we often stop remembering that they need our care. The rules of *bikkur ḥolim* apply to these people too.

❖   ❖   ❖   ❖   ❖

The Talmud tells a story about a disciple of Rabbi Akiba who became ill. When Rabbi Akiba discovered that no one was attending to the student, he himself went to the student's home, ordering his other students to sweep and clean the house for the sick student. Because of their care, the student recovered more rapidly. In gratitude, the student said to Rabbi Akiba, "My master, you have revived me." Immediately Rabbi Akiba taught that "a person who does not visit the sick is comparable to one who sheds the blood of another."

Life is full of disappointments, mysteries, and pain. While we cannot eliminate suffering completely, we do have the power to diminish its sting. By holding out our hands to one another, by providing company and comfort, we may not be able to make our world a paradise, but we shall surely make of our community a haven, a hope, and a home.

The mitzvah of *bikkur ḥolim* enables us to be fully human and fully alive to that which one human being can give to another. The time to begin giving is now.

THE POWER OF PRAYER

I'm often amazed by how people seem unwilling to let themselves go, to experience the full force of their anger or sorrow at being sick. One woman spoke in almost scientific objectivity about her illness until I took her hand and started to recite a *mi sheh-berakh*, the ancient prayer for the sick. Tears welled in her eyes, and by the end of the short prayer she was sobbing beyond control. Moved beyond words by the power of prayer, she was finally open to feel and to share, a process more healing than all the analysis and discussion that had come before.

For Further Reading

Pesach Krauss and Morrie Goldfischer, *Why Me? Coping with Grief, Loss, and Change*. Toronto: Bantam Books, 1988.

Harold S. Kushner, *When Bad Things Happen to Good People*. New York: Schocken Books, 1981.

Jane Handler Yurow and Kim Hetherington, *Give Me Your Hand: Traditional and Practical Guidance on Visiting the Sick*. Washington, DC: Adas Israel Congregation.

7 Hakhnasat Orḥim AND Ma'akhil R'evim:
Hospitality and Feeding the Hungry

All who are hungry, let them come and eat.
—TA'ANIT 20A

For Adonai your God . . . befriends the stranger, providing the stranger with food and clothing. You too must befriend the stranger, for you were strangers in the Land of Egypt.

—DEUTERONOMY 10:17-19

We live in an age of organizations. At a time of widespread homelessness, hunger, and constant mobility, we require organization and efficiency to ensure that minimal human services reach the staggering numbers of people in need. We require structures with power to counter the powerful structures that generate homelessness and hunger in the first place. Our drive to institutionalize has even infected our religious lives: Certain mitzvot have been largely abandoned to the mechanical workings of institutions.

Hakhnasat orḥim (הַכְנָסַת אוֹרְחִים, "hospitality") and *ma'akhil r'evim* (מַאֲכִיל רְעֵבִים, "feeding the hungry") are two such deeds. Although they

were once a mainstay of biblical and rabbinic religion, we now delegate feeding the hungry to soup kitchens, housing the homeless to shelters, helping tourists to the Chamber of Commerce, and integrating newcomers to "welcome wagons." While these organizations may be essential to the fulfillment of certain needs, they remain impersonal. They lack the grounding of community and friendship that can provide the emotional sustenance to accompany the food, clothes, or temporary housing that they offer.

This chapter is not an argument against institutions, but it does maintain that organization and efficiency can never replace caring and concern on a personal level. A single human hand can enter where a battalion can never reach. Our society is in need of outreached hands.

As long as we have the power to alleviate human suffering, we have an obligation to do so. Feeding the hungry is one of the simplest and most important ways of coming to the aid of a fellow human being—a concrete expression of the Jewish love of life.

❖　❖　❖　❖　❖

Why have we seen such a decline in our individual commitment and obligation to fulfilling *hakhnasat orḥim* and *ma'akhil r'evim?* Why have these mitzvot been relegated to institutions? Consider how transient our culture has become: few of us live in the place of our birth, and even those who do must call long distance to converse with childhood friends. Parents retire to warm and sunny places, often far from where their children and grandchildren live. Children leave home and attend college or serve in the military thousands of miles from their parents' homes. The price we pay for all this mobility—voluntary and imposed—is a hesitancy to make new friendships. After all, it will only hurt that much more when the time comes to say good-bye. Occupied with the more immediate chores of finding a home, unpacking, and getting one's bearings in a new location, families postpone, time and again, their life's dream or their own personal growth.

It isn't likely that we can make the kind of pervasive changes in society that would allow people to become rooted in one place. But if we can't stop the disruption, if we can't find a way to break through the

As the rabbi of a synagogue, I sit with families who wistfully remember the place they just left or who tearfully tell me they have to move because of a corporate transfer. The disruption in their lives, the difficulty of making new friends, fears about their children's adjustment to new schools—all of this takes a toll on a family's ability to cope. Moves never seem to come at a good time; they do, however, occur with painful frequency.

effects of our constant motion and our penchant for relying on institutions, an entire age will lose out on one of life's most precious treats—the comfort of communal loyalty and acceptance, the warmth of a friendship that spans the years, the sense of accomplishment in making a piece of the world a little bit better.

While we can't stop the moving from place to place, we can turn ourselves into an "extended family" along the path—little enclaves of caring and involvement that invite weary and desensitized people to join us, trust us, and share with us. We can find ways to expand our sense of community so that it will include people we have never met before or who we will see only once.

That inclusiveness is *hakhnasat orḥim,* true hospitality. By opening our homes to others, by creating a haven where strangers are welcomed (and thus shown that no one is really a stranger after all), we have the power to renew a sense of connection and belonging. By providing for the hungry and sheltering the homeless, we can offer tangible relief from the suffering of fellow human beings. By reaching out to

BIBLICAL HOSPITALITY
The tradition of hospitality and feeding the hungry goes back to the earliest roots of Jewish tradition. When three guests arrived at Abraham and Sarah's doorstep, the latter immediately sprang into action as model hosts. Abraham selected a sheep from his flock, which Sarah prepared, along with bread and other delicacies, as a meal for the visitors.

Opening our homes to our friends or to those who need a place to celebrate a holiday helps create community and allows us to share God's bounty. By giving to others, we make ourselves God's partners in the care of other human beings.

newcomers and greeting visitors with warmth, we make the world a little more intimate, a little more caring.

There are four principal areas where the mitzvot of *hakhnasat orḥim* and *ma'akhil r'evim* are central: guests, tourists, the homeless, and the hungry. In the guidelines that follow, we will consider guests and tourists first and then conclude with the homeless and the hungry.

Hakhnasat orḥim and *ma'akhil r'evim* are about welcoming people into our lives. They are about sustaining other people and deriving sustenance from the encounter. They are, through deed, affirmations of God's love and of our potential to emulate that love.

GUESTS AND TOURISTS

Many concerns about the treatment of a stranger or a distant acquaintance are not relevant to the treatment of an intimate friend or relative. The guidelines that follow pertain primarily to guests who are not close friends. While many of these suggestions are expressions of sensitivity and caring appropriate for all guests, we each develop unique ways of relating to those who are particularly close to us.

1 **Invite guests to your home for Shabbat or any Jewish festival.**
Many Jews, particularly those who grew up in observant or synagogue-affiliated families, are especially nostalgic on these days. Having been times of great warmth and togetherness in the past, these are especially difficult days on which to be alone. By inviting a Jew to join you on a festival, you assure him or her that caring continues, and you offer a feeling of connectedness. At the same time, you may derive these same benefits for yourself. (See also Chapter 12, step 10.)

Welcome Jewish tourists who are in town during Shabbat or a festival, and invite them home for a meal immediately following services. Being Jewish means being part of an international fellowship, an extended family through time and across the globe. Demonstrate that unity.

2 **Make your guests comfortable by demonstrating your pleasure with their company.** Jewish tradition can guide us in this endeavor, enabling us to make our guests feel appreciated rather than a burden. The following guidelines are taken from the Talmud:

• *Greet your guests at the door, and escort them inside.* These physical gestures communicate the sincerity of your joy at their arrival, helping them to relax and enjoy their time as guests.

• *Make an effort to remain cheerful during a guest's visit.* If you are unduly quiet or somber, guests may easily construe your silence as hostility or disappointment. This is not to say that serious discussion is off-limits or that you must mask your true feelings. The key, here as elsewhere, is to speak openly about your feelings and thoughts so that the guests are not left trying to decode your gestures and expression. Whenever possible, smile.

• *Offer food and drink.* Even if the visit is spontaneous or brief, offer something to eat and drink. Making the effort to serve food is a concrete demonstration of caring and friendship.

• *Personally serve the food, whether it is simply appetizers or an entire meal.* In this way, your guests won't worry that the helping they took is too large or that the amount they are eating might generate resentment. During the talmudic period, the rabbis made a point of serving all the courses at the same time, so that a guest's not wanting to eat a particular dish would be less noticed. This method of serving a meal also allowed the guests to pace themselves, since they wouldn't have to guess at how many more courses were yet to come. In our own day, the practice of serving all the courses simultaneously might be mistaken for an attempt to rush the meal. What matters is not the style of your service but that the guests know they are welcome and that they are made to feel comfortable.

• *Don't watch your guests too closely during a meal.* They may well mistake excessive attentiveness for stinginess or criticism of their table manners.

• *Don't rush the meal.* Let your guests take their time. As a host, you should make a point of relaxing and eating the meal slowly yourself. The point is not to finish quickly but to enjoy the companionship.

• *Ask your guests questions that allow them to speak about their own interests, activi-*

ties, and expertise. By asking questions about your guests' careers, priorities, or talents, you allow them to become comfortable with the conversation. You are also demonstrating your interest in their lives. Besides, everybody likes to be able to speak about himself or herself sometimes. When there is more than one guest, be sure to direct your questions to each one. Don't assume that just because two or more guests are part of one family, only one family member's life is worth discussing.

• *When your guests leave, escort them through the door.* Accompanying them as they leave demonstrates a reluctance to separate.

---

3 | **As a guest, help your host to relax and enjoy your time together by anticipating and addressing the host's insecurities or concerns.**

• *When you visit, ask questions about the talents or concerns of your host.* Don't keep the conversation focused on your activities and interests to the exclusion of the host's. Hosts are no less eager than their guests to discuss career, relationships, and current events. Make a point of asking questions that allow the host to talk about himself or herself. If there is more than one host (if you have been invited by a couple or a family), be sure to ask both or all of them about their activities. Don't assume that only one person present—the general assumption is that it is the man—has a career and interests and that everybody else plays a supporting role.

• *When eating, compliment the host on the food whenever possible.* Everybody likes to hear that guests have enjoyed the food that was prepared for them. But insincere compliments don't often work, and honesty is a value in itself. (See Chapter 13, step 3.) Find something about the meal or about the home itself (its decor, art work, ritual objects) that you can compliment with integrity, and then make the compliment. This is simply a specific aspect of more general

advice: show gratitude whenever someone acts kindly to you.

• *Wherever possible, comply with a host's requests.* Unless a host is extremely overbearing, keep in mind that the hospitality is in someone else's domain. At your home, it's possible to express a personal style and preference, and the host has that same right when caring for his or her guests. Unless a request is unreasonable, do as the host asks.

• *Don't overstay the host's welcome.* This last piece of talmudic wisdom may be the most important one a guest can remember. Different people wear out at different times, and a host may become tired well before the guests do. Watch carefully for signs that your host is ready for the occasion to end, and then leave when you see those signs. Few hosts feel comfortable asking a guest to leave (although there is no reason that such a request, made without malice and after a pleasant occasion, shouldn't be an accepted part of open discourse), so the responsibility for recognizing when it is time to leave remains with the visitor.

---

4 | **When visiting someone in a new house or apartment, bring a loaf of bread and a container of salt.** Bread is the biblical "staff of life," and salt was traditionally seen as an essential ingredient to any home and an agent of life itself. These two items symbolize a wish that the new home be a place of prosperity, health, and abundance for its new residents. Make a point of greeting new neighbors with this traditional welcome—it's surprising what a wonderful transformation can occur if just a few neighbors experience such a friendly welcome and associate it with the neighborhood as a whole.

---

5 | **Welcome newcomers to the synagogue.** Entering a congregation where you don't know anyone can be intimidating. If someone looks nervous or unsure, don't

wait for that person to express interest in you. Take the initiative yourself. Offer to sit with the newcomer during services, and start a conversation afterward, or invite the newcomer home for a meal. If you are the newcomer, don't be shy. Find someone to say hello to, and announce that you are new to the community and that you are interested in meeting people.

THE HOMELESS AND THE HUNGRY

It is hard to imagine the difficulty and danger faced by someone who doesn't have a regular home, who is sleeping in shelters (when lucky), on park benches, on sidewalks, and in gutters, or wherever some space can be found. Imagine never feeling clean, secure, rested, or comfortable. Imagine hunger so constant that it hurts. Imagine that the rest of humanity sees not a real person but a modern leper, the secular equivalent of an untouchable.

Hospitality that leaves a segment of humanity out on the streets not only is less than inadequate but also is a denial of the presence of God's image in all people. As long as our governments—who, after all, are our representatives—don't find a means to house and clothe and feed everyone, then our claim to being civilized rings hollow. Ultimately, the international problem of housing humanity will require serious political attention. But until then (and even afterward, most likely), our personal attention to the individuals who don't have anywhere to live will remain essential: The Torah teaches that there will always be needy people (Deuteronomy 15:11).

Care for the homeless is a recognition that in a sense we are all one another's guests. Or, perhaps, that every one of us, representing God's love to one another, must play the role of host on God's behalf. The following suggestions are meant to convey that love.

6 **Find out which local organizations work with the hungry and the homeless.** Two likely places to start such a search are the local government and the nearest synagogue. Both may have programs for helping the homeless and the hungry. If they do, they will certainly be in need of active participants. If they don't, they will be able to offer guidance to potential volunteers.

7 **Focus on concrete ways to help the homeless.** For example, help dispense food in a soup kitchen. Volunteers are always in short supply and high demand. No matter how involved one becomes in an organization, the physical act of providing food will never go out of style.

8 **Volunteer your time at a homeless shelter.** Those who run shelters need volunteers to perform a wide range of tasks. Many ask volunteers to stay overnight in the shelter in order to look after the people who are spending the evening there. Often shelters are housed within congregations, and these are especially safe. The "lucky" homeless who stay in such shelters are generally screened in advance by the local government. They are, in some sense, the cream of the crop. So give serious consideration to volunteering to spend a night at a shelter for the homeless, particularly one that is housed in a synagogue or a church.

9 **Teach job skills to homeless people who are seeking employment.** Even better, of course, would be to provide a homeless person with employment, enabling him or her to earn an income, find a place to live, and stabilize his or her life.

10 **Donate old or unused clothing to a homeless shelter.** Shelters are almost always looking for clothes for people who are out on the streets every day. This kind of giving is also an excellent application of the mitzvah of *bal tash'ḥit,* since clothing that was going to waste (by not being used) will now clothe someone in need.

11 **Volunteer at a soup kitchen or a homeless shelter on a non-Jewish holiday.** Volunteering on a day such as Christmas or Easter allows non-Jewish volunteers to enjoy their own holidays with their families and friends. It also enables the needs of the homeless and the hungry to be met even though it is a holiday.

12 **If possible, make financial contributions to the organizations that help the homeless and hungry in your community.** These groups are certainly worthy of financial support, and the members of each community must support their own—for often no one else will. It is also commendable to take to a soup kitchen or a homeless shelter food left over after a communal or private celebration. This is another practice that implements the mitzvah of *bal tash'ḥit.* (See Chapter 5.)

13 **Attack homelessness on a global level.** Jewish tradition specifically links concern for the poor and the hungry with our most sacred occasions. On the fast of Yom Kippur, in celebrating Purim and Pesaḥ, it is customary to provide food for the hungry. Today this mitzvah is often performed on a worldwide scale through organizations dedicated to fighting the widespread hunger and poverty that afflict so much of humanity. Two groups are worthy of special mention here—Mazon and American Jewish World Service—because they raise money within the Jewish community to feed and sustain the hungry and homeless of all peoples. By channeling your support to these organizations, you ensure that the recipients know that the Jewish community cares about all people, not just other Jews. You also enable these groups to continue educating the Jewish community about the needs of the hungry, and about our Jewish responsibilities to all those who are in need.

> Mazon
> 2940 Westwood Boulevard, Suite 7
> Los Angeles, CA 90064

Mazon works to provide food for the hungry throughout the United States and around the world.

> American Jewish World Service
> 15 West 26th Street
> New York, NY 10010

This organization develops ingenious ways to allow poor communities to provide for themselves. Often the AJWS will make a point of using Israeli technology, thereby fulfilling the mitzvah of *ahavat Tziyon* (see Chapter 4) as they provide for the poor.

❖　❖　❖　❖　❖

Ultimately, hospitality is a question of defining our community broadly enough so that no one is left out. Just as we demonstrate a sense of responsibility by sharing our food and companionship with those close to us, so we can cultivate a sense of family that includes the entire household of humanity. The mitzvot of *hakhnasat orḥim* and *ma'akhil r'evim* offer us a compromise: Rather than allowing us to abandon contemporary society, with its rush, its transience, and its outcasts, rather than allowing us to surrender to a faceless world of institutions and anonymity, these mitzvot reveal to us the human face in our midst and restore the caring heart to its rightful place in contemporary life.

The Jewish tradition of caring for others, part of the broader mitzvah of *tzedakah*, has always connected Jews to one another and to the rest of humanity. Shipments of food and medical aid have been an intrinsic expression of Jewish piety and involvement. The photo below, taken at New York harbor in 1919, shows rabbis assisting with the first shipment of kosher meat that was sent to the starving Jews of Poland.

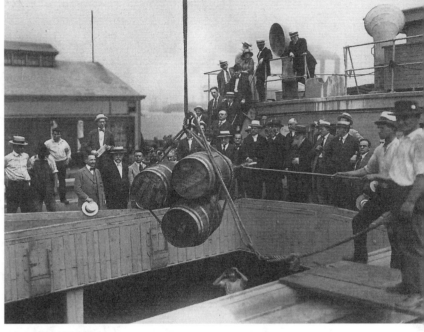

For Further Reading

Charles Kroloff, *When Elijah Knocks: A Religious Response to Homelessness.* West Orange, NJ: Behrman House, 1992.

8 *Kashrut:*
The Dietary Laws

*Don't say,
"I dislike pig
meat." Rather,
say, "I do like
it but must
abstain from it
because God
has forbidden
it for me."*
—SIFRA 11:22

*For what does the Holy One care
whether one kills an animal by the
throat or by the nape of its neck?
The purpose [of kashrut] is to refine
humanity.* —GENESIS RABBAH 44:1

For over three thousand years, Judaism has taught that how we eat and what we feed ourselves are sacred and communal matters—sanctifying us, educating us, nourishing our identity, and fortifying our morality. We need that sustenance no less than our ancestors did. Our meals can feed our spirit, too, through the same simple guidelines that have shaped Jewish eating and Jewish living since the beginning of our people.

The basic patterns of *sh'mirat kashrut* (שְׁמִירַת כַּשְׁרוּת, "observing the dietary laws") are derived from the Torah and elucidated in the Talmud. They are divided into the following general areas:

Separating milk and meat. This practice is based on the biblical commandment "You shall not

How and what we eat reflects our values and our priorities. The popularity of fast food indicates a concern for speed and efficiency. Kashrut reflects a concern for holiness, community, and decency. We may not be what we eat, but we demonstrate our values by the way we eat.

boil a kid in its mother's milk (EXODUS 34:26 AND DEUTERONOMY 14:21). According to recent scholarship, the purpose of this observance was to distinguish a Jewish focus on the living from the pagan worship of the dead. Milk symbolizes life (because it sustains an infant's life).

To eat or cook an animal in the very liquid that sustained its life would be a perversion of the purpose of the milk. By prohibiting this common pagan rite, the Torah hoped to instill in those who separated meat from milk a reverence for life and a devotion to the living. An additional benefit of this observance is that it underscores the distinctiveness of Judaism by establishing a practice unique to our people. The rabbis of the Talmud extended the biblical custom of separation to include waiting between fleischig ("meat") meals and milchig ("milk") meals and using separate "meat" and "milk" utensils, pots, and plates.

Regulating the slaughter of animals. In order to make us conscious of the value of animal life and sensitive to the sanctity of that life, there is a special requirement for the *sheḥitah* (שְׁחִיטָה, "ritual slaughter") of the animal: Blood, recognized as the symbol of life, must be drained from the animal before the meat can be eaten. By spilling out the blood, Jews symbolically acknowledge that they are not the ultimate owners of the world and its inhabitants; the earth belongs to God. By not eating the blood, we make explicit our dependence on God and on nature, and we strengthen our resolve to care for the earth as its responsible tenants.

Prohibiting certain meats. In the pagan view of the world, every aspect of nature had its own god, each in competition with the others. As a result, any overarching moral order was impossible because each god was simply acting to satisfy his or her own interests. In contrast to this amoral and anarchic viewpoint, the Torah insists that there is only one God, who passionately cares for justice and is the source of all morality. One understanding of kashrut teaches that there is a moral order to the world and it is enforced by our being permitted to eat only those animals that fit into certain archetypal categories—birds that fly and are not scavengers, mammals that chew their cud and have cloven hooves, fish that have fins and scales and are not scavengers. By restricting the Jewish diet to these animals, the

Torah imposes a sense of order on an otherwise chaotic world, thereby creating the stability necessary to cultivate a compassionate and demanding morality.

❖　❖　❖　❖　❖

THE WISDOM OF MODERATION

The ideal of Judaism is a state of harmony between all living things—a world of vegetarians. All vegetables and fruit are naturally kosher (כָּשֵׁר , literally, "fit" or "proper"); consequently, every vegetarian acts consistently with the rules of kashrut (in fact, the Torah portrays Adam and Eve in the Garden of Eden as vegetarians, and several prophetic writings view the messianic future as one of universal vegetarianism). But insisting on an impossible ideal can often force its opposite.

Saddled by inevitable failure, people flee from excessively high standards to total abandonment. Rather than imposing unattainable ideals, Jewish practice channels human urges into manageable and constructive forms. Kashrut is Judaism's brilliant compromise, teaching a sensitivity to animal life and instilling a concern for the humane treatment of animals while still allowing room for the desire for meat (as long as that desire is channeled and limited).

Kashrut harnesses the act of eating to our identity, our community, and our morality. For thousands of years, the dietary laws have created a potent bond, solidifying Jewish identity, forging a link with Jews throughout time and across the globe, and strengthening family and friends into communities devoted to a more humane order on Earth. Through the regimen of kashrut, we learn that we can discipline ourselves, enjoying the pleasures of life while affirming our highest sense of humanity. Kashrut allows us to establish a sense of control in a world that is, in many ways, random and chaotic. Finally, the practice of kashrut, motivated at its core by a recognition of the holiness of all living things, can instill in us a sensitivity to the suffering of animals and a sense of responsibility to other forms of life.

Unlike book learning, *sh'mirat kashrut* is available to us all, adult and child, scholar and beginner. By integrating the Jewish dietary laws into our lives and our communities, we follow a regimen that allows for exposure to the sacred, an affirmation of

Kashrut connects us to Jews around the world. This French kosher establishment provides a welcome home for Jews traveling from another city or nation.

our Jewishness, and a renewed commitment to the preciousness of life.

Shifting the way we eat is a challenging task, not unlike deciding to lose weight. And altering our menu to foster a sense of Jewish unity, a sense of holiness in our lives, is even more daunting. Any undertaking that has the power to renew meaning and enrich our sense of community cannot be made effortlessly. The practice of the dietary laws requires commitment, self-discipline, and striving. The key is to enjoy each new step; don't rush. Only by your progressing gradually, advancing to a new step only when ready, will it be possible to retain a sense of *simḥat mitzvah* (שִׂמְחַת מִצְוָה, "joy of the commandment") rather than feeling you are simply adding a new burden to your life. Kashrut can be exciting—an invitation to explore your Jewish identity, values, and connection to Jewish history. It can also be challenging. So go slowly; there is ample time to get there.

❖   ❖   ❖   ❖   ❖

1 **Abstain from all pig products.**
Although pork has no greater biblical significance than any other *treif* ("unkosher") meat, in later Jewish tradition the pig became a symbol of the entire dietary system. Eating pork was seen as identical to renouncing one's Judaism. Perhaps because pigs were said to wallow in filth, or perhaps because they were popular in Greek and Roman cultures, eating pork became synonymous with the abandonment of Judaism for the seductions of pagan culture. For many Jews, and for most non-Jews, abstaining from pork is still Judaism's most visible identifying feature.

As a first step toward keeping kosher, refrain from eating pig products: ham, bacon, pork chops, and so forth. While this may not seem like a gigantic step, the avoidance of pork forces you to pay greater attention to food and leads to a public identification with the dietary laws, often for the first time. This public testimony can heighten a sense of Jewish belonging and provide a sense of solidarity with other Jews who already observe some or all of the laws of kashrut.

2 **Refrain from eating shellfish.** This can serve as a second step toward observing kashrut. The Torah mentions the prohibition of all shellfish immediately after the prohibition of pork, and presumably this second prohibition is no less weighty than the first. Many theories have attempted to explain the shellfish prohibition (shellfish are the "vacuum cleaners" of the water world, sucking in the garbage that floats in the sea, or shellfish simply don't share the characteristics of the Bible's "ideal" fish, those possessing fins and scales).

The category of shellfish includes clams, oysters, mussels, abalone, crab, lobster, octopus, squid, sea cucumber, shrimp, prawn, and the like. All mollusks, crustaceans, and echinoderms count as shellfish. If you are uncertain about what fits in this category, it's a good idea to use the old-fashioned but familiar biblical standard: if it has scales and fins, it's okay. If not, then skip it.

3 **Separate milk products from meat products.** The focus so far has been on avoiding the prohibited foods. Now it's time to consider another kashrut standard, the separation of milk and meat. For purposes of the dietary laws, remember that all dairy products and any food with a dairy by-product are considered milk, and anything with a meat base or its by-products (including poultry) is considered meat. From this point forth, don't mix the two, whether in cooking or in eating. This means no more cheese on hamburgers, no cream sauces on meats, no milk with a bologna sandwich, and no meat in lasagna.

A few words of guidance may be helpful at this point: Chicken, turkey, duck, and Cornish game hen, among other kinds of poultry, are considered meat. Fish, however, is pareve (neither meat nor milk) and may be served with either dairy meals or meat meals. Mayonnaise is also pareve, as are eggs, fruit, grain, and vegetables.

While some margarine is pareve, most is dairy. If it has a kosher label, then it will indicate whether the contents are pareve or dairy. Many nondairy creamers and dessert toppings are dairy. (Kosher standards are more exacting in this instance than is the federal law.) The ingredient casein, often found in such products, is a dairy product. Again, look for a kosher label.

According to the Conservative movement, all domestic cheeses are kosher except those that have meat in them. This ruling is based on the fact that rennet (the curdling agent in cheeses, which is usually made from the stomach lining of nonkosher animals) is considered a *davar ḥadash* ("new product"). The rennet, because it is not edible, is not considered a food.

Anyone who keeps kosher knows to read even the most innocuous labels. Products that we would expect to be pareve—cookies and cakes, pie crusts, bread, and the so-called "nondairy" creamers—often contain animal or dairy products. "Look for the label" is good advice.

4 **Observe a minimal waiting period between eating a meat meal and any dairy product.** This waiting period sensitizes us to our having required an animal's life for sustenance and pleasure. Additionally, it reinforces our sense of self-control while discouraging gluttony. In most North American communities, the waiting period is three hours from the end of the meat meal.

There need not be a waiting period after a dairy meal. Before starting to eat meat, however, it is traditional to rinse your mouth with water as a way of removing any stray cheese left behind. And if you are sitting at a table, clear away the dairy foods as well as the utensils and plates that were used with them.

5 **Look at the content of food to determine whether it is kosher.**
Previously in deciding what to eat, we based the decision on a food's appearance. From this point on, look at the contents. Read the label to learn all the ingredients. This examination can take one of two forms:

• *Purchase only food that has a kosher label on it.* A kosher label tells you that the food was produced or prepared under the supervision of a specific rabbinic authority. Some examples of these are: **K** ⬛ (U)

If one or more of these labels appear on a package, the contents are kosher. Pay special attention to foods simply labeled K, however. The K implies that a rabbi who is not affiliated with any known group has supervised the preparation of the food. Consult your rabbi on the use of such products.

One instance in which everyone should insist on a rabbinic certification is in the purchase of canned tuna. Dolphin, or porpoise, natural predators of tuna, are often caught in the nets of tuna fishers. The corpses of these mammals are then generally ground in and canned with the tuna meat itself. Since dolphin, or porpoise, is *treif,* cans of kosher tuna may not contain any pieces of these sea mammals. Buying canned tuna with a rabbinic certification on the label will assure you not only that the contents are kosher but also that the tuna fishers are not making a profit from the death of these intelligent and beautiful animals. This is yet another instance in which observance of kashrut enforces a sensitivity and a concern for animal life.

• *Purchase foods without a rabbinic certification only after first checking the ingredients.* This approach is riskier than that of simply looking for rabbinic certification, but it is certainly possible. A good guide to chemical additives is essential. An excellent list is found at the back of *The Jewish Dietary Laws* by Samuel H. Dresner and Seymour Siegel (see For Further Reading at the end of this chapter); it provides information about which additives are dairy, which are pareve, and which are derived from animal products. Some natural colorings are derived from nonkosher sources (for example, the red dye cochineal, used in many fruit juices, is made from crushed insects).

Be careful to check for lard (pig fat), which is found in many baking mixes and pie crusts. If a label doesn't specify that a shortening is 100 percent vegetable shortening, then assume it is a meat derivative. These are often used in cakes, breads, cookies, and crackers.

---

6 **Ready for another leap? Eat only kosher varieties of fish.** The general guideline is the previously mentioned requirement of fins and scales. For those not expert on varieties of seafood, this excludes bullfish, eels, gars, lampreys, monkfish, puffers, sharks, rays, skates, triggerfish, and wolffish. Additionally, fish that are scavengers are generally considered nonkosher as well. Most prominently, this means no catfish. Swordfish and sturgeon are kosher, although among some Orthodox rabbis

there is a controversy about both of these fishes. For a complete list of kosher and nonkosher fishes, see Dresner and Siegel, *The Jewish Dietary Laws.*

---

7 **Avoid using eggs that contain blood.** As was mentioned earlier, the consumption of blood is prohibited because blood is a symbol of life and one of the apparent functions of kashrut is to sensitize the Jewish people to the sanctity of life. The Torah places blood off limits to emphasize the preciousness of life and to symbolize that ultimately life belongs to God, not to us. One surprising result of that restriction pertains to eggs. The egg of a kosher bird is kosher. If, however, the egg contains a drop of blood (generally as a result of the egg's having been fertilized), then it is no longer fit for consumption.

From now on, take care to ensure that there is no blood in any eggs you use. To avoid wasting eggs, break one egg at a time into a glass bowl and inspect it for drops of blood. (Glass can easily be made kosher again, so if blood is found, the bowl need not be thrown out.) Once an egg passes inspection, you can transfer it to a separate bowl containing other inspected eggs.

---

8 **Eat only "biblically permitted" meat.** This is the next step in observing a higher standard of kashrut. The only animals that can be used for kosher slaughter are noncarnivorous domestic poultry (such as chicken, turkey, duck, capon, and goose) and land mammals that have cloven hooves and chew their cud. Cattle, deer, goats, and sheep are permitted. Rabbit and pork are not (rabbits don't have hooves, and pigs don't chew their cud).

Some refer to this level of keeping kosher as biblical kashrut because it entails eating only those animals permitted in the Torah. The laws of kosher slaughtering, while essential to a full observance of kashrut and also vital for ensuring

> Kashrut sensitizes us to the sanctity of all living things by making us more aware of how we get our food and where that food comes from. The recent awareness that our desire for tuna meat results in the needless slaughter of dolphins culminated in a successful campaign to find more careful ways to catch only the tuna.

the least possible pain to the animals, are of rabbinic origin (and found at length in the Mishnah and Talmud).

In addition, a considerable number of people consider veal *treif* because of the cruelty with which the young cattle are raised. To the extent that kashrut teaches a reverence for life, eating commercially raised veal contradicts that praiseworthy goal. (See Chapter 17, step 12.)

9 **Acquire dishes to use only for milchig and pareve meals.** Follow this step once you feel comfortable separating milchig and fleischig foods. Wooden, glass, and metal utensils (including silverware), Pyrex and Corning Ware, refrigerators, dishwashers, microwave ovens, and stoves can be made kosher (see the appendix in Dresner and Siegel), so you need not purchase new ones if you are ready to set them aside and use them only for milchig and pareve products. Porcelain, stoneware, earthenware, and other ceramics cannot be *kashered* (with the exception of fine china, a talmudic concession to the financial

hardship that such a rule would impose). These must be replaced, as must Tupperware- and Rubbermaid-type containers.

After you have *kashered* what can be *kashered* and have purchased a second set of plates for dairy and pareve meals, it is now possible to serve dairy and pareve meals to people observing any level of kashrut, no matter how strictly. Your dairy food, dishes, and utensils adhere to the fullest standards of kashrut, which is quite an achievement. *Mazal tov!*

10 **The next challenge is to eat only kosher meat.** We have already seen that part of what determines the kosher status of meat is the species of animal involved. But it is also determined by the method of slaughter. The special ritual of slaughter is the pinnacle of halakhah's concern with minimizing the animal's suffering as much as possible. Kosher slaughtering involves the use of a knife that has no imperfections, so that a clean cut can be made. The cut severs the animal's sensation of pain instantly while also allowing the blood to drain from the meat. Once the blood is drained, the meat is soaked in water and salted to remove any additional blood. Only at the end of this process (established by the Talmud) is meat fully kosher.

For many people, this is a difficult step. After all, it means giving up red meat and poultry when eating in nonkosher restaurants or homes. To make this step easier, break it down into two separate steps:

• *Eat only kosher meat at home.* Because the home is a central institution of Jewish religion, beginning with a higher standard in the home makes sense. Rather than giving up nonkosher meat all at once, begin simply by raising the level of kashrut at home. In areas where there are no local kosher butchers, it is possible to order frozen kosher chicken and meat from several national corporations that will deliver to almost every area.

• *Once doing this feels comfortable, give up nonkosher meat even when eating out.* In practical terms, this means that when eating in nonkosher restaurants or in the homes of friends who do not observe the kosher laws, you become a fish-eating vegetarian. In time, this too will become second nature.

For some people, one stumbling block is the idea of having to tell a host or hostess that they no longer eat nonkosher meat. Jews are often embarrassed by having to articulate their religious needs. But try turning the picture around. Imagine inviting a Hindu friend over for a meal. Most of us would want to serve something that he or she could eat and would appreciate being told that observant Hindus don't eat meat. Far from feeling like an imposition, this wrinkle in the preparation of the meal could lead to a fascinating discussion about how Hindus see the world. Or imagine inviting a diabetic, or somebody who is boycotting a food because of a labor dispute. We would certainly want to accommodate our

Eating is more than just satisfying our hunger. It is an opportunity to be with people we love and to catch up with each other's lives and the affairs of the world.

guest. Jews can expect that same openness from others. So when invited out, speak up, and when hosting, be sure to ask whether your guests have any dietary restrictions or preferences that they would like you to respect.

Vegetarians' refusal to kill a living creature in order to satisfy their hunger may well embody one of kashrut's key values— reverence for life.

11 **Acquire kosher dishes, silverware, and pots for meat meals.** Once the only meat you eat is kosher meat, it is important to take this next step as soon as it becomes affordable so that you will be able to serve delicious meals to guests and to yourself. The procedures for *kashering* utensils are described in Dresner and Siegel.

12 **Practice the biblical tradition of "taking ḥallah."** In the biblical period, most Israelites inherited a parcel of land on which they could support themselves by farming or tending herds of livestock. The only exceptions were the *kohanim* and the Levites, who served in the Temple in Jerusalem. To provide for their sustenance, each Jew would offer these

functionaries a portion of their income, generally in the form of meat, grain, and other tithes. Since there is no longer a Temple at which animals are sacrificed, Jews no longer bring offerings to the *kohanim*. In memory of this biblical practice, however, and to incorporate a link to the Land of Israel through observation of the agricultural laws of Judaism, Jews still take a pinch from each new batch of dough they make. This is called "taking ḥallah" (in the Talmud, *ḥallah* means "loaf"). Should you bake anything from dough, take a piece of dough from each batch, pinch it off, and recite the following *berakhah* ("blessing"):

בָּרוּךְ אַתָּה יְיָ אֱלֹהֵינוּ מֶלֶךְ הָעוֹלָם אֲשֶׁר קִדְּשָׁנוּ בְּמִצְוֹתָיו וְצִוָּנוּ לְהַפְרִישׁ חַלָּה מִן הָעִסָּה.

Barukh atah Adonai eloheinu melekh ha-olam, asher kid'shanu b'mitzvotav v'tzivanu l'haf'rish ḥallah min ha-isa.

Praised are You, Adonai our God, Ruler of the universe, whose mitzvot add holiness to our lives and who commanded us to take ḥallah from the dough.

In biblical times, the ḥallah offering was given to a *kohen*. In our own time, the little pinch of dough symbolizes that ancient offering, and because it is only a symbol, it isn't holy in itself. As with the ḥallah offering of antiquity, the only requirement is that it not be used. So, after saying the *berakhah*, simply throw it out.

Like most other mitzvot, the requirement to take ḥallah pertains only to Jews. Consequently, if the dough was "owned" by non-Jews as it was being baked (say, at a non-Jewish bakery), then the bread is kosher even if no ḥallah was taken. If, however, the dough was "owned" by Jews when it was baked, then it is not kosher unless ḥallah is taken. Ḥallah can be taken at home after the loaf is purchased, by pinching off a piece of it.

❖　❖　❖　❖　❖

We cannot be Jewish alone. More than just a creed or an orientation of faith, Judaism requires a community of participants. Only in such a community can Judaism be fully expressed. As the religious civilization of the Jewish people and as the response of Jews to the commanding presence of God, Judaism can work its transforming and healing gifts only amidst people.

Don't keep kosher alone. There is no need to become isolated. As we all move up the ladder of greater involvement in kashrut, we don't need to invent the art of living with the dietary laws as though no one else had done so already. Be sure to purchase some good kosher cookbooks. Keeping kosher is a lot more than just gefilte fish! Years of experience are distilled in those collections, and it's amazing how many wonderful cuisines can be prepared in a kosher manner. Get to know some people in a nearby synagogue who can provide tips (and maybe some elbow grease!) on how to *kasher* a kitchen, where to buy kosher supplies, and how to transform favorite recipes into kosher ones. Seek out a rabbi who can be a source of advice and guidance throughout the process.

Above all, don't give up. For thousands of years, observing kashrut has been essential to Jewish commitment and Jewish identity. A way of eating that affirms our identity as a people and infuses our daily life with a touch of the sacred, kashrut has much to offer an age starved for community, spirituality, and caring. And by keeping kosher, we in turn will bring that much more meaning, self-discipline, and sensitivity to our lives, our families, and our communities.

For Further Reading

Samuel H. Dresner and Seymour Siegel, *The Jewish Dietary Laws: Their Meaning for Our Time and a Guide to Observance.* New York: Rabbinical Assembly and United Synagogue Commission on Jewish Education, 1982.

James M. Lebeau, *The Jewish Dietary Laws: Sanctify Life.* New York: United Synagogue of America, Department of Youth Activities, 1983.

CHOOSING A WINE

According to the Conservative movement, all white wines are kosher. Some red wines use the blood of oxen for fining (filtering sediment out of the liquid), rendering the product *treif* according to many rabbis. By using only rabbinically certified wines, it is easy to sidestep the dilemma of determining which are kosher. And several excellent kosher wines are now on the market. In Israel, Italy, France, Spain, and California, wines of increasingly high caliber already carry a kosher label. In particular, three California products—Hagafen, Baron Herzog, and Weinstocks—are wines worth drinking for their quality alone. For ritual purposes, however, rabbinically supervised wines must be used, and it is a good idea to use Israeli wine, as a way of strengthening the connection of the Jewish people worldwide and of helping the Israeli economy, if only in a small way.

9 *Kibbud Av va-Em:*

Honoring Parents

Rabbi Shimon Bar Yoḥai said, "…the most difficult of all mitzvot is 'Honor your father and your mother.'"

—TANḤUMA, EKEV 2

There are three partners in the creation of a person—God, the father, and the mother. When a person honors the parents, God says, "I consider it as though I lived with them and they honored Me." — TALMUD, KIDDUSHIN 30B

At every stage of life, relating to our parents is a tricky business. In our infancy, parents possess a control over us that is total. When they feed us, we eat. When they change our diapers, we are clean. When they put us in our cribs, we sleep. Our parents' schedule and priorities shape our lives. As we grow into adolescence, however, that balance begins to shift. We begin to assert authority over when we will come home, which friends we will hang out with, and which school subjects and activities we will give our greatest attention to.

That shifting balance of power is a difficult adjustment for both parent and child. One representative dilemma involved a congregant's oldest daugh-

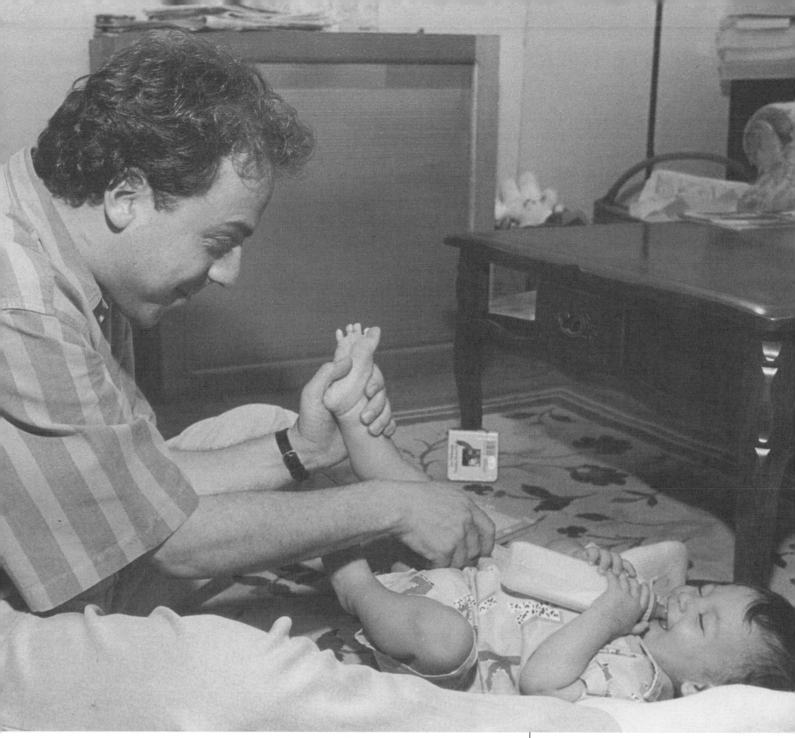

ter during her senior year in high school. The daughter had applied to a distant college that offered a program tailored to her interest in drama. Her parents had always supported her passion for drama, even paying for summer acting programs in the community. But they desperately wanted her to stay close to home and attend the local community college or the university. While both of these were fine schools, neither had the reputation or the resources that their daughter wanted. She knew that she wouldn't be as available to her parents if she attended the school of

The endless hours of love, teaching, and sharing that good parenting entails is a gift so complete that Judaism bids us to spend the rest of our lives honoring our parents with gratitude and appreciation.

her choice, but she felt that that school would give her chosen career a significant boost.

I worked with the family to try to separate the issues involved and to find ways to discuss them. What I couldn't tell the daughter or her parents was that the conflicts involved in choosing between opportunity and proximity had only just begun. Years down the road, those same conflicts would emerge around career choices: Should she take a mediocre job to be near her parents or a wonderful job that was far away? Did she owe it to her parents to remain nearby? Were they right to ask it of her?

The issue of honoring parents while living an independent life confronts anyone whose parents are still alive. That we owe our parents honor and reverence is a given in Jewish tradition. The mitzvah of *kibbud av va-em* (כִּבּוּד אָב וָאֵם , "honoring father and mother") is the fifth of Aseret ha-Dibrot (עֲשֶׂרֶת הַדִּבְּרוֹת , "Ten Commandments"), standing halfway between the first four (dealing with the relationship with God) and the last five (establishing standards of social morality). That placement reflects the insight that parents represent a bridge between God and the world, between our personal drama of Creation and our entry into the world of human interaction and expectation.

Children, struggling to establish independent personalities and lives, often need guidelines on how to love and honor their parents properly. And as they grow, they need to learn how to balance the reverence and gratitude they owe their parents with the legitimate pursuit of their own interests and priorities. Consider the following situations:

• A few years ago, a young couple called and told me they were considering marriage. I met with them several times, and we enjoyed wonderful discussions about their relationship, their dreams, and their expectations of marriage. After a month of our meetings, the young woman visited me in tears. She told me that her parents disliked the young man, and they insisted that ultimately she too would see that he

"In so many cases, it is the parents who make it impossible for
the young to obey the Fifth
Commandment. My message to
parents is: 'Every day ask your-
selves the question: What is there
about me that deserves the reverence of my child?'"
—Rabbi Abraham Joshua Heschel

was not right for her. Then they told her that they forbade the relationship. Her heart was broken. She was torn between her desire to honor her parents and her growing love for her friend.

SOARING ON OUR PARENTS' WINGS

As adults, how do we demonstrate the gratitude and respect we owe our parents for the care we received at an earlier age?

I still remember my seventh-grade science teacher asking everyone in the class to choose a science project. I decided that I wanted to study an octopus in my aquarium. No amount of discussion, pleading, or appeals to authority could move me. So my poor dad called up and down the state of California until he finally located a graduate student in oceanography willing to spare two tiny octopuses to help out one devoted father and his stubborn son.

I can recall my mother's endless love and devotion in so many instances, but one recurring example stands out. From my earliest age, my mother edited all of my school papers, none of which made it through with less than five drafts. She spent hours reading and rereading each draft, enduring my frustration and anger at having to revise the paper yet again. She was, and is, my toughest editor—but it is because of her patience and care that I am able to write with the skill that I have today.

I also remember my stepfather, Kurt, who spent hours trying to transform me into a decent tennis player (a task that, given my lack of ability, was not easy!). Endless hours of practice together eventually did help, but even more precious to me were the wisdom and humor he dispensed as we played. I still see the world from the perspective he shared with me.

Now that I am adult, how can I reciprocate the affection, concern, and care that I received from these loving parents?

- A forty-two-year-old congregant explained to me that his wife and his mother always fight when they are together. He loves and respects both, but the two of them just can't get along. He had always been able to juggle the two relationships in the past, but now his mother was no longer able to care for herself and had asked to move in with him. As her only child, he felt obliged to honor her request. His wife told him she would consent, with great reluctance, if he insisted on doing so. And now he felt paralyzed, not knowing how to balance the love he felt for each of them.

In each phase of life, as issues of autonomy and connection interact and shift, the questions of how to honor parents and whether there are any limits to that honor face every adult with living parents. Perhaps most difficult of all are the cases in which parents barely performed the minimal duties of support and love; or in which parents abused their children—through neglect, beatings, or sexual molestation. How is one to honor these parents? Does one *have* to honor them?

❖　❖　❖　❖　❖

The Jewish tradition places great emphasis on *kibbud* (כִּבּוּד , literally, "honor," the way we act) and *yirah* (יִרְאָה , literally, "reverence," our intentions) toward parents. As the people to whom we owe life itself, as the people who provided years of care, and as the link to Judaism and the Jewish past, our parents merit our honor and respect.

One of the roots for our obligation to honor our parents is their role as a preeminent source of our lives. The Talmud teaches that three partners are involved in the birth of every person—God, the mother, and the father. Parents represent God not only in their role in our inception and birth but also on a psychological level. Through the countless acts involved in raising children, parents demonstrate that the world is reliable and basically good. Each time mothers comfort screaming babies, each time fathers offer a bottle to hungry infants, children learn anew that they are not alone in a meaningless void, that their needs are met, that compassion and love are real and potent. In nurturing their children, parents establish the emotional base for a subsequent relationship between their child and the sacred.

There is also a specifically Jewish component to honoring one's parents. These people—our parents—provide the tangible link to our sacred past, our culture, and our covenant with God. The childhood memories of lighting Ḥanukkah candles, the smell of warm loaves of ḥallah on a newly set Shabbat table, the joy and love of a Passover seder—all of these connections to our Jewishness are transmitted through our parents. Even in those families where the child's Jewish commitment is more consuming or more elab-

Although younger people tend to associate old age with illness and frailty, most seniors today report that this age is, in many ways, the best period of their lives. Society owes these people the opportunity to share their wisdom and experience, and the right to continue to be productive and contributing members of the community.

orate than that of the parents, the core of the child's identification as a Jew is still a product of who the parents are and the nature of their family and friends.

Although the Torah records the mitzvah of *honoring* parents, nowhere in Jewish tradition are children commanded to *love* them. Focusing on deeds of honor, Jewish tradition says nothing about whether or not a person owes love to the people who originally gave them life. Why is this so?

Some would claim that emotions are spontaneous and uncontrollable. Yet it is simply untrue that one cannot command love. We cultivate and direct our emotions all the time—toward spouse, friends, work, and country, for example. The Torah itself commands love of God, of fellow Jews, and of non-Jews. So why doesn't the Torah or the Talmud mandate the love of parents?

I believe that the lack of such an imperative recognizes that there is no relationship as complex, multilayered, and deep as that between a parent and his or her child. Even a close spouse—the person with whom most of us share our adult lives—doesn't acquire the profound psychological significance that a parent has. Experiences of total dependency, of complete rebellion, of increasing similarity are all commonplace between the generations. Spouses can divorce and friends can separate, but a parent is forever.

Given the overwhelming variety of feelings and relationships that each individual has with his or her parents, it would be impossible to reduce that bundle of feelings to any one emotion. The entire range of human passions exists between parents and children. But behavior can be controlled, and respect and honor are legitimate demands even as emotions fluctuate and contradict one another. For that reason, Jewish tradition focuses on the practical question of how to treat parents rather than attempting to regulate (an impossible task from the start) how children feel about their parents.

A warning is necessary here: Other chapters of

this book suggest concrete actions—how to observe Shabbat, how to improve the earth, and so on. In this instance, there are so many different personalities and stages of life involved in parenting and relating to parents that this chapter can only suggest the rough outlines of a positive Jewish approach to parental relations.

Families come in all shapes and sizes, linked by mutual responsibility, love, and respect. In the context of a loving family, parents can help their children develop a sense of self-worth and trust.

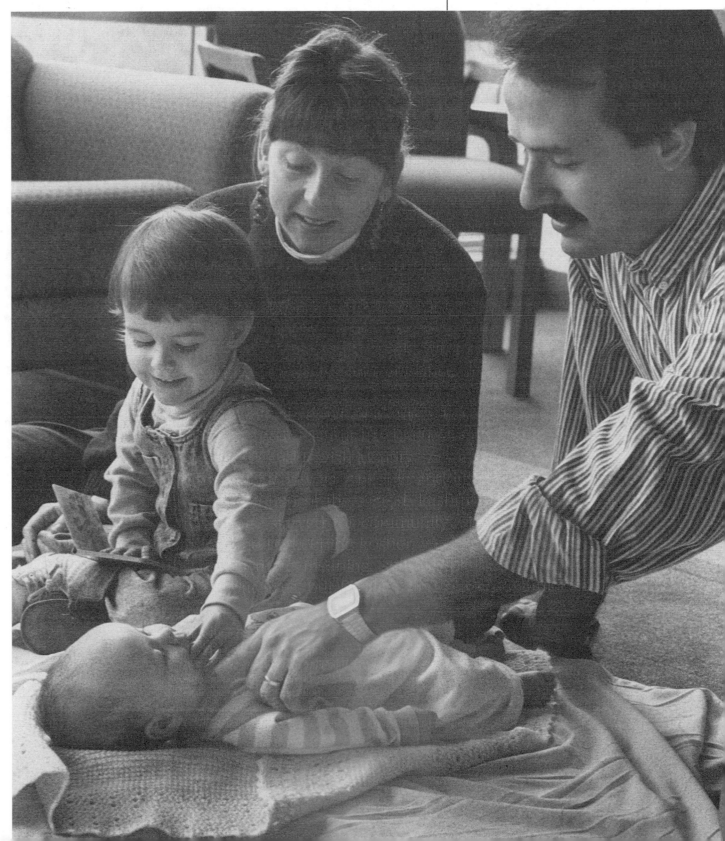

1 **Give your parents priority.** There are many people who need help in the world. Before depleting large amounts of time assisting others, it is important to make sure your own parents' basic needs have been met.

This caveat is not meant to replace other mitzvot and charitable concerns; it is simply meant to provide balance. We are our parents' primary link to the world and to the future. No one can replace our involvement. At the same time, our parents are our primary link to the past and to our own childhood identity. No one else has had such an extensive hand in our formation and growth over such a length of time.

Primacy is at the core of honoring parents. That honor may take the form of making weekly phone calls, remembering birthdays, paying regular visits, sharing meals, making shopping expeditions, and driving a parent to a doctor's office—all are different ways to demon-

Our tradition teaches that human dignity is a gift from God, something we are commanded to cultivate and venerate in each human being we encounter.

strate the centrality of our parents in our lives. What matters more than any specific deed is the attitude of caring and respect that the actions convey.

Of the two traditional modes of honoring parents, *kibbud* (our actions) and *yirah* (our intentions), *yirah* logically precedes *kibbud*, because our attitude toward our parents will permeate any behavior toward them. In fact, the Jerusalem Talmud states that one can serve parents pheasant and still deserve banishment, or on the other extreme, one can make parents grind grain and still deserve eternal life. Rashi explains this to mean that what matters is the attitude of the child as well as the reasons and context for making the request or providing the service. *Yirah* implies treating parents with a spirit of reverence, dignity, and loyalty.

2 **Preserve your parents' dignity.** According to tradition, a parent who has a special place at the table, or a favorite seat, is entitled to the dignity of retaining that place. Displacing someone is more than just a physical act; it is an assertion of that person's irrelevance, a statement that we have replaced him or her. Above all else, *yirah* is the insistence that the parent's concerns are still relevant, that the parent still matters. To this day, I remember visiting my grandparents' home, where my "Papa's" special high-backed blue chair was reserved exclusively for him. Even when he wasn't in the room, no one sat in his place.

3 **Honor your parents' views.** Strenuous public disagreement is an assertion of complete equality, of a willingness to treat someone else's opinion as trivial. To disagree publicly with one's parents runs the danger of trivializing them as well. This is not to say that parents and children cannot disagree, but the style of the dispute must itself reflect the child's reverence for the parent and the significance of the parent to the child.

This is particularly difficult in the case of an abusive parent. Jewish tradition does not intend to force a child to submit to degradation and suffering at the hands of a parent. Each person has a right to dignity and respect. How, then, apply the mitzvah of *yirah* to parents who routinely violate this right?

If *yirah* is to mean anything, it must mean that a child's relationship with a parent is not the same as his or her relationship with other people. While a child may, and should, assert his or her own self-worth and the right to decent treatment, *yirah* implies that conflict with parents should not involve unnecessary hostility—that name-calling, threats, and violence have no place even in setting reasonable limits on abusive parents. Children owe parents a respectful, restrained, and dignified presentation of their feelings. *Yirah* also implies that children should try to remain open to true regret and repentance on the part of formerly abusive parents.

---

4 **Retain a distinction between the generations.** We live in an age of militant equality. Everyone is the equal of everyone else, regardless of talent, training, and commitment. We attack hierarchy in any form. One of the few remaining areas of authority is that of parents with regard to children: Parents and children are still not equals. Although most children will become autonomous individuals with the ability to live their own lives, they will never be their parents' peers, nor should they be.

As a way of maintaining respect for their parents, children of every age should be taught not to address their parents or grandparents by their first names. This talmudic requirement also applies to addressing teachers, whether in secular or in religious school. A false egalitarianism destroys a respect for achievement that is necessary to generate growth, ambition, and accomplishment.

---

5 **Provide for your parents' health needs.** The essence of *kibbud* is to provide service to your parents and to care for their physical needs. As people age, particularly when they live alone, they may neglect their health. Jewish tradition obligates children to ensure that their parents will always have adequate food and drink. In addition, adult children should make sure their parents receive proper medical support.

---

6 **Provide for your parents' shelter and security.** The Talmud requires that children provide clothing and shelter for their parents. In essence, the Talmud makes adult children responsible for protecting their parents from the ravages of life. In our day, that may mean installing an alarm system in a parent's apartment, maintaining a yard, cleaning the home, or arranging a move to a new home, possibly even a retirement home.

---

7 **Provide your parents with access to the outside world.** The final talmudic requirement of *kibbud* is to assist parents by taking their hand and leading them as they walk. This aspect of honor involves two related roles—

> The Talmud says that one's children's children are as one's own children, but there is a unique quality to the love between grandparent and grandchild that people carry with them throughout their lives.

ensuring that parents enjoy mobility in the larger world and showing a willingness to facilitate that mobility. In the talmudic world, leading someone was a way of honoring them as well as a way of helping them go places that would otherwise have remained inaccessible. In our time as well, aging often imposes severe physical limits: an aging parent's circle of friends shrinks; opportunities for entertainment, learning, and love become fewer and more difficult. Children can break through that isolation, providing the impetus and the mobility that allows fuller participation in life.

As parents age, they become increasingly dependent on the people for whom they used to provide care. Just as infants need someone to see to their food, drink, clothing, and housing, so do many aging adults. Motivating *kibbud*, then, is gratitude and memory—a reciprocity for the many years of physical service that parents provided for their children.

8 Forgive your parents' imperfections.
Perhaps even more difficult than providing physical service for parents is according to them the same liberty that children demand for themselves. As we grow, we insist on the right to go our own way, and we expect to be forgiven for our inevitable human shortcomings. Yet children hold their parents to an impossibly high standard, expecting them to be perfect and to grow in the same directions in which the children grow.

Most parents are simply unable always to live up to their own expectations, let alone their children's. Being able to recognize that your parents are not omnipotent, that they struggle to do their best, can help you treat them with honor and respect even when you don't share their priorities or like the way they behave.

9 Allow your parents their own lifestyles and values. Just as you insist on the right to live your own life, parents retain the right to live theirs. Inevitably, two people will not always have the same concerns at the same time, particularly when the complicated dynamics of parent and child are involved. Your parents have the right to live their lives as best they understand them, just as we do. Give them that right.

10 Jews-by-choice must honor their parents' personal preferences.
Converting to Judaism means ending allegiance to any other religion, but it does not mean abandoning the family of your childhood. While religious issues (such as what to do about Christmas) may need careful resolution, the Jew-by-choice is still a member of a gentile family (as is the Jewish spouse and the couple's children), and that gentile family deserves precisely the same love, respect, and honor as the Jewish family.

❖ ❖ ❖ ❖ ❖

Halakhah's requirements for honoring our parents are a fundamental basis for much of our moral development. By recognizing the legitimate role of parents as our link to the past and to our heritage, *kibbud av va-em* educates us to value the insights of our ancestors and to recognize our own dependency on those who have gone before. In addition, by requiring our involvement in meeting the physical needs of our parents, *kibbud av va-em* sensitizes us to the needs of others and opens us to the rich reward of helping when help is needed.

With so many benefits— for the social order, for family life, and for individual growth—this mitzvah can appear to be without limit. And yet there is indeed a limit. A parent can legitimately ask for the services and attention that are directly related to the relationship between child and parent. But the child also has a right to a contented life. In those areas that do not pertain explicitly to the life of the parent or to the relationship between child and parent, the child has every right to make independent decisions. Which career to pursue, whom to love, and where to live are questions that each of us must answer for ourselves.

According to the Talmud, "When people honor their father and mother, God says, 'I consider it as if I live with them and they honor Me.'" In learning to relate to our parents as people worthy of unique respect and care yet also as real human beings with weaknesses and foibles, we negotiate nothing less than the way to live contentedly in a world that is imperfect yet also a marvel.

There is so much more that links the generations than divides them. One great advantage of living a Jewish life is that the wisdom and beauty of millennia embrace young and old in a common heritage and celebration.

For Further Reading

Gerald Blidstein, *Honor Thy Father and Mother: Filial Responsibility in Jewish Law and Ethics.* New York: Ktav Publishing House, 1975.

Lissy Jarvik and Gary Small, *Parentcare: A Compassionate Guide for Children and Their Aging Parents.* New York: Bantam Books, 1988.

Norman Linzer, *The Jewish Family: Authority and Tradition in Modern Perspective.* New York: Human Sciences Press, 1984.

10 *Pidyon Sh'vuyim:*

Redeeming the Captive

Captivity is harder than all [other forms of suffering] because it includes the suffering of all [the other forms].

—TALMUD, BAVA BATRA 8B

Cry with full throat; without restraint Raise your voice like a ram's horn! . . . Unlock the fetters of wickedness Untie the cords of the yoke. Let the oppressed go free Break off every yoke.　*—ISAIAH 58:1, 6*

My family in America had never known of any Russian relatives, so I could not possibly have anticipated my father's announcement that we had cousins in Russia.

A few months earlier, one of my American cousins, who was temporarily working in Moscow, received a phone call from a Russian Jew who informed him that they were related. My great-grandfather had arrived at Ellis Island a little after the turn of the century, and it seems that he had left a brother behind in the old country to care for their parents. The Russian branch of my family descended from that great-granduncle. My cousin sent a letter to my father, who became so excited that he arranged to spend two weeks touring Russia with the express pur-

pose of forging a relationship with our newly discovered family.

While in Russia, my dad was overwhelmed by the poverty of the people and the hardship of their lives. But he was also taken by their remarkable warmth and enthusiasm. He returned to California with hundreds of photos of smiling faces that looked just like the faces of our cousins in New York and Los Angeles. But most of the people in the pictures could speak little English beyond a simple "hello" and "good-bye."

A year after my father's return, he received a call from Vladimir, one of the Russian cousins. Vladimir was interested in coming to America, ostensibly to establish some business connections abroad but in reality to try to move with his wife and daugh-

For approximately 70 years of Communist rule, Jews and others in Russia were not free to practice their faith. Today, religious faith is once again permitted, although some fear a resurgence of anti-Semitism. The challenge now is to assist these Jews in their return to Judaism. Pictured above are the gates to the Leningrad synagogue.

ters to freedom in America. He had been studying English for years to facilitate this goal.

The first hurdle was to get Vladimir to the United States. He had no money and was entirely dependent on the response of our family—people who had never seen him. Cousins from every part of the country contributed money to buy him a plane ticket, first to New York and then to San Francisco.

A month later, I met Vladimir. A tall man with a thick black beard and sparkling eyes, Vladimir typifies, for me, the Russian Jew. Deep wells of patience, determination, and humor lend strength and perspective to his insistent efforts to find work and bring his family to America. When Vladimir arrived, he presented my wife and me with a book of paintings from the Leningrad Museum. We gave him a Hebrew-Russian Bible. He had never seen a Jewish Bible before.

Vladimir spent Shabbat with us. We lit candles, shared ḥallah, and recited Kiddush over the sweet, red wine. On Saturday morning, we took him to the synagogue, where he was called to the *bimah* to dress the Torah. After services, we all took a walk in the hills near our home. Vladimir described his life in Russia. He told of the danger of being a Jew in the Soviet Union, of the permanent sense of being an outsider. He explained that his non-Jewish friends had a difficult time understanding why being a Jew is important to him. He spoke of how moving it was to be able to be in a synagogue, to celebrate Shabbat freely, and he revealed that that morning was the first time he had held a Torah scroll. Vladimir spoke of his determination to raise his daughters in freedom, where they would have a greater knowledge of their Jewish identity. He also spoke of his own desire to learn about Judaism and its values.

Demonstrations, marches, and picketing are important tools to put pressure on despotic governments that oppress their Jewish populations and to mobilize public opinion for their defense.

In Vladimir's presence, I felt small and spoiled. How easy my life seemed in comparison to his: synagogues in every neighborhood, Jewish books sold in bookstores. Comfort and safety characterizes our communities while Vladimir and two million Soviet Jews had to maintain an almost secret Jewish identity, unable to rely on the protection of their government or the decency of their fellow citizens. For decades, the Jews of Russia were imprisoned for the crime of teaching or learning Hebrew; they were fired from their jobs for applying to move to Israel and then thrown in jail for parasitism, the crime of not working. Quotas kept Jews out of Russian universities and graduate programs. Synagogues were shut down, and the few that remained open were under government surveillance.

Despite the full force of Soviet secret police and government disapproval, many Jews found the courage to build a Jewish underground. They cherished smuggled Hebrew books, tefillin, prayerbooks, and books on Israel. They surrounded American Jewish tourists, urging them to protest their treatment when they returned to the West. They made Simḥat Torah an annual celebration of Jewish identity; for them, it expressed their scorn for the Soviet system and its anti-Semitism.

The Jews of the former Soviet Union are only one of the Jewish communities that have suffered the fear of violence and the pain of poverty. The Beta Yisrael, "the Jews of Ethiopia," known for too long as Falashas (a Geez word of disdain meaning "stranger" or "exile"), are also heirs to a long legacy of oppression and abuse. For millennia, these people lived in northern Ethiopia with a distinct culture and tradition. In fact, during the medieval period, they maintained a proud and separate kingdom. Unaware of the writings or practices of Rabbinic Judaism, the Jews of Ethiopia had practiced a Judaism in many ways reminiscent of the Judaism described in the Bible, and they burned with a passionate love for Zion.

Large numbers of Russian and Ethiopian Jews

FREE THE HOSTAGE

Captive Jews are nothing new. As long as Jews have dwelled among a hostile majority, the mitzvah of *pidyon sh'vuyim* (פִּדְיוֹן שְׁבוּיִים, "redeeming the captive") remained a central obligation of every Jewish community. Throughout the Middle Ages and even into modernity, Jewish organizations would establish special funds to pay for the freedom of Jews held hostage simply because they were Jews.

have now settled in Israel. Operation Moses transferred some ten thousand Ethiopian Jews to Israel—the first time in the history of the world that a large number of blacks were voluntarily settled as equals in a predominantly white country. More recently, Israel successfully transported all but some two thousand of Ethiopia's remaining Jews to their new homes in Israel. Similarly, once the Russian government permitted its Jews to make aliyah, Operation Exodus was created to provide the funds and organization to translate that permission into reality.

The miracle is within our grasp. For the first time since the destruction of the Temple, some two thousand years ago, we can procure the freedom of almost a million Jews; we have the ability and the power to restore countless Jews to their homeland. The vast Diaspora community of Russian Jews stands on the brink of reunification with their people and their heritage.

Of course, the situation in the republics of the former Soviet Union and in all of Eastern Europe is

Jews from Ethiopia have already enriched Israeli society through service in the defense forces, enrollment in schools and universities, and the use of their talents in Israel's diverse workforce. The Ethiopian Jews' devotion to the Land of Israel is an inspiration for Jews everywhere.

highly unstable. As of this writing, several former Communists have won reelections, and a resurgent anti-Semitism has become part of the public discourse in Russia and elsewhere. Despite such troubles, freedom is possible for these Jews. All it takes is a steady stream of flights to bring them to Israel, apartments for them to live in, training for their employment in a modern economy, clothing, food, and schools to teach them Hebrew. Many already have permission to emigrate.

Yet, adding complication to the status of Russian Jewry is the refusal of many to immigrate to Israel. Like so many other Jewish communities, many Russian Jews would rather struggle to cultivate their lives and their Judaism where they are. So part of our task is to provide these people, separated from their heritage by years of Communist indoctrination and dictatorship, with teachers, textbooks, and the resources necessary to establish the synagogues and schools in their homeland that are so vital to a meaningful Jewish life.

The only impediment to that sacred goal is a shortage of funds, energy, and involvement. This is not the first time that American Jews have been tested. In 1943, in a cynical gesture to extort money from an embattled world, the government of Romania offered to liberate its Jews for a significant sum of money. In America, a Jewish organization ran an ad in *The New York Times* proclaiming: FOR SALE TO HUMANITY: 70,000 JEWS GUARANTEED; HUMAN BEINGS AT $50 APIECE. When the money wasn't raised, those Jews were murdered in the Nazi death camps.

Once again, although in a different context, we are being tested. Once more, the well-being of our fellow Jews is in our hands. If we demonstrate sufficient heart, generosity, and courage, they will be free, and we will have established our decency as practitioners of the venerable mitzvah of *pidyon sh'vuyim*.

This time, we dare not fail.

❖　❖　❖　❖　❖

1 **Join organizations that focus on specific groups of Jews.** Redeeming captive Jews sometimes requires publicizing their plight, and so it also requires an acute sensitivity to whether or not publicity will help. In some cases, as with Russia, public pressure is precisely what will most benefit the Jews living there. In other cases, however, such as with Ethiopian Jewry, publicity was what prevented their freedom in the first place. It is impossible to become an expert in the intricacies of diplomacy. As loose cannons we can do little good, and there is the real possibility of causing harm. Each of us must rely on the government of Israel and on private Jewish organizations to keep us informed and to direct our actions.

The organizations below can provide relevant information about the current status of each local Jewish population and how we can help them most effectively. Some of the principal groups are

> North American Conference on
>   Ethiopian Jewry
> 165 East 56th Street
> New York, NY 10022
> 212-752-6340

> National Conference on Soviet Jewry
> 730 Broadway, Second Floor
> New York, NY 10003-9596
> 212-780-9500

> Union of Councils
> 1819 H Street, NW, Suite 230
> Washington, DC 20006
> 202-775-9770

2 **Donate clothing, pots, dishes, and furniture to a nearby synagogue or to the Jewish Family Service Agency.** There are a growing number of Jewish immigrants from countries in which Jews have suffered oppression—Russia, the Arab nations, and Ethiopia are just a few. As refugees from these places settle into life in America, they need our help. They also need to learn English and to

make friends. Our gifts and our time will make a great difference in their feeling welcome and supported.

3 **Send telegrams and letters and even make phone calls to the governments and embassies in whose lands Jews are oppressed.** This is a crucial way to remind them that we are watching and that more needs to be done. Despite the leniency of the new Russian government, there are still several issues that remain unresolved. The pertinent addresses to which to direct your concerns are these:

> Embassy of the Republic of Russia
> 1125 16th Street, NW
> Washington, DC 20036
> 202-628-7551

> Russian Mission to the United Nations
> 136 East 67th Street
> New York, NY 10021
> 212-861-4900

> Consulate General of the Russian
>   Federation
> 2790 Green Street
> San Francisco, CA 94123
> 415-202-9800

• *Write to the Russian government, urging it to allow more Israeli consuls in Russia with greater working space.* Although many more Russian Jews now have permission to leave Russia, the shortage of staff has often delayed the processing of their emigration forms. In addition, the number of Israeli consuls and the size of their facilities are limited by Russian regulation.

• *Also, urge the Russian government to increase the number of customs officials examining containers bound for Israel.*

4 **Through letters and phone calls, encourage the newly democratic governments in Eastern Europe to provide transit visas for Jews seeking immigration to Israel.** The more avenues open to Jewish immigration to Israel, the more quickly large numbers of Jews can leave and live in safety.

Political action is always for a serious purpose, but it can also be fun. These children lead a race on behalf of Russian Jews, raising consciousness and money at the same time.

5 **Become politically involved.** A great deal of credit for the success of opening up Russian immigration goes to American politicians who formed a powerful lobby on behalf of the Russian refuseniks. They have also worked with foreign countries on behalf of Jews in Ethiopia, Syria, Yemen, and elsewhere.

The need for political involvement is still pressing. We cannot hope to help the Jews of Ethiopia, for example, without the active support of the administration in Washington, as well as that of senators and representatives of Congress. Their involvement will continue only if we educate our politicians and demonstrate our own tenacity. Below are several ways of achieving these goals:

• *Maintain a correspondence with both state and federal elected officials and inform them of needed action as new issues arise.* Keep your letters short, neat, and positive. And don't issue threats—nobody likes to be intimidated.

• *Find out when Congress and the state legislature adjourn, and schedule a meeting with your legislator during his or her recess.* When not in session, most legislators head back to their local districts to try to shore up support among their voters. Use the allotted time to thank the legislator for any previous support, to sketch out what is happening now, and to describe what action is required. Keep the meeting brief, and stick to the main point. At the end of the meeting, ask whether members of the legislator's staff will be assigned to the issue.

Remember to send a thank you letter summarizing the discussion and reminding the legislator of whatever political intervention or position should emerge as the next step. And keep in contact with any relevant staff members; they often have the power to speak and intervene on the legislator's behalf.

• *When visiting Washington, DC, or your state capital, make an appointment with each of your elected representatives.* Such a meeting can be even more effective than one in the legislator's district office because it shows your greater effort to meet the legislators on their own turf.

Following any meeting with an elected official, notify the appropriate Jewish agency. It will want to know whether the representative made any commitments or stated any positions that it could then build on.

---

6 **Participate in (or start) a program for welcoming Jewish immigrants into your community.** Many congregations have special committees for helping new immigrants as they make the transition to American life. Not only will this involvement help the new Americans, but it will also teach the local community the importance of reaching out to others.

• *Many congregations offer a year's free membership to any Russian Jew.* Suggest this policy, as a minimum, to the rabbi and synagogue president. Another idea is to provide Russian Jews with candlesticks and a Russian transliteration and translation of the Shabbat blessings.

• *An even more demanding commitment, but one that is also more rewarding, is to adopt a Russian family.* In many larger Jewish communities, this program has successfully linked recent arrivals with more established families. By inviting recent Russian emigres to share a Shabbat meal or the celebration of a Jewish holiday, by guiding them in their search for work, by introducing them to the intricacies of shopping in America, and by helping with other technical details, you can make their transition much less frightening. In the process, you will learn about life under totalitarian rule (a good source for our own gratitude!) and help touch the lives of another family.

---

7 **Give generously to the special funds established (primarily through the Jewish Community Federation) to assist Jewish immigrants and refugees.** With *pidyon sh'vuyim*, as with any social change, progress is expensive. It costs a lot to fly a Jew

Like the United States and Canada, Israel is a nation of immigrants from around the world. Democracies are enriched by the rich symphony of cultures and peoples, each adding to the nation's human resources, diversity, and wisdom. Pictured here are the Jews of Yemen who suffered under an oppressive government for hundreds of years. In 1950, the Israelis brought almost the entire Jewish population of Yemen to Israel, approximately forty-three thousand people.

to Israel (or America), to provide him or her with shelter, clothing, and instruction in language and a trade. Yet a commitment to the freedom of all Jews means nothing if it doesn't include a willingness to foot the bill. To be one people must translate into mutual support. The Talmud says that "all Jews are responsible for one another." To liberate and sustain the many Jews who have known suffering, fear, and poverty is surely a worthy investment and a lofty ideal. It is also our responsibility to act quickly; the opportunity may never come again.

❖　　❖　　❖　　❖　　❖

Alla Khazova, a Russian Jew, was visiting her relatives in New Jersey. While staying with her family, she overheard her daughter ask her American cousin why he wore a Star of David. She remembered his simple response: "I'm a Jew." Alla Khazova told a reporter for *The New York Times,* "I'm emigrating because my daughter is afraid to say that. I want my children to live in a free country where they can calmly say, 'I'm a Jew.'"

We all want that. We are a hand's grasp away from our people's freedom, a possibility so compelling precisely because it was impossible for so long. Once before, within this very century, we were offered a similar opportunity, and we turned our backs on our own. Now, through the liberation of others, we have the chance to redeem ourselves and to redirect our destiny as a people.

If we will it, it is no dream.

Do not stand by the blood of your fellow, I am Adonai.
—LEVITICUS 19:16

For Further Reading

Martin Gilbert, *The Jews of Hope.* New York: Penguin Books, 1985.

David Kessler, *The Falashas: The Forgotten Jews of Ethiopia.* New York: Schocken Books, 1985.

Howard M. Sachar, *Diaspora: An Inquiry into the Contemporary Jewish World.* New York: Harper and Row, 1986

Natan Scharansky, *Fear No Evil.* New York: Random House, 1988.

11 *Rodef Shalom:*
Seeking Peace

The whole Torah exists only for the sake of shalom.

—TANḤUMA, SHOFTIM 18

"Seek peace, and pursue it" (Psalm 34:15). The Torah does not obligate us to pursue the mitzvot, but only to fulfill them at the proper time, at the appropriate occasion. Peace, however, must be sought at all times; at home and away from home, we are obligated to seek peace and pursue it.

—NUMBERS RABBAH 19:27

In 1968, when I was almost ten, my mother threw out my toy guns. That was the year Senator Robert Kennedy was assassinated while campaigning in California for the presidency. My mother was watching the newscast of his speech and saw him fall. To this day, I remember the view of her shaking back as she sat before the television and wept.

Soon after that tragedy, she announced that she was taking away every toy gun, every symbol of violence I had. I was beside myself. How can you play GI Joe if there are no guns? What were my cowboys and Indians supposed to do with one another if their arrows, spears, and rifles had been confiscated by my outraged mother?

The ban encompassed more than just toys of war. Anytime she heard the sound of gunfire on television, she would turn the set off. There were no questions, and there was no appeal. Reacting as any other nine-year-old boy would, I was furious. With a single act, my mother had taken away my favorite games and trivialized my most powerful toys. But even in my anger and frustration, I knew I was face-to-face with something of supreme importance. My mother's zeal, her sudden lack of accommodation, lent urgency to the insight that violence, killing, and war were intolerable. One didn't play at butchering another human being; execution was not a game. Her indignation and pain, her love and guidance, were never stronger than on the subject of peace.

Violence is pervasive in our culture: on television, in movies, in children's games, and in toys. We must teach our children that what they perceive as glamorous in their games and television shows often leads to death and tragedy in the real world.

Peace in the world is inseparable from peace in the family. We build world peace one home at a time, as we reap the blessings of peace through the people we love. As the ancient midrash, *Avot de-Rebbe Natan,* explains: "Those who make peace in their own homes are as if they made peace in all Israel."

My mother knows that peace, along with justice, embodies humanity's greatest blessing. Without consciously articulating Jewish tradition, she is an accurate reflection of this Jewish priority, a passionate *rodef shalom* (רוֹדֵף שָׁלוֹם, "pursuer of peace").

The Jewish religion itself reveals the centrality of shalom. Every major Jewish prayer ends with a petition for peace. The first book of rabbinic law and wisdom, the Mishnah, ends with a prayer for peace. And one of the minor volumes of the Talmud is called *Perek ha-Shalom* (פֶּרֶק הַשָּׁלוֹם, "The Chapter of Peace")—shalom is the only ethical topic to receive exclusive consideration in a talmudic volume.

Symbols of shalom became a dominant thread in Judaism, uniting many distinct practices and festivals around a common theme. Consequently, Shabbat is known as a day of peace, celebrating the harmony among humanity, God, and nature. The Temple in Jerusalem was a monument to peace, where Jews would pray for their own well-being and that of the nations of the world. Finally, the most prominent religious leader in biblical Judaism, the *kohen gadol* (כֹּהֵן גָּדוֹל, "high priest"), became a symbol of peace and an instrument for its achievement.

❖　❖　❖　❖　❖

In an age of increasing violence—in the streets, in the schools, and on television—our world and our souls are desperately in need of shalom. At its core, this lack of shalom may well reflect an insecurity and a neediness within the human psyche. But it is not possible even to begin attaining inner peace without first acquiring public tranquility. Having lost the ability to enjoy quiet contemplation, harassed by the intrusions of a rude and ruthless world, where can we retreat for our own solace? When is there time for our own renewal?

The complexities of our age will not go away. Shalom comes about not through escape but through the understanding and transformation that will allow us to confront our demons and restore sanity and compassion to public life and private aspiration. In turning to shalom as a value and, even more, as a way to behave, we seek a tool potent enough to reduce discontent at the personal and social levels.

SHALOM IS MORE THAN "PEACE"

Language itself hints at the centrality of peace in Jewish traditions. The ancient Greek word for peace simply means the opposite of war, and the Roman goddess Pax ("Peace") was a minor deity until the time of the Roman Empire. But from the time of the Bible onward, the word "shalom" has carried a wealth of positive meanings. Not merely the absence of war, "shalom" means "safety," "wholeness," "completion," "fulfillment," "prosperity," "health," and "peace of mind and heart." In English, "peace" is often understood to be the absence of something—a lack of conflict. In Hebrew, "shalom" is understood to be the presence of something—a sense of well-being and fulfillment.

Because of the complex interplay among different aspects of shalom, this chapter will distinguish five categories: inner peace within individuals (step 1), our homes (steps 2-3), our community (steps 4-6), our nation (step 7), and our world (steps 8-9). By examining how to make shalom a part of our own daily work and a part of our commitment to *tikkun olam* (תִּקּוּן עוֹלָם, "repairing the world"), we are actually revealing what is of prime necessity: the confidence that a solution is possible.

While the building block of our society may well be the family, we are part of a larger community, linked by proximity and by shared destiny. Learning to live in harmony with our neighbors and friends is one way to build a more peaceful and stronger community.

1 Seek *naḥat ru'ah* (נַחַת רוּחַ , literally, "repose of the soul")—a tranquility and sturdiness within. This is the most personal area of shalom and one that eludes brief description. There is no single place to go, no one person or group that can confer the gift of inner peace. But by gradually opening yourself to self-awareness and to the perceptions of others, you can grow to love yourself and to enjoy your own company. The ability to love oneself is an indispensable prerequisite for compassion and for relationships with others. Paradoxically, it is generally true that the more patient and loving we are toward others, the more love and care we will have for ourselves.

• *Find a quiet corner, and read through the Psalms.* When I feel the pressures of daily life becoming too insistent, when the demands of my work or the disappointments of my hopes begin to overwhelm, I turn to *Sefer Tehillim* (סֵפֶר תְּהִלִּים ,"the book of Psalms"). These beautiful poems, ancient and profound, provide the eloquence to express my pain and cleanse my heart. For thousands of years, Jews (and, later, Christians) have derived great comfort from this tiny book. Gradually cultivate your personal favorites. Some of mine are Psalms 19 ("The heavens declare the glory of God"), 20 ("May Adonai answer you in time of trouble"), 86 ("Incline Your ear, Adonai"), 91 ("You who dwell in the shelter of the Most High"), 121 ("I turn my eyes to the mountains"), 130 ("Out of the depths I call You, Adonai").

• *Another opportunity to open a window into one's soul is to keep a diary.* Record random thoughts, reactions, dreams. A diary or journal is a useful tool for tracing one's personal growth in a way that is safe, private, and honest.

2 Build a home that nurtures and sustains children, spouses, parents, and friends. The origin of peace is in the home; consequently, Jewish tradition stresses the centrality of *sh'lom bayit* (שְׁלוֹם בַּיִת , domestic harmony). By learning to live peaceably with those you love (which is more difficult than it sounds), you establish a pocket of shalom that can spread beyond the confines of your home.

Like inner peace, *sh'lom bayit* requires mutual respect and a willingness to respond to the feelings of family members. Human beings inevitably disappoint one another (as we do ourselves) because of our shortcomings, moods, and distractions. As long as we can restrain ourselves enough to listen to the loving complaints of our families and work sufficiently hard to change our behavior to accommodate their needs, as long as we are willing to translate our feelings into words and use words that can nurture better understanding, then *sh'lom bayit* remains a realistic goal.

One key point in establishing *sh'lom bayit* is to remember that parents and children, siblings and spouses or lovers, do not exist solely to please others. All people have their own agendas and needs, including a need for independence and seclusion. While it is tempting to expect those we need most to focus on meeting our needs, both children and parents are remarkably resistant to abandoning their own lives and aspirations. We can grow together, but we can not ask others to substitute their identity for ours.

3 Shield yourself and your loved ones from witnessing destructive and hateful acts. This is a priority in establishing a home of shalom. Every day in almost every American home, countless human deaths, beatings, explosions, kidnappings, and other horrors permeate family rooms, dens, and living rooms through our television stations.

According to a study at the University of Illinois, the children's shows of twenty years ago showed an average of twenty violent acts per hour. The average today is forty-eight. The American Academy of Pediatrics notes that children's shows are three times more violent than prime-time programs and that the average child witnesses at least twelve thousand acts of crime, bloodshed, beating, or killing each year.

And the effect of witnessing this mayhem? In a review of thirty-three studies on the effect of televised violence, thirty-one of them demonstrate that children behave more aggressively after viewing violence. They are more likely to hit other children, call people names, and refuse to obey classroom or parental instruction. As Senator Paul Simon has explained, "The evidence that televised violence contributes to aggressive and destructive behavior is overwhelming."

Consider taking the following steps:

• *One simple act to protect* sh'lom bayit *is simply to follow my mother's precedent: if there is violence on television, change the channel or shut the set off.* There is no substitute for direct action.

• *Write to your congressional representative and senators, expressing your disapproval of the level of violence on network and cable television.* Toy companies often sponsor violent programs in order to boost sales of their war toys. Our government should have a pressing interest in making sure that the sale of war toys doesn't dominate the agenda of children's television. Urge your government representatives to support legislation (currently sponsored by the National Coalition on Television Violence) that would curtail the link between war toys and war cartoons.

While you may have serious concerns about the centrality of free speech and a wise mistrust of censorship, it is important to remember that the amount of television time is limited. Decisions about which shows to air are often based on a show's ability to attract the most

commercials at the best rates, rather than on which will contribute to a healthy and involved citizenry. As a result, many worthwhile shows are simply not put on the air. Choices about which shows to air should reflect the concerns and priorities of the people watching them, not just the concerns and priorities of the toy and television industry.

• *Write to the Federal Communications Commission, urging it to investigate the connection between children's programming and the sale of violent toys.*

Federal Communications Commission
1919 M Street, NW
Washington, DC 20554

• *Subscribe to* NCTV News, *which is published by the National Coalition on Television Violence.*

NCTV News
P.O. Box 2157
Champaign, IL 61820

---

4 **Volunteer at a local park, school, soup kitchen, or other public organization.** There is no more effective way to transform society. The core of Jewish identity is the community—the link between people that provides purpose, context, and value. Certainly the shalom of a community—its well-being and prosperity—is the essential component of our own contentment. Our local communities can be only as vibrant and as healing as we allow them to be; through our volunteerism and support, we can nurture a network of care and encouragement.

Such a commitment need not consume an inordinate amount of time. Groups such as Big Brothers, Big Sisters, Boy Scouts, and Girl Scouts require a fixed and ongoing involvement. Activities such as cleaning a park or a beach, painting the wall of a school, bringing clothing to a shelter, or participating in a synagogue's social-action projects take only an occasional effort.

Many of the other mitzvot in this book also involve ways of helping the community: See especially the chapters on *bikkur ḥolim* (Chapter 6), *hakhnasat orḥim* (Chapter 7), Shabbat (Chapter 12), and *sh'mirat ha-lashon* (Chapter 13).

---

5   **Greet people with a message of peace.** When speaking to Jews, start the conversation not with "hi" but with "shalom." My stepfather routinely welcomes people by saying "peace," which he repeats before they part.

---

6   **Begin a dialogue with non-Jewish communities in order to foster greater understanding.** As a member of a minority, and a frequently misunderstood one at that, you must be willing to help non-Jews revise their opinion of Jews and the Jewish people. Heirs of two thousand years of anti-Semitism, we carry the scars of persecution, pogroms, and beatings. While a sensitivity and a willingness to confront hatred are important, an obsession with Jewish persecution can generate paranoia—the sense that every non-Jew is, at best, an anti-

Semite in training. Just as non-Jews need to revise their opinions of Jews by meeting us, we need to learn how to trust again by meeting them. Two principal paths to organized dialogue are well worth pursuing:

• *The National Conference of Christians and Jews organizes local interfaith groups and programs all over North America.* These are always marked by a balance of candor and mutual respect. To get involved, contact their national office:

National Conference of Christians and Jews
71 Fifth Avenue, Suite 1100
New York, NY 10003
212-206-0006

The NCCJ also produces an interfaith calendar listing the symbols and holidays of several faith traditions, and this is a great resource.

• *The Jewish Community Relations Council is devoted to creating a dialogue between diverse groups.* Judaism is far more than just a religion, even though it is centered on religious values and institutions. Our history as a people has produced both a culture and a tradi-

By feeding the hungry, we allow our fellow humans to feel their own dignity and to enjoy a sense of connection to others. Connection and dignity are the essential tools of *rodef shalom.*

tion, so it is important for Jews to meet as Jews, not only with members of other faiths but with representatives of other ethnicities. Many groups of people face misunderstanding and hostility from the general population (in that regard they share a common experience with the Jews). Unfortunately, we are not exempt from imposing those stereotypes and biases. One of the most direct ways to diminish prejudice is through personal contact. Make an effort to get to know members of groups that face hostility and bias—African Americans, Asians, Latinos, gays, and lesbians. For those who live in areas that have a large number of Jews, the Jewish Federation sponsors a Jewish Community Relations Council, which organizes small, informal discussions among different religious and ethnic groups. The Federation's address and phone number are in the phone book.

7 **Support organizations that seek to publicize government abuse.** Power corrupts (almost as much as powerlessness does!), and governments possess a power that claims to be supreme. The only way we can keep governments under any restraint is by supporting those who are willing to publicize government abuse.

In the United States, one organization that supports whistle blowers is the Government Accountability Project, which assists federal employees who have the courage to oppose dishonest, fraudulent, and illegal or wasteful projects by the government. We, in turn, have a role to play by ensuring the safety and jobs of those patriots who publicize government abuse. For information about how to get involved, contact

> The Government Accountability Project
> 25 E Street, NW, Suite 700
> Washington, DC 20001
> 202-347-0460

8 **Become aware of the issues involved in bringing about peace on an international level.** Even though humanity has divided itself into a few hundred nations, the astronauts' photographs of Earth remind us that we are, ultimately, one. We all live on the same planet, and we are linked by a shared future. Increasingly, the problems and frustrations that paralyze any single nation become issues in every nation. Overpopulation, world hunger, pollution, and illiteracy are just a few of the issues that touch the life of even the most affluent and the most secure.

Bringing peace to the world is the fitting culmination of any program of shalom. But bringing about peace on an international scale requires one to be well informed in order to address the complex issues involved. The most informative newsletter on issues of war and peace comes from the Center for Defense Information, an organization in Washington, DC. Get on their mailing list, and subscribe to their newsletter, *The Defense Monitor.* Each issue addresses a specific topic in depth. It also summarizes what its authors hold to be a reasonable response based on the facts and America's security needs. The organization's address is

> Center for Defense Information
> 1500 Massachusetts Avenue
> Washington, DC 20025

Another excellent organization, one that also advocates action in addition to providing information, is the Union for Concerned Scientists. It publishes a variety of useful fact sheets on a range of issues involving nuclear weapons and policy questions. For copies, write to

> Union for Concerned Scientists
> 1384 Massachusetts Avenue
> Cambridge, MA 02238

9 **The next step in helping to increase international peace is to become active, either through political action or through human contact.** Both are vital.

• *Consider the two political organizations described below.* Each has a distinct approach to issues of international harmony and

Deep enmities give way before the power of hope, faith, and courage. The fragile peace between Israel and Jordan, launched by Prime Minister Rabin and King Hussein, and nurtured and guided by President Bill Clinton and the people of the United States, is a testimony to the impact that persistence and goodwill can make in the world.

suggests concrete actions that can change the direction of government action.

An innovative group is 20/20 Vision. Each month, it mails to its members a postcard asking that they take a specific action—make a phone call or write a short letter. It summarizes the issue and the points to make and provides the name and address of the person or organization to contact. The cost of membership is twenty dollars per year, and the organization promises that it will require only twenty minutes of your time each month.

This kind of focused and personalized lobbying can prevail when the random letters of unorganized constituents get ignored. It is hard to imagine a more interesting or useful expenditure of twenty dollars. Write to one of two locations:

20/20 Vision
Eastern Office
69 South Pleasant Street, Suite 203
Amherst, MA 01002

20/20 Vision
Western Office
1181 C Solano Avenue
Albany, CA 94706

Amnesty International USA addresses the issue of people imprisoned because of their beliefs, color, sex, ethnicity, or religion. The organization calls for fair and prompt trials and an end to torture and executions. Amnesty International is active throughout the world and works hard to maintain impartiality and effectiveness. Its clout comes from the large number of letters it can generate, all written by volunteers. Since its founding in 1961, Amnesty

International has worked to help more than twenty-five thousand "prisoners of conscience." To find out more about this fine group and how to participate in the liberation of prisoners of conscience, write to

Amnesty International USA
322 Eighth Avenue
New York, NY 10001

• *Become personally involved with people from other countries.* If we rely only on political change, the prospects for world peace and human understanding remain dim. Although political action remains essential, it can change only the contour of the discussion. It does not touch the more stubborn realm of feelings, bias, and perception. Personal contact is the only tool for molding opinion and touching human hearts. How can we reach out to the world? By contacting one person at a time.

• *Get a pen pal.* Establishing a correspondence with someone in another country puts a human face on a distant part of the globe—and shows the humanity in our own little corner.

• *Support exchange students.* Wonderful programs operate in nearly every community, placing foreign high school students in American homes for a weekend, a semester, or a year. By living with an American family, the students see American life from the inside, and Americans get to know and love the students as members of their families. To get involved in hosting an exchange student, phone the American Field Service at 1-800-AFS-INFO.

• *Support the Peace Corps.* This government agency sends American volunteers to distant parts of the globe to assist in humanitarian projects and to foster goodwill. For more information, contact your U.S. senator or your congressional representative.

As important as family and community may be, a world at peace requires political involvement as well. Only through the hard work of activism, donations, and use of the ballot can we translate the lofty and profound vision of Judaism, and the world's faiths, into reality.

❖ ❖ ❖ ❖ ❖

We cannot be true to our ancient covenant, we cannot begin to reorient our lives to God's perspective, without actively involving ourselves in the quest for shalom. Through our efforts, we can bring greater harmony to our families, greater cooperation to our communities, and more peace to the world. Shalom, that greatest of blessings, is wholeness. As we work toward that day when humanity will be united, we advance toward a time when the abundance of our joy and curiosity and playfulness is finally free to enrich our lives and our loves, to plant rather than to uproot, and to fashion ourselves and our world anew.

For Further Reading

Bradley Shavit Artson, *Love Peace and Pursue Peace: A Jewish Response to War and Nuclear Annihilation.* New York: United Synagogue of America, 1988.

Victor Frankel, *Man's Search for Meaning.* New York: Pocket Books, 1959.

Jeffrey Hollender, *How to Make the World a Better Place: A Guide to Doing Good.* New York: William Morrow, 1990.

The book of Psalms.

12 Shabbat:
Day of Rest and Renewal

What was created after it was already Shabbat? Tranquility, serenity, peace, and quiet. —GENESIS RABBAH 17:7

Remember the Shabbat day to keep it holy.
—EXODUS 20:8

I grew up not knowing that Shabbat could be a special day. My week was punctuated by going out on Friday and Saturday nights and by working during the day on Saturday and Sunday. It was only in college, as I began to learn about Judaism, that Shabbat began to grow in importance in my life. The requirements of my classes and the demands of my extracurricular activities easily exceeded whatever time I allotted to them. No matter how much I studied, no matter how many hours I spent in the library, there was always more to be mastered, more I could do. Sometime during my junior year, I decided to set a limit to my work. I resolved not to write or to read any assignments from sundown on Friday night to sundown on Saturday.

I remember breaking the news to some of my friends. One particularly accomplished friend, astounded at my declared intention, exclaimed, "How can you afford to take off twenty-four hours a week?"

Most of us spend our time running from task to task, cramming appointments, carpools, and activities into each minute of our day. Opportunities to slow down and simply be with our loved ones are rare and precious. Shabbat is one such opportunity, and it arrives every week.

How could I afford to take off twenty-four hours a week? How could I afford not to? How could I afford not to take time for a leisurely meal without having to worry when the library would close? How could I afford not to spend time enjoying the beauty of the world and the pleasure of my friends?

❖ ❖ ❖ ❖ ❖

Very few of us work for mere necessities. Most American Jews are far wealthier than their grandparents. We aspire to elegant cars, beautiful homes, luxurious vacations, and powerful careers. And, gener-

---

THE GOOD SHIP SHABBAT

As a rabbi in an American suburb, I am involved in helping non-Jews convert to Judaism. After extensive study, the final steps in the process are a ritual immersion in a *mikveh*, a ritual circumcision for men, and an interview before a board of three rabbis or three knowledgeable Jews to ensure each convert's sincerity and to determine whether each knows enough about Judaism to make an informed choice. One time, as a part of the normal questioning, one of the rabbis asked a young woman to name her favorite Jewish ritual or holy day. Without hesitation, she said, "Shabbat." The rabbi then asked her to compare Shabbat to some physical thing and to explain the comparison. After a moment of concentration, she announced that Shabbat is like a vacation cruise.

"Imagine," she said, "taking a twenty-four-hour cruise each week. Once on board, there are no chores because it isn't possible to bring any work on board. There are no ringing phones, no blaring announcements, no driving, no congested freeways, no deadlines. All meals have already been prepared and will be served with elegance. Whatever the passengers desire has already been placed on the ship before it embarked. The vessel sets sail as the travelers gather to sing and to savor a candlelit dinner, embellished with shimmering red wine and a bread so rich it tastes like cake. Surrounded by family and intimate friends, with nowhere to rush off to afterward, each traveler can slowly relish the sumptuous dinner in peace.

"The next morning, as was true the night before, there are no chores, no tasks, no deadlines. So everyone fills his or her time by gathering with other passengers, by talking about matters large and small, the questions and interests that tend to get lost in the shuffle of daily life. They sing a little, meditate a bit, even take some time to study some aspect of Jewish history or religion. People take walks around the deck or play their favorite games together.

"After eating another elegant meal for lunch, the passengers retreat to their cabins for a nap or perhaps to read simply for pleasure. At the end of the cruise, as the yacht approaches its berth, everyone gathers on deck to hold a candle-lighting ceremony to mark the end of this restful, lovely time."

ally, we have attained them. What we often lack is the time to enjoy our possessions, to relax with those we love, and to nurture our souls.

We possess things in abundance. But we are constantly short of time. This shortage of time often distances us from our spouses or lovers, our friends, and our children. Our constant mad rush can erode our connection with who we are and what we value. Too tired to absorb any human contact, we steal brief naps, squeeze in an hour of exercise, and return to work undernourished in mind and spirit. The strain of work follows us to our homes, our recreation, and our bedrooms. Without quiet time, we have no chance to renew our energy, to remember what all the rushing and labor are for.

The remedy to all this busyness and pressure already exists; it has been tested over the years, and it is readily available wherever Jewish communities nurture their identities. The remedy is Shabbat, שַׁבָּת.

Each week, just before sundown on Friday until an hour past sunset on Saturday, the entire Jewish people are invited to sail on just such a voyage. The luxury liner *Shabbat* provides for the needs of its passengers, offering a period free from mundane concerns, free from stress, and free from the demands of career, achievement, and activities.

Shabbat, however, represents more than just freedom from obligation. The seventh day is also an opportunity for a deeper freedom. It grants us the liberty to spend undistracted time with those we love and the freedom to gather with other Jews to remember what being Jewish is all about. Protected from the need to produce or to do, we engage in the possibility of learning to live and to be. Shabbat teaches us how to celebrate living and how to dedicate that existence to making the weekday world a more compassionate, more humane, and therefore more Godly place.

❖　❖　❖　❖　❖

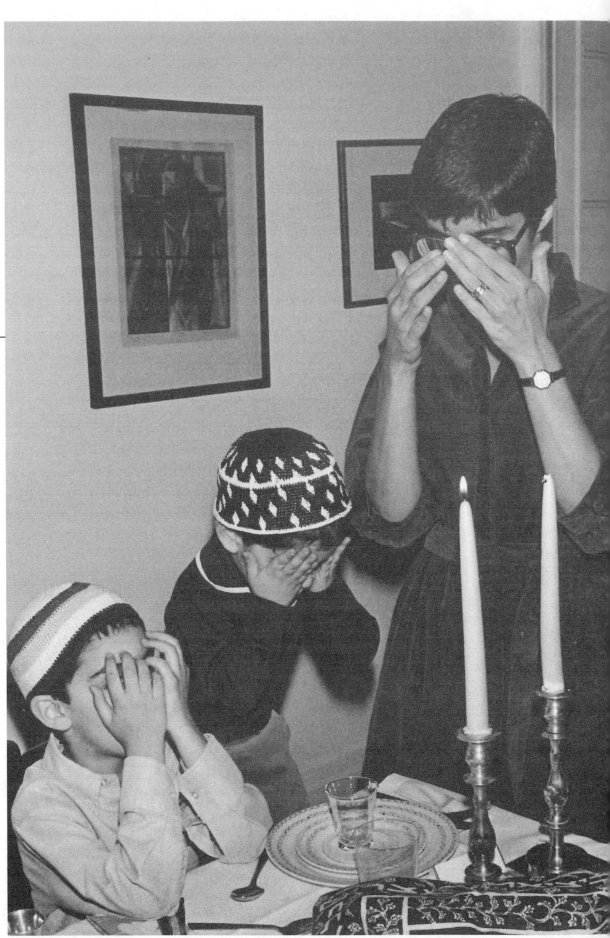

Shabbat adds a sweetness and a rhythm to the week, and all that is needed to begin observing this day of rest are two white candles, a glass of wine, two loaves of bread, and a tasty meal with friends or family.

1 **Because of its simplicity and beauty, candle lighting is a good way to initiate Shabbat observance.** Make this lovely ritual the cornerstone of every Friday night. No matter what other plans the evening may include, start it by placing two candles in a pair of your favorite candlesticks. (Use any candlesticks and any candles, provided that the candles burn for at least an hour.) Set the candlesticks wherever they will remain safe and undisturbed for the rest of Shabbat. Gather family or friends together, and light both candles. Circle your hands around the lights three times and cover your face with your hands. Once the candles are lit, you should not move them, and you should let them burn out completely. (Later in the chapter we will consider the traditional time when the candles ought to be lit.) After lighting the candles, recite the following blessing:

בָּרוּךְ אַתָּה יְיָ אֱלֹהֵינוּ מֶלֶךְ הָעוֹלָם
אֲשֶׁר קִדְּשָׁנוּ בְּמִצְוֹתָיו וְצִוָּנוּ
לְהַדְלִיק נֵר שֶׁל שַׁבָּת.

Barukh atah Adonai eloheinu melekh ha-olam, asher kid'shanu b'mitzvotav, v'tzivanu l'hadlik ner shel Shabbat.

Praised are You, Adonai our God, Ruler of the universe whose mitzvot add holiness to our lives and who commanded us to kindle Shabbat light.

After concluding the blessing, take a moment to reflect on the events of the week, on the people who make life worth living, and on the warmth and beauty of the candles. Enjoy the glow.

2 **Make your Friday night meal special.** The center of the Friday night experience is the Shabbat dinner. The dinner starts with a few simple rituals and then proceeds to the joys of good food and friendly companionship. During the summer, it follows immediately after candle lighting. During the winter, when candle lighting is quite early (often around four-thirty in the afternoon), most people eat dinner at a later hour.

Set the table with a white tablecloth. Add flowers to the table. On the center of the table, place two *ḥallot*—two loaves of ḥallah, חַלָּה—on a decorative platter. There should be at least one special goblet—the Kiddush cup—for the blessing over the wine. (Some people prefer giving each person his or her own Kiddush cup, while others use one cup that is shared by everyone.) The wine should be kosher, made from grapes, and preferably Israeli (as a way of supporting and identifying with the Jews of Israel). Finally, place a cloth or silk cover over the *ḥallot*. Such covers are generally embroidered, but any material, even a napkin, will do.

• *The meal begins with those present singing "Shalom Aleikhem,"* שָׁלוֹם עֲלֵיכֶם. This song is based on a talmudic story about two angels, one good and the other evil. According to the legend, if the angels see that a family is enjoying a loving Shabbat meal, then the good angel can coerce the bad angel into wishing that all future Shabbat meals will be this wonderful. This song can be recited while the singers are holding hands as a group or forming a circle around the table, with each person's arms on another's shoulders.

• *Special blessings are recited for children and for one's spouse.*[1] They offer a lovely opportunity to express our love for our closest companions. These blessings also remind us what a gift that love can be.

• *Once everyone has finished the traditions above, proceed to the Kiddush* (קִדּוּשׁ, literally, "Sanctification").[2] This prayer sanctifies the beginning of Shabbat. The Kiddush recalls the Creation of the world and the liberation of the Hebrew slaves from Egypt. Both themes—cosmos and freedom—pervade all of Shabbat, exemplifying the Jewish conviction that God is the source of both life and justice.

Fill the Kiddush cups with kosher wine
or grape juice, ask everyone to stand, and hold
the cup in your palm, with your fingers pointing
upward. This pose represents the awareness that
joy and sustenance come from God (the hand
holding the cup is in the position of one receiving wine from heaven) and replicates the shape
of a rose, the mystical symbol of the Jewish people. Immediately after reciting the Kiddush
blessing, everyone present sits and sips wine
from the cup.

    • *After reciting the Kiddush, perform the
ritual of washing the hands and reciting Ha-
Motzi.* Many contemporary Jewish rituals are
designed to remind us of our biblical heritage
and of the central biblical institution of worship,
the Temple in Jerusalem. In the Temple, the
kohanim (כֹּהֲנִים ,"priests") used to perform the
sacrifices in a state of ritual purity. They attained
that level of holiness in part by performing the
ritual of *netilat yadayim* (נְטִילַת יָדַיִם, "washing
the hands"). Today the home is a central institution of Judaism, and the Shabbat table is the
modern symbol of the Temple altar. The *ḥallot*
symbolize the two Shabbat sacrifices offered in
the Temple—the daily sacrifice and the special
sacrifice for Shabbat. By performing the same
action the *kohanim* performed before blessing
the bread, we recall their loving service and
remember our responsibility to be a "nation of
priests and a holy people."

    Provide a cup or pitcher by the sink,

preferably one with two handles, although any will do. Fill it with water, and then pour the water over each hand three times, beginning with the right hand and alternating hands with each pour. It is traditional to recite the blessing while drying the hands.[3]

Because washing the hands is considered preliminary to reciting Ha-Motzi (הַמּוֹצִיא , the blessing over bread) and the two are considered a single act, no one should speak between the two rituals. Once everyone has completed the blessing for washing the hands and has returned to the table, uncover the bread, hold the two loaves together, and recite Ha-Motzi.

בָּרוּךְ אַתָּה יְיָ אֱלֹהֵינוּ מֶלֶךְ הָעוֹלָם
הַמּוֹצִיא לֶחֶם מִן הָאָרֶץ.

Barukh atah Adonai eloheinu melekh ha-olam ha-motzi leḥem min ha-aretz.

Blessed are you, Adonai our God, Ruler of the world, who brings forth bread from the earth.

After reciting Ha-Motzi, pass the ḥallah around so everyone can tear off a piece. Lightly salt the bread in memory of the Temple sacrifices, which were also salted. Then eat the piece of ḥallah. At this point, the rituals preceding the meal are over. Enjoy the company and the meal.

3 **Wear clothing that is particularly attractive, particularly comfortable, or both.** As a preliminary Shabbat activity, take a shower or a bath. If it is appropriate, shave.

It is hard to understand why we put so much effort into looking our best for total strangers or work acquaintances and then, for those we love, look worn and faded. Shabbat can be a time to share our best looks with the people we care about most.

4 **Attend Friday night services.** The next step in Shabbat observance involves community. It is practically impossible to be a Jew alone. Community is a central aspect of

Jewish identity and Jewish spirituality. Recall that the giving of the Torah at Mount Sinai happened in the presence of the entire Jewish people, not to any particular individual. So, find a nearby synagogue whose style and worldview agree with your own, and begin attending Friday night services.

Many congregations now have a late Friday night service to provide time for a Shabbat meal first. These services often have more responsive readings in English and more singing than do the more traditional Saturday morning services, so they are an ideal introduction to the synagogue and to the public observance of Shabbat. There are two possible ways to make this attendance habitual:

• *Commit yourself to going to services every Friday night for two months.* At the end of the two-month period, meet with the rabbi to assess your feelings about the services and to

Wine is a symbol of joy as well as a symbol of our partnership with God—God's bounty causes the grapes to grow, but it takes human ingenuity and effort to transform those grapes into wine.

chart future levels of participation and learning.

• *Base your decision on what feels comfortable, perhaps attending Friday night services only every other week or once a month.* The advantage of this approach is that it imposes a less immediate burden. The disadvantage is that it dilutes and postpones the exposure needed to become truly comfortable with the service and friendly with the congregants. In any case, if this option feels more comfortable, try to increase the rate of attendance as quickly as possible.

---

5 | **Begin incorporating the prohibition of** *melakhot* **into your growing pattern of personal Shabbat rituals.** This is the next logical step in growth toward a full Shabbat observance. Until now, we have focused on building a Friday night experience of Shabbat through positive additions—beautiful rituals, a festive meal, a short prayer service. These mitzvot are called positive commandments because they involve direct action: "You shall do . . . ." While certainly significant, positive commandments are only one aspect of a full observance. Now we will progress to a different aspect of Shabbat observance.

In the Torah, the Ten Commandments are recorded twice. In one instance, we are told to *shamor* (שָׁמוֹר ,"guard") the Shabbat, and in the other we are told to *zakhor* (זָכוֹר ,"remember") the Shabbat. Remembering Shabbat involves taking direct action, doing something. Equally important, however, is the restraint of guarding against the encroachment of the week's normal preoccupations. These mitzvot of enforced restraint are often termed negative commandments, not because they are immoral or improper but, rather, because they are expressed as a negative: "Don't do . . ." or "You shall not . . . ." Your first expression of a negative mitzvah will be on a Friday night. But before we consider the specifics, it is necessary to discuss one of the principal features of Shabbat.

On Shabbat, Jews traditionally refrain from any activity that turns our creative powers outward, since Shabbat commemorates the day on which God rested from the work of creation. Any permanent intervention in the world of nature is prohibited. Such an activity is called a *melakhah,* מְלָאכָה , commonly translated as "work" but not to be mistaken for contemporary, individual notions of what constitutes work. Just because a labor induces sweat doesn't mean that it's *melakhah.* And just because the task is effortless doesn't mean it isn't *melakhah.* The Torah records that all *melakhot* are prohibited on Shabbat. Rabbinic interpretation defines what exactly constitutes a *melakhah.* (See the list at the end of this chapter.)

And so, the prohibition of *melakhot* is to be incorporated into your growing pattern of personal Shabbat rituals. Begin on Friday night. Light the Shabbat candles, and put aside all chores or unpleasant tasks. This means no preparing for an assignment due in the coming

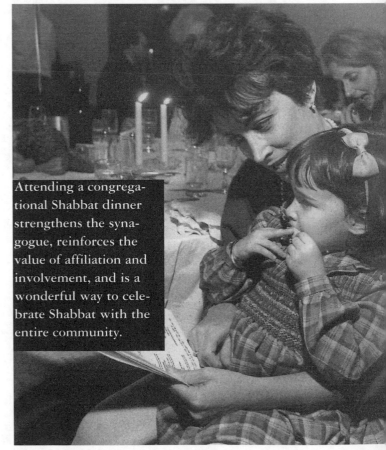

Attending a congregational Shabbat dinner strengthens the synagogue, reinforces the value of affiliation and involvement, and is a wonderful way to celebrate Shabbat with the entire community.

week, no writing of checks, no taking of notes as a reminder of something to do later, no making of phone calls to rent a car or reserve a plane ticket. By doing these things, we take from the present to invest in a tenuous future. Instead, put aside all forms of work. Only by doing so can you truly live in the moment.

One *melakhah,* by the way, is the lighting or extinguishing of a flame. So plan your candle-lighting ritual for no less than eighteen minutes before sunset. After that time, candle lighting is not a permissible activity. The precise time of the Friday night sunset can be found in the local Jewish newspaper or by calling a nearby synagogue.

As this new aspect of Friday night becomes increasingly comfortable, the experience of Shabbat rest will simultaneously deepen and expand. Once writing, gardening, and puttering with tools have been set off limits, the pressures of work necessarily recede—what we cannot alter, we often forget. Everyone deserves a night off, and those we love deserve at least one evening a week of our full attention, playfulness, and interaction.

---

6 Observe the Havdalah ceremony.

Shabbat lasts from just before sundown on Friday night to an hour after sundown on Saturday. Just as Shabbat begins with a candle-lighting ceremony, so, too, it ends with one. The ceremony of conclusion is called Havdalah (הַבְדָּלָה , literally, "distinction"). The ceremony is short and provides a beautiful way to enter the new week. It is also a summary of the biblical-rabbinic view of our place in the world. Although there is still much more to Shabbat observance than has been considered so far, the brevity, beauty, and simplicity of Havdalah make its observance a natural next step in extending the spirit and practice of Shabbat.

Havdalah stresses the importance of making distinctions. Part of any healthy identity is knowing what we are not. If we thought that we were everyone, we would be unable to retain any sense of our self-definition. The need for distinctiveness holds true in the realm of the holy as well. To be a Jew means to be distinct—not superior, not holier, but distinct. We remind ourselves of our distinction by recalling that the seventh day is distinct from the rest of the week, that light is distinct from darkness, and that Israel (the Jewish people) is distinct from other peoples. Note, however, that both Shabbat and the weekdays are vital and good, that light and darkness are both blessings. Israel is no better than other peoples; each people possesses a unique relationship to God and a distinct insight that may be contributed to the world. We are truest to ourselves and most giving to humanity when we retain and cultivate distinct traditions rather than blend aspects of different traditions into a homogeneous and bland mush.

For the Havdalah ritual, purchase a braided candle with at least two wicks (special Havdalah candles are sold in synagogues and in Judaica shops). You will also need a spice box and at least two spices (cloves are one of the spices used most frequently, although any pleasant smelling spices are fine), some kosher wine or grape juice, and your Kiddush cup.

Everyone stands to recite Havdalah while one person holds the cup of wine in his or her right hand.[4] After the blessing over wine, it is customary to set the goblet down without drinking from it.

Next is the blessing over the flames of the candle. As the blessing is recited, everyone cups his or her hands so that the light casts a shadow image of their fingers onto their palms. Why is this done? Every *berakhah* should correspond to a concrete use or deed, not simply to an abstract conception. Rather than just praising God for light in general, we link our ritual of gratitude to a deed that "benefits" us—in this

Shabbat is more than just an idea—it offers the joys of touch, smell, sight, and sound. While these children enjoy helping to make the ḥallah, they are also building a positive Shabbat experience that will remain with them throughout their lives.

case, seeing the flame and making a shadow on our hands. One ancient midrash notes that we create a shadow using our fingernails because of their special quality: just as our fingernails continue to grow throughout our entire lifetime, so Judaism offers us the opportunity to continue to grow spiritually throughout our lives. Another lovely interpretation asserts that since our fingernails are the fastest growing part of our bodies, we pray that our moral and ethical stature may grow as quickly as our fingernails.

The concluding blessing reiterates the central theme of Havdalah and of Shabbat itself—the distinctive identity of the Jewish people, which corresponds to the unique identity of the seventh day. Lift the glass of wine again and hold it during this prayer. At the end of the prayer, pass around the wine. Each person should take a sip.

Conclude Havdalah by extinguishing the flame in the wine remaining in the cup. The new week has now begun.

---

7 **Expand the prohibitions of *melakhot*.**

We have already seen that traditionally no *melakhah* ("work") is permitted on Shabbat and that this prohibition eliminates all writing, cooking, gardening, building, cutting, and carrying. As a result of this prohibition, activities such as humanity's millennial struggle to achieve dominance over nature stop for an idyllic moment. On Shabbat, according to the Torah, God rested from the work of Creation. On Shabbat, we, too, learn to act as though our labor had been completed and as though all our needs were provided for automatically. On this day, our struggle for survival is suspended. In the armistice of Shabbat, we can experience unity with the world and with the world's Maker. This restraint allows us to refocus our creative energies. Rather than concentrating on dominating the outside world, for one day a week we can focus on making ourselves live up to our own holy potential—to reflect the divine image within each of us. Cultivating that image requires more than determination. It also requires advance preparation.

• *Shop for and prepare Shabbat dinner in advance.* As soon as you feel comfortable doing so, extend this practice to Saturday lunch as well. Make a point of having the necessary food on hand before Shabbat begins. Preparing two fully cooked meals on Friday may feel burdensome, so consider a cold lunch (tuna sandwiches, a salad, and so forth). This new practice will affect your Thursday nights and possibly your plans for Wednesday as well. Shopping for the weekend now becomes a Wednesday-Thursday activity, and cooking for Shabbat may begin on Thursday and conclude on the following day.

This transformation of the week is intentional. Traditional sources advise that the commandment to remember Shabbat means that we should remember the seventh day even on the other days of the week. By initiating our preparations on Wednesday, we extend Shabbat so that its *kedushah* (קְדֻשָׁה , "holiness") and purpose permeate all our days. We carry a little of Shabbat with us wherever we go.

• *Purchase a hot plate (for example, the kind made by Salton) or a* blekh *and a coffee percolator.* One of the central prohibitions of Shabbat involves cooking. Because cooking is one preeminent way in which humanity transforms the natural order, we demonstrate our unity with nature on Shabbat by abstaining from this activity. In addition, the kindling, transferring, or extinguishing of a flame is also a *melakhah* and therefore forbidden throughout Shabbat. With the above-mentioned appliances in place before Shabbat begins, it becomes possible to enjoy a warm dinner and lunch as well as hot water for tea, coffee, or your favorite hot drink.

One of Judaism's most beautiful—and brief—ceremonies is Havdalah. The braided candle, wine, and spices all strengthen us for the tasks of the coming week and give us one last opportunity to come together before we disperse to our Saturday night activities.

A word about heating: It is permissible to heat food that has already been cooked, because you are not permanently altering the food. But be sure to set up the percolator and hot plate before Shabbat begins. And remember that boiling water constitutes a form of cooking just as cooking solid food does.

It is also possible to use a stove and an oven as a hot plate, however. Simply set the oven and a few burners to the desired level, and turn them on before the onset of Shabbat. Then leave them on until after Havdalah is concluded. To remind yourself not to touch the dials or turn off the stove, you can use a *blekh*, a metal sheet which covers the burners, extends over the front of the stove, and covers the dials as well. This device serves to highlight the distinctiveness of Shabbat while preventing anyone from mistakenly tampering with the stove and oven.

Having prepared your meals in advance, and having armed yourself with the *blekh* or a hot plate and a percolator, it is now realistic and possible to abstain from all cooking during Shabbat.

• *Avoid driving on Shabbat.* Sitting in traffic, or worrying about needing a refill, or spending money (even on a broken car) makes it almost impossible to maintain the Shabbat spirit. It is difficult, however, for most people to enjoy Shabbat together or to attend services at a synagogue without using a car. Try to use your car only to attend and return from synagogue services. It may take time before this practice seems feasible and feels comfortable, but ignoring your car for twenty-four hours is a significant step toward achieving a more peaceful Shabbat, cleaner air, and a more restorative day.

| **8** | **Limit your Shabbat activities to those that fall under the category of** |

menuḥah (מְנוּחָה , "rest"). There are several kinds of *menuḥah*. One form is leisure, during which we fill the time with pleasant and unde-

manding activities. Another form is sleeping, a venerable and wonderful Shabbat practice. A nap on Saturday afternoon, either alone or with a loved one, can add immeasurably to a sense of rejuvenation and satisfaction. Indeed, our sages taught that Friday night was a particularly meritorious time for marital sex. After all, Shabbat is a time of delight and joy, and what could be more joyous than the love between committed and devoted spouses, each receiving and providing pleasure?

Another form of *menuḥah* is the customary Shabbat stroll—with children, friends, or extended family. Enjoy a leisurely walk as you explore a nearby neighborhood. Talks that occur while walking have an uncanny way of focusing on truly important issues and concerns, perhaps because the strollers are free from the distractions of the phone, the bills, the car, and the chores. Walking is also a good way to avoid the claustrophobia that can result from sitting at home for twenty-four hours, even if much of that time is spent eating and sleeping.

Consider also playing a ball game near your home, throwing a Frisbee, going for a run with a friend, or any number of athletic activities. The advantage of participating in athletics on Shabbat is that your focus is limited to pleasure and health. Competition and concern for status, which so often motivate athletic performance on other days, are less feasible on Shabbat because it is harder to keep score or to play in organized teams. The focus of the day is one of pleasure for its own sake.

Yet another form of *menuḥah* involves pleasurable learning, either together or individually. Shabbat afternoon is an ideal time to read and discuss the weekly Torah portion. Many books stimulate family discussions or provide issues to consider. Use the time to read a book of Jewish history, Jewish philosophy, an aspect of Jewish religion, or try studying the Talmud or midrash with a friend. For suggested books, see the titles listed in For Further Reading at the end of Chapter 14.

9 Attend a Saturday morning service.

Another aspect of *menuḥah* is a reorientation and a return to a sense of belonging to a community, a return to a sense of the *brit* (בְּרִית, "covenant") linking the Jewish people and God. The two values of community and holiness come together in the Saturday morning service. There the Jewish people gather to pray together, to read and study Torah with one another, and to socialize as a religious community. Saturday morning in the synagogue is still the central address of the Jewish people.

There are two possible ways of making Saturday morning services a focal point of your Shabbat. Depending on your personality and temperament, one may feel preferable to the other:

• *Commit yourself to attending synagogue one or two Saturday mornings each month.* Schedule particular Saturdays for this purpose rather than waiting until there is time. (Hillel, a sage from the first century, used to teach: "Don't say, 'When I have leisure, I will study,' for you may never have leisure.") For example, block out the first or the first and third Saturdays of each month for going to synagogue. Gradually increase the number of times until Shabbat morning always (at least as a rule) involves synagogue services.

• *Some people find it easier to establish a new practice simply by doing it. If that description applies to you, then commit yourself to attending services every Saturday morning.* By establishing this priority and knowing that this commitment remains each week, you may find it easier to reschedule other commitments.

A word about intention: Unfortunately, our lives and our nature conspire to reduce our best intentions to ideals that may never be translated into action. Other, seemingly more pressing commitments generally relegate our resolutions to the back burner. Think about how many times we begin a diet to lose extra pounds, how many times we have resolved to get in shape, to read more, to stay in touch with a friend or relative. All these lofty ideals remain mere ideals because there is no structure through which to express them or by which to persevere in them.

We need rules and structures in order to actualize our own highest aspirations, including our religious aspirations. Merely keep Shabbat attendance a goal, and its only effect may be periodic feelings of guilt when you fail to attain it. Make Shabbat attendance a regular commitment, and it can transform your life and your community.

A community of Jews is eager for your company. Millennia of Jewish sacred writings are waiting for your attention. Experiences of shared joy, wonder, comfort, and timelessness all wait for your energy, insight, and participation. All are inside a synagogue, waiting for you. Seize the opportunity.

10 Invite guests home for the afternoon.

Pick someone from the synagogue who looks like a potential friend, someone who seems lonely, who needs comfort, or even someone who is already a good friend, and invite that person to your home for a Shabbat lunch. Shabbat won't feel isolating if it becomes a time to share with other people, to cement ties to the community, or to establish new friendships.

The rituals to be followed before a Shabbat lunch are similar to but simpler than those for Friday night. Kiddush begins with two quotations from the Torah that refer to Creation and freedom.[5] After reciting these passages, sing the one-line blessing over wine, perform the ritual of washing the hands, and say Ha-Motzi.

Shabbat, despite its prohibitions against writing, cutting, and cooking, is not a prison. The luxury of free time can allow people to play in the park, take a walk, exercise, read together, nap, and eat. There is so much to do on Shabbat that it often feels like the day simply isn't long enough to fit everything in!

11 **Give up writing on Shabbat.** We have talked about the need to refrain from activities that permanently alter the world. Another way of looking at the same issue is to recognize that we act as though most of our efforts, and the bulk of our self-worth, derive from what we do rather than from who we are. All week long, we expend energy on doing as a way of increasing self-esteem, creating an identity, and seeking prestige and approval. Yet if each of us is made in God's image, then our ultimate value derives not from what we do but simply from our existence. Part of the lesson of Shabbat is that we must perceive human worth in all human beings, ourselves included, exclusively because we are all human. So, on Shabbat we avoid doing, and we emphasize being.

Writing is the quintessential human activity, distinguishing us from all other life on Earth. It is also one of the most significant methods by which we assert control over nature. Difficult though it may be, it is time to give up writing on Shabbat.

As a corollary to not writing, and as a way to remember not to write, avoid even touching any writing implements. This practice of not moving or touching any object that is normally connected to an activity prohibited on Shabbat is called *muk'tzeh* (מֻקְצֶה , "set aside"). Writing implements, money, tools, cigarette lighters, matches, and many other objects fall under this category.

12 **Recite the *Birkat ha-Mazon*.** The Torah contains the mitzvah "to eat, be satisfied, and bless Adonai your God." The practice of saying grace after meals is called *Birkat ha-Mazon* (בִּרְכַּת הַמָּזוֹן , "blessing for nourishment"). It is also sometimes referred to as *bentsching* (from Yiddish, meaning "bless").

Saying the *Birkat ha-Mazon* is a way of reminding yourself that nourishment is itself a miracle and a gift. Along with the practice of kashrut (the dietary laws; see Chapter 8), it serves to elevate the act of eating to a sacred deed.[6]

While *Birkat ha-Mazon* is appropriate after every meal, first make it a Shabbat practice, both as a way of learning it and as a way of making Shabbat special. Linked to the mitzvah of *Birkat ha-Mazon* is the custom of singing *zemirot* (זְמִירוֹת , special Shabbat songs). This adds to the joy of the meal and provides an activity that individuals of all ages can participate in together. Various *zemirot* are found in the books listed in For Further Reading at the end of this chapter.

13 **Attend Minḥah and Arvit services.** A full Shabbat starts on Friday night, continues with services on Saturday morning, and includes a festive lunch while still leaving time for a nap, a walk, and some games. But before Havdalah, there are three more elements to make the day complete: an afternoon service, Minḥah (מִנְחָה , corresponding to the name of the grain offering in the biblical period); a special meal, the *se'udah sh'lishit* (סְעֻדָּה שְׁלִישִׁית , "the third meal"); and the evening service, Arvit, עַרְבִית .

These three events shift the mood of Shabbat, preparing for its conclusion and for the resumption of weekday activities. Look to a nearby synagogue for the times of Minḥah and Arvit. *Se'udah sh'lishit,* traditionally a much lighter meal than the other two, is often held between services at the synagogue itself.

❖   ❖   ❖   ❖   ❖

The Thirty-Nine *Melakhot* Forbidden on Shabbat, According to the Mishnah

1. Plowing	13. Bleaching	21. Tying a knot	33. Erasing
2. Sowing	14. Combining raw materials	22. Untying a knot	34. Building
3. Reaping	15. Dyeing	23. Sewing	35. Demolishing
4. Binding sheaves	16. Spinning	24. Tearing	36. Kindling a fire
5. Threshing	17. Weaving	25. Trapping	37. Extinguishing a fire
6. Winnowing	18. Making two (or more) loops	26. Slaughtering	38. Finishing a product
7. Selecting	19. Weaving two (or more) threads	27. Skinning	39. Carrying from the public to the private (and from the private to the public)
8. Sifting	20. Separating into threads	28. Tanning	
9. Grinding		29. Scraping pelts	
10. Kneading		30. Marking out	
11. Baking		31. Cutting to shape	
12. Shearing sheep		32. Writing	

❖ ❖ ❖ ❖ ❖

In a world that often doesn't know how to rest, Shabbat can offer a haven that is more than simply dozing. In a society filled with loneliness, Shabbat provides the structure to build community, to nurture families, and to comfort individuals. In an age searching for meaning, Shabbat offers access to values and traditions that cultivate the best that we can be, that reach beyond the ages, and that link us to God.

Shabbat can be a seventh of our lives, time spent renewing suppleness of spirit and love of life. A sign of love between us and the Holy Blessed One, its transforming powers await our desire to set sail. Our cruise awaits.

WHERE TO FIND IT IN THE PRAYERBOOK

1. Blessings Recited Over Children

Siddur Sim Shalom. New York: Rabbinical Assembly, 1985, pages 722-25.

Gates of the House. New York: Central Conference of American Rabbis, 1977, page 32.

The Complete Artscroll Siddur. Brooklyn, NY: Mesorah Publications Ltd, 1984, page 354.

Likrat Shabbat. Bridgeport, CT: Media Judaica, 1992, Section II, page 8.

2. Friday Night Kiddush

Siddur Sim Shalom, page 726.

Gates of Prayer. New York: Central Conference of American Rabbis, 1975, page 719.

Kol Haneshamah. Wyncote, PA: The Reconstructionist Press, 1994, pages 116-19.

The Complete Artscroll Siddur, page 360.

Likrat Shabbat, Section II, page 11.

3. Blessing for Washing Hands

Siddur Sim Shalom, page 726.

The Complete Artscroll Siddur, pages 14 and 224.

4. Havdalah

Siddur Sim Shalom, pages 700-3.

Gates of Prayer, pages 633-36.

Kol Haneshamah, pages 520-27.

The Complete Artscroll Siddur, page 618.

Likrat Shabbat, Section II, pages 73-75.

5. Kiddush for Shabbat Lunch

Siddur Sim Shalom, pages 734-35.
Gates of Prayer, page 720.
Kol Haneshamah, page 464.
The Complete Artscroll Siddur, page 492.
Likrat Shabbat, Section II, page 16.

6. Birkat ha-Mazon

Siddur Sim Shalom, pages 784-85.
Gates of the House, pages 6-18.
The Complete Artscroll Siddur, page 182.
Likrat Shabbat, Section II, pages 19-25.

Recommended Reading

Samuel H. Dresner, *The Sabbath.* New York: Burning Bush Press, 1970. A poetic and philosophical approach to the Shabbat.

Abraham Joshua Heschel, *The Sabbath: Its Meaning for Modern Man.* New York: Farrar, Straus and Giroux, 1951. Another poetic and philosophical approach to Shabbat.

Ron Wolfson, *The Art of Jewish Living: The Shabbat Seder.* New York: Federation of Jewish Men's Clubs and the University of Judaism, 1985. An excellent how-to, complete with the tales of a variety of Jews who recount how they make Shabbat their own.

13 Sh'mirat ha-Lashon:

Guarding Your Tongue

*My God,
keep my
tongue
from evil,
my lips
from lies.*

*—TALMUD,
BERAKHOT 17A*

Our ability to speak is one of the glories of being human. We are able to use our mouths to communicate a stunning array of information, feelings, and perceptions. Yet speech is also easily subject to abuse. We cover our own sense of insecurity by speaking ill of a competitor; we entertain our friends with funny stories that may be deeply embarrassing to a third person (who is generally not present); we lie out of convenience or out of laziness—and we have come to find this kind of speech socially acceptable.

Not only do we routinely pass false information ("Tell him I'm not home") or tell jokes at the expense of others, but we also worry that our friends might consider us stodgy and dull if we don't gossip, if we don't relate incidents that make others look foolish or

bad. Our own fears of becoming the butt of someone else's jokes and aspersions, our own desire for
social acceptance, and the sheer weight of convention
(after all, everybody does it) conspire to keep us
speaking in ways that corrode our character. Perhaps
our ability to abuse speech is the reason the midrash
says, "God loves and hates Israel's voice."

   Ultimately, we all pay a price for our network
of slander, innuendo, and deception: We lose the ability to trust those around us, and we begin to look at
others with a skepticism that borders on hostility. In
addition, we expect less from others and from ourselves and tend to interpret every action in the worst
possible light. The negative effects of these practices
impose on us all a significant degree of unhappiness,
alienation, and mistrust.

There is a delicate bal-
ance between an interest
in the lives of others and
an indulgence in gossip
and slander.

A cousin of mine related an uncomfortable dilemma. Her niece was going to her first junior high school dance. The girl previewed the outfit she planned to wear, sporting the ugliest hat my cousin had ever seen. She knew that her niece had selected it by herself—the first significant piece of clothing that her parents had had no say in. Eyes bright with expectancy, the girl turned to her aunt and asked her for her opinion. What should she have said?

The Torah itself provides examples in which God lies to spare human feelings. For example, when Sarah hears that she is going to become pregnant, she laughs and says that her husband, Abraham, is too old to produce children. Abraham overhears her laughter and asks God what she said. God tells Abraham that she laughed because she thought she was too old to bear children. By altering Sarah's statement, God maintains *sh'lom bayit* (peace in the family).

• Late one evening, having sat through my class on Jewish ethics, a middle-aged mother approached me with a question that had been bothering her. After being overwhelmed by paying a month's worth of bills, she had heard the phone ring. Her child answered it. It was a call from someone she had been dodging for the past several days, and she really didn't want to get into a long, drawn-out conversation, especially since she was finally catching up on her household paperwork. She quickly passed her child a note with the instructions, "Tell him I'm not home." Now she wants to know whether she did the right thing. Or, she wonders, is she merely teaching her child to lie?

• Another congregant complained about an incident at work. He was lunching with some of the workers in his office when the conversation turned to the subject of their new boss. One colleague commented that the new boss wasn't wearing a wedding ring, and that comment led to speculation about whether the newcomer was gay. A series of jokes about not turning their backs on him ensued. My congregant was outraged by the conversation but at the same time had become unable to stop thinking about the boss. How, he wondered, did that conversation affect his own judgment of the new boss? And could he have done anything to prevent the conversation or to stand up for his boss or for gays?

• When I was in college, a fellow student was once telling a group of students a rumor he had heard involving possible sexual misconduct between a professor and a few undergraduates. The professor had never been formally charged. Several of the students became indignant and promised to send protest letters to the school administrator. How did the repetition of these rumors change the way the students thought of this professor? Was their change in attitude fair or just?

• Ever hear the joke about three Poles in a boat?

L'shon ha-ra (לְשׁוֹן הָרַע, literally, "the evil tongue") is the practice of making a derogatory, deceptive, or damaging statement that is not motivated by a constructive or beneficial goal. Even honest information that results in the deprecation of an individual or group is *l'shon ha-ra,* provided that the primary intent in sharing the information was negative. Consequently, a joke about an ethnic group, a story about a foolish or stupid or repugnant deed, a deception—all are examples of *l'shon ha-ra.*

Unlike many of the other mitzvot described in this book, this one strikes at the heart of social popu-

Just as we cannot regather the dandelion seeds we blow to the wind, so too our words, once spoken, can never be recalled. And because our words are invisible, we must be careful how we use them since we may never know the extent of their audience or their damage.

*Who is eager
for life?
Who desires
years of good
fortune?
Guard your
tongue from
evil, your lips
from deceit.*

—PSALM 34:13-14

larity and human insecurity. A community in which *l'shon ha-ra* is common practice is one in which people cannot afford to trust one another; it is a community in which we can expect our deeds to be construed in the most unflattering light. For this reason, the Torah relates several prohibitions about *l'shon ha-ra:*

• Do not go about as a talebearer among your people (LEVITICUS 19:16).

• Do not carry false rumors (EXODUS 23:1).

• Do not insult the deaf or place a stumbling block before the blind (LEVITICUS 19:14).

• Do not take vengeance or bear a grudge against your countrymen. "Love your fellow as yourself; I am Adonai" (LEVITICUS 19:18).

As commendable as it may be to eliminate *l'shon ha-ra*, the fact is that its practice can be fun, it builds a sense of belonging (although by humiliating someone else), and it is generally perceived as harmless. Restraint in speech (שְׁמִירַת הַלָּשׁוֹן , *sh'mirat ha-lashon*) is often perceived as boring, sanctimonious, and humorless. So pervasive is the practice of *l'shon ha-ra* that even otherwise kind and caring people presume it to be acceptable. The Talmud notes that "many are guilty of robbery, a minority is guilty of lewdness, but all are guilty of slander."

How, in such a context, can we begin to make a change? Once again, the method advocated here is slow and incremental. There is no easy way to stop *l'shon ha-ra,* but we can each take a first step, and then another step, toward its containment. And with each new step, we will have a notable effect on those around us as well as on ourselves. Each step will become progressively easier and will feel more natural.

Controlling *l'shon ha-ra* takes courage and discipline. Yet the rewards are a more compassionate community, a greater sense of inner calm, an enhanced ability to trust and to care. Surely these goals are worth our effort.

❖　❖　❖　❖　❖

1 **Elevate your awareness of *l'shon ha-ra* by reciting the following prayer each morning.** It is based on a prayer by the nineteenth-century Polish rabbi Israel Kagan.

Gracious and merciful God, help me to restrain myself from speaking or listening to derogatory, damaging, or hostile speech. I will try not to engage in l'shon ha-ra, *either about individuals or about an entire group of people. I will strive not to say anything that contains falsehood, insincere flattery, scoffing, or elements of needless dispute, anger, arrogance, oppression, or embarrassment to others. Grant me the strength to say nothing unnecessary, so that all my actions and speech cultivate a love for Your creatures and for You.*

2 **When speaking about an individual, omit his or her name, and disguise the details of the event.** Be sure the event would not be identifiable even to the person involved. When describing a case to a colleague, doctors and psychotherapists generally follow the precaution of omitting the patient's name and details of his or her life, in order to protect the patient's anonymity. This practice emerges from the conviction that everyone has a right to privacy and to decide who may know the details of his or her life. If doctors and therapists employ this technique for a constructive purpose, imagine how much more careful the rest of us ought to be when we are simply gossiping or indulging in scorn and hostility.

3 **Become aware of when you are listening to the *l'shon ha-ra* of others and when you are speaking deceitfully yourself.** Once you become conscious of derogatory speech, you are better able to control it. Analyze your words before speaking about someone by asking the following three questions:

- Are they true?
- Are they well intentioned?
- Are they unlikely to harm anyone?

If a statement about someone does not receive a "yes" to each of these three questions, then refrain from saying it. Let us consider each question in more detail:

- *Are they true?* While telling the truth in every case may not be ideal, generally it is better to tell the truth than to lie. Only in cases where the truth would precipitate immediate danger or where the truth is needlessly callous (telling a child that you think her drawing is not beautiful) should you waive a general preference for truth-telling.

- *Are they well intentioned?* Repeating defamatory information about another person is *l'shon ha-ra* only when it is not meant for a constructive purpose. When two teachers discuss a student, when a therapist discusses a patient with another therapist, or when an employer is called on to write a letter of recommendation, they are not engaging in *l'shon ha-ra*. In each case, the motivation is to help the person involved. So long as the motive is to be helpful and the discussion is limited to providing only the information necessary to achieve a positive resolution, then the discussion is not *l'shon ha-ra*.

- *Are they likely to harm anyone?* Truth is not the only goal. It isn't even the highest goal. Above the generally commendable concern for truth is the concern for the dignity of other human beings. The Mishnah states that altering the truth is permissible *mip'nei darkhei shalom* (מִפְּנֵי דַרְכֵי שָׁלוֹם, "for the sake of peace"). The highest standard, therefore, is that no one may be harmed by the discussion. If harm is possible, then even if the information is true, it is wiser to avoid the discussion.

We spend the largest block of our time with the people with whom we work. This extensive time together often generates an excessive interest in their foibles and personal lives. As a result, particular care is necessary in the work place to restrain the urge to gossip. Awareness of this weakness in ourselves should also foster a healthy skepticism about what other people report to be true about their co-workers.

4 **Cultivate a sense of skepticism and disbelief about the negative reports of others.** Knowing that each of us often makes statements that are untrue or exaggerated, that express rage, bitterness, or jealousy, we can assume that the critical comments that others make may be tainted. Therefore, if you overhear someone making hurtful statements about someone else or if someone tells you of something dishonorable that another person supposedly did, you might question how free of hostility, insecurity, or embitterment that report really is. A measure of skepticism about critical remarks can go a long way toward blunting their effect and a long way toward reminding you just how influential such remarks can be.

5 **Select the two or three most aggravating people in your life and refrain from speaking about them in public.** As pleasurable as it may be to belittle these people during lunch or a coffee break, it is possible to withstand that temptation. Generally, these discussions are motivated by a sense of anger or a sense of being a victim or simply for the fun of embarrassing someone unpleasant. Although it will be difficult to begin to curb these discussions, if you select a few likely individuals to place off limits, you can make a significant start.

6 **Stop repeating jokes that degrade others.** All too often, social conversation ultimately degenerates into jokes whose humor depends on disparaging another group of people. Jokes about ethnic or religious groups, women, and gays all humiliate members of those groups and give a false sense of superiority to those listeners who are not in the categories being joked about. Such jokes degrade everyone.

In addition, stop laughing or smiling when others tell you such a degrading joke. If possible, mention that such jokes depend on disparaging different groups of people and are not funny. At the very least, when friends and colleagues see that you are not amused, they will be discouraged from telling jokes that demean their fellow human beings.

While the human failings of other people may seem funny, few of us enjoy having people laugh at our own misdeeds or errors. Simple compassion would dictate that we not delight in the suffering of others.

7 **Another way of increasing sensitivity to *l'shon ha-ra* is to try this simple test: Substitute the name or identity of someone close to you for that of the person or people you are describing.** Instead of making a comment about a neighbor, make the same comment about a best friend. Does the statement still feel neutral or well intentioned? If so, then it is probably also all right to make it about someone else. A similar standard would be to ask, "Would I make this comment in the presence of the person I am speaking about?" If you wouldn't be comfortable making the remark in front of that person, then perhaps you shouldn't make it at all.

8 **Balance a negative comment with a positive one.** You may find yourself having said something negative about another person, with the purpose of the remark not being to help the person or to further some constructive goal. It may not always be possible simply to undo a remark just made. If it isn't, try immediately to balance the negative comment by following it with an appreciation of some positive trait. The follow-up comment should, of course, be honest, focusing on some admirable characteristic or talent.

If each time we said something negative about someone, we also said something positive, we would soon become aware of our need to deride that person. That heightened awareness would lead to a greater ability to control both the harmful speech and the need to articulate it.

9 **Vent your anger on, or report harmful information only to, a spouse, a companion, or a very close friend.** Recognize that we have a drive to let off steam and that the sharing of certain information can have an important benefit—in allowing us to regain a balance and an ability to go on with life. Not expressing any negative comments at all may simply be "too much." By limiting whom we will speak to in this way, we limit the harm done to others and remove *l'shon ha-ra* from the realm of social entertainment.

10 **When others start to gossip, remain silent.** Try to minimize *l'shon ha-ra* in the conversations of others. A good beginning is to remain silent when others start to gossip. At first, this restraint may feel difficult. It will become easier over time, however, particularly as it becomes clear just how pervasive gossip is. By not contributing to *l'shon ha-ra,* you may be able to diminish its appeal. Through silence, you can lessen the momentum that such a conversation normally acquires.

11 **Avoid praising someone to his or her enemy, for doing so is an invitation to *l'shon ha-ra.*** If it is clear that a friend dislikes someone, then praising that person will only invite the friend's negative comments to support his or her hostility. Simply avoiding conversation about individuals obviates the need to shift the topic once it has already started to go in the wrong direction.

12 **If a conversation slips into *l'shon ha-ra*, ask if anything can be done to help the person being criticized to overcome his or her fault.** It is often difficult to shift gears or abruptly call a halt to the practice of *l'shon ha-ra,* even if those involved admit in theory that their conversation constitutes harmful gossip. So move from criticizing to being a source of help, thereby making yourself a sympathetic advocate, helpfully underscoring the humanity of the person being discussed.

As difficult as it may seem, expressing anger, disappointment, or sorrow directly to the one who provoked it is the only way to restore trust and honesty, the only way to allow for apologies and improvement. Speaking to each other is always better than speaking about each other.

13 **If all attempts to steer a group away from *l'shon ha-ra* fail, then there may be no alternative but to make an explicit statement.** Consider asking that the group change the subject, explaining that talking about other people in a dehumanizing way doesn't feel entertaining. Or perhaps less directly, just change the subject. Of course, in criticizing the gossip, be careful not to disparage the members of the group or cause them to respond by redoubling their gossip. Self-righteousness can result in others' stubborn insistence on continuing gossip. A simple statement of your personal preference to avoid *l'shon ha-ra* might be most effective in getting people to change the topic.

❖   ❖   ❖   ❖   ❖

Imagine a community in which people speak of others with a desire to help them, a community in which jokes do not feed on our fear of difference and our need for acceptance, a world in which we can trust the integrity of our public figures and our neighbors, a world in which we leave a room knowing that those remaining will not start discussing our shortcomings or faults once we are beyond earshot. We may never succeed in creating such a universe, but the mitzvah of *sh'mirat ha-lashon* is a possible pathway toward that beautiful ideal. And each step we take, whether or not we ever reach the destination, creates a world that is that much more harmonious and supportive of human beings and the human community.

According to the Talmud, the tongue is like an arrow. Once it is unsheathed, it is able to harm both near and far. Once it is in flight, there is no guarantee where it will land. Guarding our tongues, however out of fashion in our culture, is a matter of human survival. While an arrow can strike only one target, the midrash teaches that slander injures three: the one who speaks it, the one who listens to it, and the one about whom it is spoken. We all have an interest in a civilized tongue.

For Further Reading

Unfortunately, there is no adequate English translation or summary of Rabbi Israel Meier Kagan's *Hofetz Hayyim.*

Sissela Bok, *Lying: Moral Choice in Public and Private Life.* New York: Vintage Books, 1978. A secular discussion of harmful speech.

There are short discussions of *l'shon ha-ra* in the three books below:

Louis Jacobs, *The Book of Jewish Belief.* West Orange, NJ: Behrman House, 1984, pages 208-20.

Allan Mintz and Everett Gendler, "Dissonance and Harmony: *Lashon Ha-ra.*" In *The Third Jewish Catalog,* eds. Sharon Strassfeld and Michael Strassfeld. Philadelphia: Jewish Publication Society, 1980, pages 94-103.

Dennis Prager and Joseph Telushkin, *The Nine Questions People Ask About Judaism.* New York: Simon and Schuster, 1975, pages 178-81.

14 *Talmud Torah:*
Study and Learning

*You shall
teach them
diligently
to your
children.*
—DEUTERONOMY
6:7

*It is for our own good that we learn
Torah and forget it; because if we studied Torah and never forgot it, the people
would struggle with learning it for two
or three years, resume ordinary work,
and never pay further attention to it.
But since we study Torah and forget it,
we don't abandon its study.*

—KOHELET RABBAH 1, 13:1

Every Friday morning, I speak with my synagogue preschoolers: sixty children ranging in
age from three to five. I tell them a story and
discuss an approaching holiday, their families, or events in the community. Generally, I prepare
much more than we cover, because our encounters
may begin with my outline but rapidly become a conversation that the children themselves direct.

One year as Ḥanukkah was approaching, I
decided to talk about the idea of freedom. I wanted

The survival of Judaism depends on something as frail
and resilient as learning and teaching. Whether in a
classroom, a synagogue, or a home, we add our voices
to the process that is Torah by studying our sacred
writings and traditions, by joining in discussion and
debate with our fellow Jews.

to give the children a sense of what the Festival of Lights reveals about Jewish values. I started our discussion by asking why we celebrate Ḥanukkah. "To get presents," the chorus chanted. One dissenter insisted that we celebrate Ḥanukkah to light candles. When I asked, "*Why* do we light candles and get presents?" no one reacted at all. I realized I would have to adopt a different strategy.

I asked the children what it means to be free. This open-ended question was better received. A little boy informed me that it means being able to drink milk. A girl next to him added that being free means leaving your room whenever you want to. A third child revealed that freedom is playing with Mommy and Daddy.

There you have it: the nursery school perspective on freedom—milk, Mommy and Daddy, and the liberty to leave your room. With this in mind, I described the Maccabees as people who insisted that Jews should have the right to be who they are and to play with their own toys and with their own friends. By the end of the morning, both the children and I had learned something from the exchange: I learned about what freedom can mean—nurturance, caring, and the liberty to determine one's own identity. And the children learned to connect their understanding of freedom to the passionate deeds of the Maccabees.

❖   ❖   ❖   ❖   ❖

Learning is exactly that process by which we incorporate new experiences into the way we understand the world, our place in it, and ourselves. It is, for example, the interaction that occurred between the preschoolers and me that year before Ḥanukkah. Learning happens all the time, in every place, not just in a classroom. We learn when we attend a concert, visit a museum, or walk along the beach. Figuring out how to assemble a piece of furniture or how to build a sukkah is an act of learning, as is baking a cake or leading a Havdalah service for the first time.

This Torah shall not depart from your lips.
—JOSHUA 1:8

Every encounter with another person, with nature, or with a job provides us with the opportunity to change ourselves, to add depth and layers of meaning to our identity.

According to a story in my family, each summer my stepfather, Kurt, and his mother would spend a few weeks with Kurt's grandfather in Poland. The first words from Kurt's *zayde* were always, "Yankele, can you read yet?" When Kurt was five years old, he enrolled in a *ḥeder,* where the rabbi taught him the Hebrew letters and coached him to read from the Torah and then to translate the Hebrew into Yiddish.

Imagine Kurt's excitement at the age of six, when he went for his annual visit to his *zayde,* knowing that this time he would be able to respond to his grandfather's question with a proud yes. As he had every summer before, *Zayde* asked Kurt, "Yankele, can you read yet?" This time, when little Kurt answered "Yes!" *Zayde* took a Hebrew Bible and opened it to *lekh lekha,* the verse in Genesis where God instructs Abraham to "Go forth from your native land and from your father's house to the land that I will show you." Kurt eagerly read the sacred script and translated the Hebrew into Yiddish. Kurt's *zayde* beamed, catching a glimpse of eternity in the moment.

What Kurt recalls from that powerful moment is the glory of being able to transform black marks into letters and the letters into words that tell something about people and their lives. To this day, Kurt glories in his *zayde's* pride and in his own.

This blend of book learning and personal exploration that Kurt experienced, this linking of the generations through a shared body of literature, practice, and identity, characterizes *talmud torah* through the ages. Jewish learning provides a knowledge of Jewish thought, ritual, and history even as it permits self-exploration, the search for deeper meaning, and the clarification of values. The mitzvah that includes all others, that leads to all others, is the mitzvah of *talmud torah,* תַּלְמוּד תּוֹרָה.

❖   ❖   ❖   ❖   ❖

THE GREATEST COMMANDMENT
The Talmud teaches that the mitzvah of *talmud torah* (Jewish learning) is the greatest of all mitzvot. Because study leads to action and because understanding and information are prerequisites for performing mitzvot, *talmud torah* contains the potential for all the other mitzvot. What we learn is who we become.

Jewish learning is democratic: old
and young, men and women, all can
come together to learn from a master
teacher. As disciples of the wise, we
transform a normal moment into
another Mount Sinai, an occasion for
us to hear God's voice.

1 **Find a good teacher.** The first step in *talmud torah* is to get a good teacher. This person need not be a rabbi or a professor. Often, simply another learning Jew is more than adequate (although the more one has learned and lived, the more questions one will be able to answer satisfactorily). In any case, a knowledgeable and passionate teacher is a must. Find one and latch on.

Many synagogues, seminaries, boards of rabbis, and Hebrew colleges offer an introduction to Judaism. Such courses are generally designed for adults—Jews who want an adult understanding of their own history and faith, and gentiles who want to know more about Judaism or are considering conversion. The classes vary widely in content. Find one that seems rigorous enough to meet your interests and whose teacher shares your approach to life and your values (although not necessarily your understanding of religion or Judaism). Such a class is your portal to the lifelong process of *talmud torah*.

2 **Find a study partner.** In urging a process of learning, the Mishnah counsels, "Select a rabbi for yourself; acquire a colleague for study." This second step is essential. Find a colleague to study with—a friend, lover, spouse, child, or someone taking the same course you're taking. This traditional Jewish method of team learning is called *ḥavruta,* and the participant is called a *ḥaver* (חָבֵר , "colleague," "friend").

The benefits of team study are many: it encourages preparation, regular meeting times, and the articulation of insights (hence, a better understanding and a more thorough retention of the material); it discourages the glossing away of difficulties. Additionally, it places learning in the context of a relationship: both participants learn to question, to challenge, to justify, and to support their own assertions and beliefs.

3 **Set aside a fixed time each week for your studies.** Learning takes time and persistence. When you confront Jewish scholarship and history for the first time, you may find yourself confused and discouraged by the sheer bulk of material. There is simply so much of it! But don't let the magnitude dissuade you. Break the task down into manageable bits, and learn a little at a time, in regular increments. The only way to do this is to commit yourself to short, regular learning sessions. Set aside a fixed amount of time every day, three times a week, or twice a week—just as you would (or do)—for an exercise program. (The brain needs exercise too.) Even if you start with only a half-hour twice a week, make the commitment, and keep it.

4 **Read the Ten Commandments each day.** The Ten Commandments possess a checkered past. In antiquity, they were a part of the morning prayer service (in both the Temple and the ancient synagogues), but they were removed in order to counter sectarian assertions that they were the only binding commandments in the Torah. In order to demonstrate that the *entire* Torah reverberates with the will of God, the rabbis of the Talmud instituted public Torah readings on Monday and Thursday mornings, in addition to the more widely known Shabbat readings.

Although no longer read publicly, the private contemplation of the Ten Commandments has always been encouraged, no less so now than in the past. The Ten Commandments are found in the Torah (Exodus 20:2-14) and in most siddurim.

5 **Begin studying Hebrew.** However knowledgeable about Jewish history and values one becomes, a Jew who can't read the Hebrew letters is an outsider once the prayers begin. If you cannot read Hebrew, a synagogue service is a spectator sport, a chance to watch a rabbi, a cantor, and a few congregants reading and singing words beyond your grasp. As the synagogue is still the center of Jewish communal life, a Jew who doesn't know Hebrew must feel peripheral in the midst of the religion's core institution.

Opportunities to learn Hebrew are abundant. Courses at synagogues, community colleges, Jewish community centers, and universities abound. Tapes and textbooks for private study also proliferate; advertisements for them appear regularly in every Jewish newspaper. Until you have read and understood the Psalms in the original Hebrew, you cannot fully appreciate the beauty of their language. For more information on learning Hebrew, see Chapter 4, step 11.

6   **Build your own Jewish library—for reading and for reference.** For over three thousand years, the Jewish people have put in writing a record of their relationships with God, humanity, and one another. Thousands of books are available, on every Jewish subject. These books can provide a home education. A shelf or two of Jewish books will set a tone for your home and provide the content for evolving religious practice and a sense of identity.

At the end of this chapter, a list of more than forty books serves as a useful bibliography and a basis for a home library. It is a supplement to the books listed in For Further Reading at the end of the other chapters in this book. Taken together, these books represent excellence, breadth, and a significant body of knowledge. It could (and should) take several years to digest their contents.

I have tried to give preference to paperbacks that are still in print and to limit myself to a reasonable number of selections. When people ask what to get you for birthdays and holidays, suggest a particular title, or even a gift certificate from a bookstore that will order specific books.

One way we show respect for Jewish books that contain God's name and are no longer usable is to give them a ritual funeral. This ritual is a recognition that our soul as a people is transmitted and contained in words passed from one generation to another.

7   **Treat sacred books in a way that reflects and shows respect for their significance.** Ever since Muhammad, Jews have been known as the people of the Book because of their special relationship to the Book of books, the Torah. While other ancient peoples worshiped by sacrificing people or animals, Jews developed a form of worship that centered on reading as a sacred act. To this day, the Shabbat morning service includes the practice of carrying a book (the Torah scroll) around the sanctuary while the congregants reach out to touch and kiss it. Below are two additional ways to show respect for our sacred books:

• *Never place a sacred book on the ground.* Instead, put the book on a chair or a table, or hold it in your lap. Similarly, never use a sacred book as a mat for some other object (in other words, don't put a coffee mug on top of the Bible!).

• *Should a book fall on the ground by accident, kiss the book while retrieving it.* This traditional response demonstrates to all who are watching that the dropping of the book was not a deliberate display of contempt. It also reaffirms the preciousness of the book's contents.

---

8 **Read Jewish magazines, journals, and newspapers.** There are so many thoughtful Jewish writers and so many pressing topics that it is impossible to read books on all of them. The only way to try to follow the range of Jewish thought today is to read Jewish magazines, journals, and newspapers.

• *Read* Sh'ma. Of the tremendous number of magazines available, this one stands out for its excellence and its uniqueness. *Sh'ma,* an eight-page weekly magazine, was founded by Rabbi Eugene Borowitz and is currently edited by Rabbi Nina Beth Cardin. It does not follow any party line. Instead, it carefully presents a range of responses so that everyone will find affirmation and aggravation in each edition. I know of no magazine that packs as much content and vitality into such little space. *Sh'ma* is simply a must. Subscribe by writing to

Sh'ma
99 Park Avenue, Suite S-300
New York, NY 10016

• *Subscribe to a Jewish journal.* While magazines are helpful, their format almost always requires a slick approach. For a more thoughtful treatment of serious issues, journals are essential. Each religious branch of Judaism publishes its own, as do many private and political groups. Of all the available journals, my favorites for depth, relevance, and range are

Judaism
15 East 84th Street
New York, NY 10028

Conservative Judaism
3080 Broadway
New York, NY 10027

Jewish Spectator
4391 Park Milano
Calabasas, CA 91302

Subscribe to and read at least one of these, and then save the issues for future reference. (Journals add a scholarly touch to any bookshelf.)

• *Subscribe to at least one Jewish newspaper.* Every major Jewish community prints its own local paper. While many are excellent, my favorites are

New York Jewish Week
1501 Broadway
New York, NY 10036

Los Angeles Jewish Journal
3660 Wilshire Boulevard
Los Angeles, CA 90010

Baltimore Jewish Times
2104 North Charles Street
Baltimore, MD 21218

Northern California Jewish Bulletin
88 First Street, Suite 300
San Francisco, CA 94105-2506

---

9 **Spend a summer studying Judaism full-time.** Studying full-time for a month or two will enable you to reach new levels of knowledge. By enrolling in a summer program, you will have access to excellent libraries and to a vibrant Jewish community, and you will have the chance to live among people whose inclinations are similar to yours. For information about summer programs sponsored by the Conservative movement, contact

Jewish Theological Seminary of America
3080 Broadway
New York, NY 10027

University of Judaism
15600 Mulholland Drive
Los Angeles, CA 90077

Programs sponsored by the Reform movement are organized through the Hebrew

Union College–Jewish Institute of Religion at one of the following locations:

Hebrew Union College–
Jewish Institute of Religion
1 West 4th Street
New York, NY 10012

3077 University Avenue
Los Angeles, CA 90007

3101 Clifton Avenue
Cincinnati, OH 45220

Programs sponsored by the Reconstructionst movement are organized through

Reconstructionist Rabbinical College
Church and Greenwood Avenues
Wyncote, PA 19095

Programs sponsored by the Orthodox movement are organized through

Orthodox Union
333 Seventh Avenue
New York, NY 10001

For those unable to afford the luxury of studying full-time for a month or two, consider the several excellent programs in the United States and abroad that offer a shorter course of Jewish study. One excellent program is offered by the Brandeis-Bardin Institute in Los Angeles. Its Brandeis Camp Institute Program attracts groups of young adults in extremely effective programs of Jewish study in the summer, and excellent weekend programs for all age groups. The national network of Ramah Camps (affiliated with the Conservative movement) offers a range of adult retreats throughout the year. The national office can provide more detailed information about the local offerings:

Camp Ramah
3080 Broadway
New York, NY 10027
212-678-8881

The United Synagogue of Conservative Judaism has also developed several opportunities for learning and spiritual growth.

United Synagogue of Conservative Judaism
155 Fifth Avenue
New York, NY 10010-6802

As we join in the study of Torah—the basis for our identity as Jews and the guide for our lives—we make God's Torah into our Torah and help Judaism to live on through our words and our deeds.

Reform Jews seeking a course of study tailored to their movement should contact

> Union of American Hebrew
> Congregations, Camping Department
> 838 Fifth Avenue
> New York, NY 10021-7064

Those seeking programs from an Orthodox perspective should contact

> Orthodox Union
> 333 Seventh Avenue
> New York, NY 10001

---

10 **Join a weekly Torah study group.** This is one of the most effective and pleasant ways to study Torah on a regular basis. The Torah is divided into weekly selections (called *parashat ha-shavuah,* פָּרָשַׁת הַשָּׁבוּעַ), and most synagogues have some form of organized study (the one in my synagogue is called the *ḥevrah Mikra,* חֶבְרָה מִקְרָא, literally, a "Bible society"). Generally these groups meet just before or after Shabbat morning services. They provide a lovely way to learn about the Torah in a religious context, with a community examining how the Torah is to be lived in the present, not just how it was understood in the past.

---

11 **Teach others.** The best way to learn is to teach. Preparing to present material clearly and accurately is the surest test of mastery. In answering the probing challenges and questions of my own students, I've often discovered that I hadn't known something as well as I had presumed. I've also seen new insights emerge from the encounter between a good teacher and a lively class. If you want to teach, there are two avenues available, each requiring a different level of knowledge and amount of time:

• *If you have children, take the time to teach them.* This commitment may involve a weekly family discussion of the Torah portion or your reading each child's religious school assignment and talking it through with the child.

Schools cannot substitute for the home, they can only provide the tools and material to empower Jewish families to be Jewish. The more parents are involved in their children's Jewish education, the greater the impact of that education. No one can buy an identity or memories. They can only be experienced.

• *Teach in a synagogue religious school.* The vast majority of American Jewish children attend supplemental Jewish schools (afternoon programs that hold classes a few days a week and are generally linked to a congregation), and the schools almost always face an abysmal shortage of teachers. Teaching in a synagogue school sharpens the teacher's knowledge and provides the children with a valuable role model. Even if it's possible to teach only once a week, or even once a month, there is a religious school nearby that needs help. The ultimate performance of *talmud torah* is one in which you share the joy of learning with the next generation and build a stronger community at the same time.

---

12 **Support the institutions that educate Jews.** We can't all be scholars, but we all need scholars. We can't all be full-time students of our Jewish heritage, but we can enable others to do what we perhaps cannot do—educate children and rabbinical students. Giving *tzedakah* to institutions of Jewish learning, whether synagogue schools, community day schools, or rabbinical seminaries, is a worthy fulfillment of the mitzvah of *talmud torah.*

• Most afternoon schools cannot cover their expenses with tuition alone. These schools need the support of the larger Jewish community.

• Not every family will choose to send its children to a Jewish day school, but those schools also need our support—and they offer us something in return. We are all enriched when the children in our community know about their heritage and practice their religion with comfort.

• The different branches of Judaism

have their own rabbinical schools, each producing rabbis for their particular movement. All rabbinical schools are in need of assistance. The bulk of the rabbis in the Conservative movement are educated at two American Institutions: Jewish Theological Seminary in New York City and University of Judaism in Los Angeles. The Conservative movement also sponsors two rabbinical schools abroad, one in Israel (the Seminary of Judaic Studies) and one in Buenos Aires (Seminario Rabbínico Latino Americano). The Reform movement educates its rabbis at Hebrew Union College–Jewish Institute of Religion, which has campuses in New York, Cincinnati, and Los Angeles and has a program for the ordaining of Israeli rabbis at its Jerusalem campus. The Reconstructionist movement's seminary is located in Wyncote, Pennsylvania. The Orthodox movement's seminary, Yeshiva University, is located in New York.

To provide financial support to these institutions, contact

The Development Office of the Jewish
 Theological Seminary of America
3080 Broadway
New York, NY 10027

Spending time with children, enjoying their curiosity and intensity, and giving them the gift of Jewish identity is a richly rewarding experience. Volunteering with a religious school is a gift—for both recipient and giver.

The Development Office of the
  University of Judaism
15600 Mulholland Drive
Los Angeles, CA 90077

The Development Office of Hebrew
  Union College—Jewish Institute of Religion
1 West 4th Street
New York, NY 10012

The Development Office of the
  Reconstructionist Rabbinical College
Church and Greenwood Avenues
Wyncote, PA 19095

The Development Office of
  Yeshiva University
500 West 185th Street
New York, NY 10033

The seminaries also train educators, cantors, and community leaders and have long offered graduate study for scholars. Supporting these programs is a way of ensuring the Jewish future. Speak to your rabbi or educator about how you can support the training of rabbis, and then make a commitment to include Jewish education, at all levels, in your charitable contributions. If we don't support them, no one will. And in supporting a new generation of Jewish leaders and thinkers, we are ensuring our own spiritual and cultural future as well.

❖　❖　❖　❖　❖

Only humans are able to absorb the experiences and ideas of those they have never met, people who died before they even began to live. Through study and learning, we join a dialogue that spans the generations. The youngest Jew becomes a contemporary of Abraham and Sarah, Moses and Miriam, Hillel and Maimonides. Through the accumulated writings of the past, their legacy and their insights are not lost. Our voices become instruments in the symphony of Jewish expression, the latest link in a vast chain.

Talmud torah provides us with another connection as well—one to God. In study, we encounter the mysterious and indefinable. Rabbi Louis Finkelstein often used to observe, "When I pray, I talk to God; when I study, God speaks to me." Through study, we can hear God's voice echoing in encounters long concluded. By participating in the give and take of the mind, we can decipher from ancient words God's will for our own time.

Through *talmud torah*, we can share the warmth and the passion of a call that sounded in our ancestors' study and is present in ours as well. If during our learning we open our souls as well as our hearts, we, too, can hear that still, small voice. It is a voice calling us home.

❖　❖　❖　❖　❖

BUILDING A JEWISH LIBRARY

Jews have been reading and writing for at least three thousand years. As a result, it is impossible to present a complete or objective list of significant Jewish books in a short space. Instead, this list presents my selection of significant and readable books, almost all of which are still in print. Books listed at the end of other chapters are not repeated here. Hardcover books are marked with an asterisk.

INTRODUCTIONS TO JUDAISM

Michael Fishbane, *Judaism.* San Francisco: Harper and Row, 1987. A marvelous introduction by a great scholar. Fishbane looks at the history of Judaism, interprets its beliefs and practices, and gives examples of religious individuals and typical practices.

Milton Steinberg, *Basic Judaism.* San Diego: Harcourt Brace Jovanovich, 1947. A classic. A beloved Conservative rabbi presents a warm understanding of the essence of Jewish religion.

GENERAL REFERENCES

*Isaac Klein, *A Guide to Jewish Religious Practice.* New York: Jewish Theological Seminary of America, 1979. The indispensable guide to the wealth of Jewish ritual practices: prayer, holidays, dietary laws, menstrual purity, and the life cycle.

*Cecil Roth and Geoffrey Wigoder, eds., *Encyclopedia Judaica*, 16 vols. Jerusalem: Keter and MacMillan, 1972. The complete record of Jewish history, religion, thought, culture, and politics.

THE BIBLE
Primary Source

Tanakh: The Holy Scriptures. Philadelphia: Jewish Publication Society, 1988. This is the definitive English translation of the Hebrew Bible, produced by professors of Bible at secular universities and by representatives of the three major religious movements within Judaism.

Understanding the Bible

Norman K. Gottwald, *The Hebrew Bible: A Socio-Literary Introduction.* Philadelphia: Fortress Press, 1985. An excellent guide to the times and context of the *Tanakh*, Israelite society, and contemporary scholarship on biblical study.

Jon D. Levenson, *Sinai and Zion: An Entry into the Jewish Bible.* San Francisco: Harper and Row, 1985. The best introduction to the core ideas of the *Tanakh*.

RABBINIC JUDAISM
Primary Sources

Jacob Neusner, ed., *The Mishnah: A New Translation.* New Haven, CT: Yale University Press, 1988. A clear translation of the first compilation of rabbinic law and lore, with a marvelous introduction by one of the leading living scholars of rabbinic Judaism.

*I. Epstein, *The Babylonian Talmud.* London: Soncino Press, 1948. A somewhat dated translation of the fundamental rabbinic work, on which all subsequent Judaism is based. There is no other accessible translation of the entire Talmud.

Judah Goldin, *Aboth de Rabbi Nathan.* New York: Schocken Books, 1974. An excellent translation of *Pirkei Avot*, the Mishnah's *Sayings of the Sages* and the accompanying midrash.

Understanding Rabbinic Judaism

Gary G. Porton, *Understanding Rabbinic Midrash: Text and Commentary.* Hoboken, NJ: Ktav, 1985. The best guide available. Contains extensive samples of midrash and guides the reader through them.

Morris Adler, *The World of the Talmud.* New York: Schocken Books, 1958. Somewhat dated but still an excellent introduction to the social and intellectual context of the Talmud.

Adin Steinsaltz, *The Essential Talmud.* New York: Basic Books, 1976. A passionate presentation of the relevance of Talmud and its worldview by one of the great Orthodox rabbis and teachers of Talmud in world Jewry.

Jacob Neusner, *Invitation to the Talmud: A Teaching Book.* San Francisco: Harper and Row, 1973. The great scholar and teacher presents examples of Mishnah, *Tosefta*, the Jerusalem Talmud, and the Babylonian Talmud along with a running commentary and sound introductions.

HISTORY

*Leo Schwartz, ed., *Great Ages and Ideas of the Jewish People.* New York: Modern Library, 1956. This book is readily available and affordable. It is a wonderful collection of essays by some of the greatest scholars of its time, laying out the richness of Jewish religious civilization and thought in every age.

H. H. Ben-Sasson, *A History of the Jewish People.* Cambridge, MA: Harvard University Press, 1976. A sound and solid textbook by professors from Hebrew University in Jerusalem. Used in college courses. The maps are very helpful too.

ZIONISM AND ISRAEL

Amos Elon, *The Israelis.* New York: Holt, Rinehart and Winston, 1971. Presents the people of Israel, not simply the headlines that often hide the flesh-and-blood reality.

One way to engage in *talmud torah* is to support those institutions, such as rabbinical seminaries, which educate and train Jewish religious leaders. Pictured here is a graduating class at the Rabbinical School of the Jewish Theological Seminary in New York.

Arthur Hertzberg, ed., *The Zionist Idea: A Historical Analysis and Reader.* New York: Atheneum, 1977. A masterful anthology of the founding ideologies of Zionism as well as an incisive introduction by a leading Conservative rabbi and professor of modern Judaism and Jewry.

CONTEMPORARY JEWISH MOVEMENTS AND COMMUNITIES

Howard M. Sachar, *Diaspora: An Inquiry into the Contemporary Jewish World.* New York: Harper and Row, 1985. The best introduction out.

Eugene B. Borowitz, *Reform Judaism Today.* West Orange, NJ: Behrman House, 1983. Rabbi Borowitz, probably the greatest living Reform theologian, teaches at the Hebrew Union College-Jewish Institute of Religion. This is close to a definitive presentation of Reform Judaism.

Neil Gillman, *Conservative Judaism: The New Century.* West Orange, NJ: Behrman House, 1993. An accessible and lively history of the Conservative movement. Illustrated with many photographs.

Elliot N. Dorff, *Conservative Judaism: Our Ancestors to Our Descendants.* New York: United Synagogue Youth, 1977. In this clear and passionate book, Rabbi Dorff of the University of Judaism, scholar of Jewish law, theologian, and master teacher, here demonstrates that Conservative Judaism is the modern continuation of traditional Judaism. He summons many biblical and rabbinic texts to show the continuity of method and conviction.

Samuel C. Heilman and Steven M. Cohen, *Cosmopolitans and Parochials: Modern Orthodox Jews in America.* Chicago: University of Chicago Press, 1989. A scholarly and insightful assessment of modern Orthodoxy and its challenges.

BY AND ABOUT JEWISH WOMEN

Rachel Biale, *Women and Jewish Law: An Exploration of Women's Issues in Halakhic Sources.* New York: Schocken Books, 1984. A sensitive, scholarly, and comprehensive presentation of Jewish law as it pertains to women and their lives.

The Memoirs of Gluckel of Hameln. New York: Schocken Books, 1977. The most exciting diary to come out of the medieval period. You will fall in love with Gluckel, whose guts, wit, energy, and enthusiasm account for her success.

Susannah Heschel, *On Being a Jewish Feminist: A Reader.* New York: Schocken Books, 1983. A remarkable anthology of contemporary viewpoints on why many modern women feel excluded or diminished within traditional Judaism, and an array of responses to remedy that imbalance.

Susan Weidman Schneider, *Jewish and Female: Choices and Changes in Our Lives Today.* New York: Simon and Schuster, 1984. Just what it says, the "Jewish catalog" for Jewish women. It presents a remarkable array of information and practical advice on ways of becoming involved and educated in every aspect of Jewish living and organization.

JEWISH PHILOSOPHY
Primary Sources
Isadore Twersky, *A Maimonides Reader.* New York: Behrman House, 1972. The great Harvard scholar of Maimonides has compiled a wonderful selection of the medieval sage's writings.

Mordecai Kaplan, *The Meaning of God in Modern Jewish Religion.* New York: Reconstructionist Press, 1962. Written by the founder of Reconstructionist Judaism and one of the dominating Jewish thinkers of the twentieth century, this book poses an important challenge to the way we think of God.

Nahum N. Glatzer, *Franz Rosenzweig: His Life and Thought.* New York: Schocken Books, 1961. Rosenzweig, a German existentialist philosopher, articulated the approach of gradual growth that permeates this book and much of contemporary Jewish pedagogy. This book collects his best writing and significant insights.

Abraham J. Heschel, *Between God and Man: An Interpretation of Judaism*, ed. Fritz A. Rothschild. New York: Free Press, 1959. My principal guide in matters of Jewish spirit, thought, and faith, Rabbi Heschel exemplified in his life and writings that passion for justice and yearning for holiness that pervade rabbinic Judaism. He taught at the Jewish Theological Seminary, and this is an anthology of his writings. Read anything he wrote whenever possible.

*Joseph B. Soloveitchik, *Halakhic Man.* Philadelphia: Jewish Publication Society, 1983. One of the great contemporary Orthodox thinkers, for many years a professor at Yeshiva University. This is one of his key works.

Understading Jewish Philosophy
Julius Guttman, *Philosophies of Judaism* New York: Schocken Books, 1973. The principal text for clarifying the whirls and eddies of Jewish philosophers and their systems of thought. Particularly strong for the medieval period.

Eugene Borowitz, *Choices in Modern Jewish Thought: A Partisan Guide.* West Orange, NJ: Behrman House, 1983. This does for modern Jewish philosophy what Guttman did for medieval Jewish philosophy.

JEWISH LAW AND ETHICS
*Robert Gordis, *The Dynamics of Judaism: A Study of Jewish Law.* Bloomington: Indiana University Press, 1990. Consummate rabbi, professor of Bible at the Jewish Theological Seminary, and editor of *Judaism Quarterly*, Robert Gordis wrote as beautifully as he spoke. With passion, intelligence, and sophistication, he presents the way in which Jewish law has worked to inspire and educate people to goodness throughout history and into the present. Worth every penny.

*Louis Jacobs, *A Tree of Life: Diversity, Flexibility, and Creativity in Jewish Law.* Oxford, England: Littman Library, 1984. A marvelous and well-documented presentation of the flexibility and creativity of Jewish law by one of the leading rabbis of our age.

*Abraham P. Bloch, *A Book of Jewish Ethical Concepts: Biblical and Postbiblical.* New York: Ktav, 1984. A sound if somewhat dull presentation. Read it for the information it contains.

JEWISH ART
*Cecil Roth, *Jewish Art: An Illustrated History.* Greenwich, CT: New York Graphic Society, 1971. A history of Jewish art from the earliest stages of antiquity to 1970. Lots of illustrations. A big book.

JEWISH MYSTICISM
Zohar: The Book of Enlightenment, ed. Daniel Matt. New York: Paulist Press, 1983. A beautiful, poetic translation of sections of the Zohar, the basic text of Jewish mysticism. The commentary and introduction are wonderful guides, written by a great scholar of the Jewish mystical tradition.

Gershom G. Scholem, *Major Trends in Jewish Mysticism.* New York: Schocken Books, 1961. Scholem is the father of Jewish mystical studies. As a professor at Hebrew University, he made the study of kabbalah respectable, even necessary. This is his major work.

Adin Steinsaltz, *The Thirteen Petaled Rose.* New York: Basic Books, 1980. A beautiful portrayal of a kabbalist's concerns and language, a chance to feel kabbalah from the inside.

PRAYERS AND HOLIDAYS
*Abraham Millgram, *Jewish Worship.* Philadelphia: Jewish Publication Society, 1971. A sound, complete introduction to the meaning of prayer, the history of Jewish worship, and a guide to the specific prayers of Shabbat, the weekday, and the festivals.

*Evelyn Garfiel, *Service of the Heart: A Guide to the Jewish Prayer Book.* Northvale, NJ: Jason Aronson. Just what it claims to be, and very good at it, too.

Abraham Joshua Heschel, *Quest for God.* New York: Crossroad, 1990. A poetic and soul-filled exploration of the world of prayer and praying by its master practitioner.

Michael Strassfeld, *The Jewish Holidays: A Guide and Commentary.* New York: Harper and Row, 1985. The best one-volume guide to the Jewish holiday cycle. This book blends abundant information about history and symbolism with a respect for contemporary reality and a guide to "living" the festivals. The marginal comments, by a range of religious and scholarly leaders, are a great bonus.

15 Tefillah:
Prayer,
Tallit, Tefillin, Mezuzah

The problem is not how to revitalize prayer; the problem is how to revitalize ourselves. —RABBI ABRAHAM JOSHUA HESCHEL

TALLIT! TEFILLIN! ACTION!

A good play requires props, costumes, stage directions, good lighting, the right backdrop, and a little music at the proper moment. All these elements contribute to the process of allowing the actor to live the life of the play. So, too, with worship. The prayerbook, the pageantry, and the ritual objects are, in part, tools to allow a more complete identification between actor and part, a more complete participation in the will of the Director, our God.

Why pray?

The answer to that question is not found inside synagogues or prayerbooks. It is not found in meditation or in the right techniques. The issue of prayer is not a technical problem, not simply a question of learning Hebrew or the right melody or the proper posture. The problem of prayer is the problem of God: Will we let God into our lives? Are we comfortable being uncomfortable in the presence of the Creator of the universe? Do we dare address God?

Why pray? Because that's what we do when we stand in the presence of the unknowable. It is our response to an awareness that God is with us and will not abandon us. Prayer is a bridge, linking our outstretched hand to God.

❖ ❖ ❖ ❖ ❖

God is everywhere, but we don't know how to identify our encounters with God. The first step in learning to pray requires learning how to label our experiences. Each of us could easily list moments in which we encountered an inexplicable sense of wonder, awe, or marvel. But we cannot name the emotions we experienced during those moments. We have no vocabulary for them and are thus unable to evoke them. We don't even seek out others to share the experiences with. And we *certainly* wouldn't discuss our sense of awe in sophisticated company! So

Prayer is not limited to any one place. A synagogue and a lovely lake both provide a setting to experience the wonder of being alive, God's power and wisdom, and a sense of gratitude that leads us to reach out to our Creator. Prayer is what we do with our wonder.

the first step in learning to pray is to begin cultivating an awareness of our encounters with God.

The second step in learning to pray is learning how to develop our experiences of God into words and deeds. Prayer is the vehicle that provides words for our wonder and solace for our sorrows. It lends us the script we need to express righteousness, piety, and goodness. In the process of the drama of prayer, we actually become the part that we perform. We are both actor and spectator, and the story emerges in the unfolding of our lives. Under God's direction, our souls, hearts, and minds provide the stage for transformation and renewal.

Withdrawal from prayer makes God's presence sporadic, private, and uncertain. Prayer lets God into the world; prayer lets humans into God's presence. Prayer allows us to become truly human.

❖   ❖   ❖   ❖   ❖

While it is possible to pray anywhere, attending services at a synagogue has the advantage of allowing one to experience the warmth and beauty of Jewish traditions in the company of other Jews.

1 **Pause long enough to cherish the marvel of being.** Prayer is a response to wonder. Yet modern men and women often don't have the time, or the inclination, to appreciate living. Try the following steps:

• *Cultivate an awareness of the world's beauty by imagining the world without one of its pleasures.* I imagine, for example, that in five minutes I will be blind. I shut my eyes and think of the faces I will never see again, the beautiful places and pieces of art I will miss. After letting the sorrow of that loss sink in, I open my eyes and let in the rush of colors, shapes, and patterns. This exercise reminds me of what I most take for granted: the beauty of the world and how wonderful it is to be able to see and experience everything in it.

• *Make time for the experiences you generally miss.* Wake up before dawn, and find a place from which the sunrise will be visible. Notice the colors, the way the street takes on a range of tones and lights. Doesn't the warmth of the sun feel great? Watching the sun rise or set at a beach, by a lake, in the mountains, or in a field can be a powerful reminder of the majesty of the world.

• *Attend a synagogue service.* Don't worry about following every prayer or understanding every word. Instead, close the siddur and sit in silence. This quiet space can become a haven for contemplation, for thoughts of gratitude, and for a sense of connection. With closed eyes, breathe deeply several times. Let the music, the *davening* ("praying"), the singing, and the ancient Hebrew words permeate the moment. Consider the miracle of Jewish survival across the millennia, the profundity of the message of Judaism, the remarkable fact that we are the latest links in a community that transcends generations and borders.

2 **Wear a *kippah* (** כִּפָּה **, "yarmulke") during prayer.** According to Jewish tradition, the act of covering the head is a way of demonstrating humility in the presence of God; it is an acknowledgment that God is everywhere and sovereign. Judaism often expresses and encourages an inner orientation, or attitude, by fashioning a physical deed that both instructs and, by requiring a specific action, serves as a reminder. For example, we interpret the biblical metaphor of

"bind these words" upon our hearts and upon our doorposts to mean we should make the value of Torah study concrete by wearing tefillin and affixing mezuzot to our doorposts. And so the biblical and rabbinic value of cultivating an awe for God (known as *yirat shamayim,* יִרְאַת שָׁמַיִם) is both nurtured and expressed through the act of wearing a head covering.

In antiquity, it was common practice for all peoples to cover their heads. But with the conquest of the ancient Near East, first by Hellenistic culture and then by Roman might, the new custom of appearing bareheaded began to spread. Whereas Western culture considers it an act of modesty and respect to remove one's cap in the presence of a figure of authority, in Judaism it is considered an act of brazen impudence and superficiality (קַלּוּת רֹאשׁ , *kallut rosh*). In Judaism, then, the custom of covering one's head has always been associated with modesty, respect for one's fellow human beings, and reverence for God's presence. Additionally, the head covering is yet another way of creating holy space with our bodies, a way of dressing solely for the purpose of aligning our focus with the sacred.

In ages past, it was traditional for all males and married women to cover their heads. A growing number of communities, however, have expanded the practice to allow for equal participation. With privilege comes responsibility, so in many congregations all women are asked to cover their heads, for precisely the same reason as the men. In addition, many Jews cover their heads at all times, not just when they are in the synagogue, as a sign of respect for God, to show their modesty and humility of spirit, and to provide an outer sign of solidarity with the Jewish people.

3 **Pray spontaneously.** According to Jewish tradition, "The gates of prayer are always open." The Bible and the Talmud record numerous times when people simply spoke to God, pouring out their pain, joy, needs, or hopes to their Maker and Redeemer. Prayer can include complaints, criticism, rage, or they can focus on love, gratitude, and happiness. Like most personal relationships, the connection between God and you involves the full range of emotions and expression.

4 **Recite the morning and evening Sh'ma.** One of the central Jewish acts in the creation of a sense of the sacred is reciting the morning and evening Sh'ma, the biblical verse that proclaims, "Hear O Israel: Adonai is our God, Adonai alone." Spoken at the beginning of consciousness and just before sleep, this verse reminds Jews of one of the central messages of Jewish religion—that God is unique and single, that we have a relationship with God, that God cares about us.

This recitation takes but a moment and can easily become part of a daily regimen. Upon awakening, recite the one line:

שְׁמַע יִשְׂרָאֵל יְיָ אֱלֹהֵינוּ יְיָ אֶחָד.

Sh'ma Yisrael, Adonai eloheinu, Adonai Eḥad. When that recitation feels natural and comfortable, add the three biblical paragraphs that follow, which constitute part of K'riat Sh'ma (the recitation of the Sh'ma). Finally, include the rabbinic verses, which were added in the time of the Talmud as an editorial comment on the biblical text.[1] Each of the three rabbinic paragraphs reiterates a significant aspect of the Jewish understanding of God: as creator of the natural order, as source of social morality and justice, and as the redeemer of the Jewish people and all humanity. In the evening, recite the Sh'ma in bed just before turning out the lights.

5 **Affix a mezuzah to a doorpost of your home.** Jews affix a written version of the Sh'ma to the doorposts of their homes. The presence of the mezuzah (מְזוּזָה, which in Biblical Hebrew means "doorpost" and has come to refer to the piece of kosher parchment on which the Sh'ma is written) reminds the residents of their commitments to God, to the Jewish people, and to Jewish values while reinforcing the notion that the home is central to the Jewish religion and is a holy place. Take care in purchasing a mezuzah. Many stores sell nonkosher parchments at a much cheaper price, yet according to Jewish law, these false mezuzot do not fulfill the mitzvah of affixing a mezuzah.

While the rules governing the *klaf* (קְלָף, "parchment") are exacting (it must be kosher, the ink is a special ink, and it must be handwritten by a *sofer*, a "scribe"), there are virtually no regulations for the case containing the parchment. Mezuzah cases can be humorous, elaborate, colorful, wooden, stone, or of any variety that appeals to the imagination.

• *Affix a mezuzah to the outer door of your residence.* To fit inside the case, the mezuzah is generally rolled tightly, and the word שַׁדַּי, Shaddai, is left showing. The case is installed on the right doorpost, as one enters, the top tilting toward the house at a 45-degree angle (if possible) and placed in the upper third of the doorway.[2]

•*Begin adding mezuzot to the doorway of each room, with the exception of the bathroom.* You might choose to start with the room you spend the most time in, the room where you eat, or your bedroom. With some creativity, you can make your own mezuzah cases, or purchase one new case each year until you have covered every doorway in your home.

---

6 **Recite a blessing before and after each meal.** One of the principal functions of prayer is to teach a feeling of gratitude. Learning to be thankful, to appreciate the blessings that so often are simply taken for granted, provides rich benefits for both the one who prays (who becomes more conscious of all the goodness that goes into every day) and those around him or her.

No prayer of gratitude is more basic or typically Jewish than the blessings before eating. The Talmud reminds us that one who eats without saying a *berakhah* (בְּרָכָה , "blessing") commits an act of theft, stealing what belongs to God. There are different *berakhot* to be recited before eating different types of foods.[3] All of them emphasize our reliance on the beneficence of Creation and instill thankfulness for God's abundance. Begin each meal or every snack by reciting the appropriate *berakhah.* Because eating involves several mitzvot (saying a *berakhah,* keeping kosher), it is appropriate to wear a *kippah* at every meal.

In addition, the Torah tells us that after we have eaten and are satisfied, we should express our gratitude to God with *Birkat ha-Mazon* (בִּרְכַּת הַמָּזוֹן , the grace after meals).[4] This beautiful prayer thanks God for the earth's bounty, for the land of Israel, for the city of Jerusalem, and for the promise of a messianic future of peace, harmony, and well-being.

At first, it may feel overwhelming, and socially awkward, to recite this prayer at each meal, so consider picking one meal each day after which to recite it, or begin by reciting it after each meal on Shabbat. But gratitude is a spice that can enhance every meal, and *Birkat ha-Mazon* is Judaism's way of saying thank you to God. Eventually, it should become a part of every meal.

---

7 **Use prayer to contribute a sense of the sacred to occasions that might otherwise seem mundane or secular.** Judaism is a way of living that brings people into contact with God at all times. The judicious use of formal prayer can transform simple moments into glowing ones, taking an everyday activity and turning it into a chance to emerge closer to God and closer to the best of human potential.

• *Practice the Sheheḥeyanu,* שֶׁהֶחֱיָנוּ , *and recite it whenever it is appropriate.*[5] At any happy occasion or whenever enjoying something new, it is helpful to have a script suitable for the occasion. For Jews, the prayer that says it all is the Sheheḥeyanu. This brief *berakhah* thanks God "for granting us life, for sustaining us, and for helping us to reach this day." By reciting the Sheheḥeyanu, you can lend a deeper meaning to the purchase of a new sweater, the eating of a delicious piece of fruit for the first time in a season, or the celebration of a birthday.

• *Begin study sessions with a prayer.*[6] Jewish tradition offers a special prayer to be recited for study. Generally this prayer is recited as part of the morning service. It thanks God for giving us the mitzvah of studying Torah and asks that the process of study be sweet to us and to our children.

Talmud torah, the mitzvah of religious study, need not be limited to the study of religious or Jewish texts. When learning contributes to building character, deepening integrity, or heightening sensitivity, then it constitutes a religious act. If you don't yet participate in a morning minyan (מִנְיָן, the quorum of ten adults required for the recitation of certain prayers), or if you don't recite the Shaḥarit (morning) service on your own, then start any study session with the prayers for learning. Remember to wear a *kippah* throughout the time you spend studying. The combination of prayers and *kippah* may help to remind you that the ultimate purpose of learning is not simply amassing more facts or mastering a new skill (although these may be worthy tools that contribute to the achievement of the ultimate goal). The ultimate value of learning lies in the power of knowledge to transform, humanize, and strengthen integrity.

---

8 **Attend Shabbat services regularly for two months.** As an undergraduate, when I was questioning the existence of God, I approached the Hillel rabbi to ask for his help. Rabbi Gold responded that there was no neutral place from which to consider the question, and he suggested that I try living as a believer and see how that worked out for me. He offered a deal: I would attend Shabbat morning services for two months, and at the end of the period, we would talk again.

Those two months hooked me for good. Even though I couldn't read any Hebrew (and the service was entirely in Hebrew) and even though I didn't know any of the melodies (and most of it was sung), I loved the traditions, the warmth, and the wisdom of the Torah and its commentaries. Rabbi Gold recognized that the only way to judge whether or not attending ser-

vices can be meaningful is by doing it regularly for long enough to feel comfortable with it. After two months, even though I still didn't know Hebrew, I knew I loved Jewish prayer.

If you attend Shabbat services, the experience will, at the least, provide you with a vast amount of knowledge about what goes on inside synagogues. And there is a good chance that the services will seem compelling, inviting, and worthwhile just as they did (and still do) to me.

---

9 **Take advantage of the many talented Jewish musicians and composers active in the United States and Israel.** Many musicians record lively renditions of traditional prayers and melodies, and some also create their own modern melodies for ancient prayers. Becoming familiar with the content and spirit of Jewish prayer through this music is certainly one of the most enjoyable ways to become an expert in the prayers.

Great Jewish talents from years gone by, such as Ernest Bloch, Jan Peerce, and Leonard Bernstein, have left us recordings that can still inspire us with their beauty and their majesty. Some of the talented groups and composers alive today are Beged Kefet, Debbie Friedman, Parvarim, Safam, Craig Taubman, Yad B'Yad, and the annual Israel Chassidic Song Festival, which tours the world each year. Start building a collection of these artists' recordings. Use it as an opportunity to enjoy Jewish music and to become familiar with the prayers of the synagogue service.

---

10 **Add additional ritual practices to your recitation of the morning Sh'ma.** The transition from sleep to wakefulness is a time to set a tone that can last throughout the entire day.

• *To set the mood for morning prayer, purchase (or make) a tallit.* What is distinctive about the tallit (טַלִּית, the ritual prayer shawl) is the knotted fringes at the corners, known as tzitzit (צִיצִית, literally, "blossoms"). These special tassels were worn by Jews as early as the biblical period, signifying that every Jew is a partner in a special covenant with God. Additionally, the tzitzit remind us of the mitzvot of the Torah (since the total number of knots and threads, like the number of mitzvot in the Torah, equal 613). The tallit itself may contain any colors and generally is made of wool.

• *Begin wearing tefillin,* תְּפִלִּין, *during your morning prayer.* Tefillin are leather boxes containing the same kosher parchments and bib-

lical verses as the mezuzah case. The Torah instructs the children of Israel to bind these on their arms and heads as a sign of fidelity to their sacred traditions, and Jews (particularly Jewish men) have been doing so since antiquity.

Once you are comfortable with the tallit and the way it is worn, make an investment in a set of tefillin. Although they may seem bizarre at first, there is no better way to create a sacred space than with tallit and tefillin. They come to us from the era of the Torah itself and carry with them a sense of antiquity, of connection, and of difference. If only for a moment, they lift the mood—and the person praying—beyond the demands of the working world and above the limits of time.

• *Add additional prayers to your recitation of the Sh'ma.* The number of prayers required to meet the halakhic obligations for morning prayer is surprisingly few. The Psalms, readings, and meditations were added by subsequent generations, often to inspire greater devotion. By starting with the minimum, it is possible to attain competence and a sense of mastery while still having time to get to work. The required prayers are the three paragraphs of the Sh'ma, to be recited morning and evening, and the Amidah, עֲמִידָה, to be recited morning, noon, and evening. While this is a bare-bones beginning, it does fulfill the minimal obligations of prayer.

11 **Carry a small edition of the siddur (in a purse, knapsack, or briefcase) wherever you go.** The siddur, סִדּוּר, is the collected thoughts and worldview of the Jewish people. There is no better introduction to Judaism or to the Jewish people. In addition to the regular prayer services, it contains other wonderful prayers and readings. On many occasions during the day, instead of simply waiting and wasting time, you can explore the pages of the prayerbook. About one third of the Psalms are scattered throughout the prayerbook , in addition to a chapter of the Mishnah, *Pirkei Avot*, which contains remarkable gems of rabbinic wisdom and insight, and a collection of readings, poems, and meditations.

12 **Attend a morning minyan.** There is no experience quite like a weekday morning prayer service. The minyan generally consists of the regulars who know the service well, so don't expect responsive readings or regular announcements of the page number. For the first few times, just watch and imitate. In no time, the service will feel completely natural.

13 **Recite the Traveler's Prayer, *Tefillat ha-Derekh*, תְּפִילַת הַדֶּרֶךְ, before taking a trip.** Moments of transition attract a ritual response, whether with words or with objects. So it is that the transitions of life—birth, puberty, marriage, and death—become focal points of prayer and ritual. The borders of the home–the doorposts–also attract ritual attention, through the mezuzah. Another transition that summons a need for prayer is the act of travel, of going from one place to another.

Tefillat ha-Derekh (Traveler's Prayer) is a poignant prayer for putting travel within the context of Jewish values.[7] Recite *Tefillat ha-Derekh* before any long trip. With this quiet and quick act, you will emphasize the miracles of being able to stay in touch across long distances and of

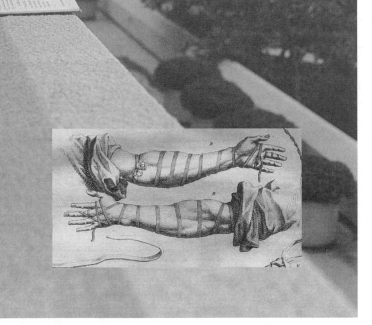

14 **Recite Arvit, עַרְבִית, before getting into bed.** Darkness is often frightening. In the nighttime darkness, our minds tire and grow cloudy. Lacking the energy of morning, we experience loneliness, depression, or exhaustion.

Jews have created a context of security and connection through the Arvit (evening) service. Take a moment to recite Arvit before getting into bed.[9] At first, simply say the Sh'ma and the Amidah. That is the bulk of the service. Gradually, add the other prayers and reflections. This recitation is a great way to end a day. A local synagogue may have an evening minyan, offering the added benefit of company and guidance.

15 **Wear an *arba knafot*, אַרְבַּע כְּנָפוֹת .** Many Jewish acts are public statements: people see a *kippah* and know something about the values and identity of the person wearing it. They witness someone refusing to eat pork and they know that person is making a public statement about his or her priorities and sensitivity. Yet there is also an important place within Judaism for a private relationship with God.

One of the most powerful tools for heightening that awareness of such a relationship is wearing the *arba knafot* (or *tallit katan*, טַלִּית קָטָן), the small tallit that goes underneath the shirt. The *arba knafot* creates a distinction between the home and everywhere else: At home, I wear the tzitzit of the *arba knafot* loose, letting them flop around; everywhere else, I tuck them in to preserve the privacy of these special links to my biblical heritage and to God.

The difficulty of wearing *arba knafot* is not financial (they're pretty cheap) or an issue of embarrassment (they're virtually invisible underneath a shirt), but psychological—you are always aware of their presence. They are meant to remind you that you are standing in the presence of God, and they call you to do a better job of

being secure and safe at home and away. *Tefillat ha-Derekh* is a way to focus on the miracle that giant pieces of metal filled with human beings actually fly through the sky, float on the sea, or hurdle across narrow rails at remarkable speeds. *Tefillat ha-Derekh* may not guarantee the safety of the voyage, nor does it replace the skill and attention of the pilot or engineer, but it does provide Jews with an opportunity for wonder, reflection, and gratitude.

After a long trip, especially one that involves crossing the sea, it is customary to ask to receive an aliyah to the Torah and to recite a special *berakhah* of gratitude for a safe return, *Birkat ha-Gomel,* בִּרְכַּת הַגּוֹמֵל .[8]

loving humanity and caring for the world. So don't rush to fulfill this mitzvah. Wait until you feel the pressure to experience that awareness and you feel the possibility of being able to sustain it so that this mitzvah will be a positive step upward. Then start wearing *arba knafot.*

---

16. Recite Minḥah, מִנְחָה, each afternoon. The most difficult prayer service to make time for is Minḥah (afternoon prayers). Like Arvit, Minḥah is brief, requiring only a few minutes. But midday is the time for lunch, meetings, perhaps an exercise break. In the rush of contemporary schedules, this is the busiest period. For precisely that reason, however Minḥah is important. As a reminder of the tone established in the morning, as a way of taking time out to breathe, appreciate, and seek balance, Minḥah is invaluable.[10]

❖　　❖　　❖　　❖　　❖

JOIN THE CLUB

My first reaction to attending a morning minyan was shock—I had never seen tefillin, and they looked completely alien to me. Everyone seemed to know exactly what to do, and people were mumbling so quickly that I was convinced there was no way they could possibly be sincere in their prayers.

In the years following, I, too, have become one of the speedy mumblers. As a congregational rabbi, I am used to newcomers complaining about the apparent lack of conviction or reflection on the part of those who sustain the daily minyan. I have seen the newcomers' confusion as they flip through pages, lost in a siddur they thought they knew, unable to follow the service or keep up with the *sh'liaḥ tzibbur* (שְׁלִיחַ צִבּוּר, prayer leader).

The point, though, is not to judge the old-timers for their lack of decorum or their speed, nor the newcomers for their hasty judgments. The gap between the two groups simply shows that the morning minyan is a culture of its own–everywhere around the world, from Morocco to Brazil to San Francisco to St. Petersburg, it has a unique ambiance and feel. Without that special quality, it wouldn't deliver a sense of soaring above time, of standing in the presence of the holy, of the warmth and eternity of the Jewish people. The minyan can evoke all those experiences—I sense God more at the morning minyan than at any other single time.

The issue, then, is how to become a member. How can you learn the equivalent of the secret handshake and password that make the doors open, the inner circle give way? The reality is that the minyan is not a private club; every minyan would love an infusion of new people, no matter their level of knowledge or personal commitment. Pick one day a week on which to attend a nearby minyan. Every Orthodox congregation and most Conservative congregations have a daily minyan (some meet only on Monday and Thursday mornings, which are Torah-reading days); some Reform congregations also offer a morning minyan. Some synagogues have a Sunday morning tallit-and-tefillin group, which meets for minyan and then provides breakfast and a speaker.

As you begin to feel more comfortable, increase your attendance accordingly.

When I was applying for the position of rabbi at Congregation Eilat, I spent a Shabbat there. I led the service, taught some classes, and met with the community. During one of my classes, someone asked me to summarize Judaism. I responded by quoting from Psalm 16, "I will set Adonai before me always."

Every deed can be a sacred deed; every moment, an encounter with God and a reaffirmation of meaning. Nothing is so trivial or irrelevant that it can't be worked into a tool for strengthening our humanity, community, and holiness. In our hands is the power to harness random acts and instinctual drives, to mold them into a network of moral rigor and emotional depth, forging mute facts into values that affirm and restore our own humanity.

In transforming our routine, we renew ourselves; we begin to encounter God in areas that used to seem mundane. Prayer is the key to that transformation, for it adds a layer of depth and resonance to otherwise random moments and habitual patterns of behavior. Focusing attention on the daily miracles of life—a new day, an old love, life itself—prayer can intensify and restore our commitment to repair the world under the sovereignty of God. And isn't that potential—the inner power of prayer—itself a miracle worthy of gratitude?

For Further Reading

Nahum N. Glatzer, *Language of Faith: A Selection from the Most Expressive Jewish Prayers*. New York: Schocken Books, 1975.

Abraham Joshua Heschel, *Quest for God: Studies in Prayer and Symbolism*. New York: Crossroad, 1954; reprint 1990.

Siddur Sim Shalom, ed. by Jules Harlow. New York: Rabbinical Assembly and United Synagogue of America, 1989. One of Conservative Judaism's prayerbooks, this is the finest siddur available, because of its masterful translations and because of its fidelity to the traditional text and to the insights of contemporary Jews. It is available in a pulpit edition (large and hardcover), a regular edition, and a personal edition (hardcover or paperback).

WHERE TO FIND IT IN THE PRAYERBOOK

1. Morning Sh'ma

Siddur Sim Shalom. New York: Rabbinical Assembly, 1985, pages 100-105.

Gates of Prayer. New York: Central Conference of American Rabbis, 1975, page 33.

Kol Haneshamah. Wyncote, PA: The Reconstructionist Press, 1994, page 277.

The Complete Artscroll Siddur. Brooklyn, NY: Mesorah Publications Ltd, 1984, page 84.

2. Blessing for Affixing a Mezuzah

Siddur Sim Shalom, page 712.

Gates of the House. New York: Central Conference of America Rabbis, 1977, pages 103-107.

The Complete Artscroll Siddur, page 226.

3. Blessings Before Eating Food

Siddur Sim Shalom, pages 714-15.

Gates of the House, pages 19-23.

The Complete Artscroll Siddur, page 224.

4. Birkat ha-Mazon

Siddur Sim Shalom, pages 784-85.

Gates of the House, pages 6-18.

The Complete Artscroll Siddur, page 182.

Likrat Shabbat. Bridgeport, CT: Media Judaica, 1992, Section II, pages 19-25.

5. Sheheḥeyanu

Siddur Sim Shalom, page 712.

Gates of Prayer, page 451.

Kol Haneshamah, page 355.

The Complete Artscroll Siddur, page 230.

Likrat Shabbat, Section II, page 67.

6. Prayer Before Studying

Siddur Sim Shalom, pages 6-9.

Gates of Prayer, page 52.

Kol Haneshamah, page 168.

The Complete Artscroll Siddur, page 16.

7. Tefillat ha-Derekh.

Siddur Sim Shalom, page 713.

Gates of the House, page 23.

The Complete Artscroll Siddur, page 222.

8. Birkat ha-Gomel

Siddur Sim Shalom, page 402-403.

Gates of the House, pages 125-27.

Kol Haneshamah, page 400.

The Complete Artscroll Siddur, page 142.

Likrat Shabbat, Section II, page 72.

9. Arvit

Siddur Sim Shalom, begins on page 200.

Gates of Prayer, begins on page 31.

The Complete Artscroll Siddur, begins on page 256.

10. Minḥah

Siddur Sim Shalom, begins on page 164.

Gates of Prayer, begins on page 111.

The Complete Artscroll Siddur, begins on page 232.

Likrat Shabbat, Section I, begins on page 286.

16 *Teshuvah:*
Repentance and Turning

For there is no one on earth who does only good and doesn't err.

—ECCLESIASTES 7:20

God creates anew those who repent.

—PESIKTA RABBATI

No one is perfect. Being human necessarily entails limited energy, limited intelligence, and limited ability. As a result, it is nearly impossible for anyone always to attain his or her own ideals, let alone the high expectations of others. Many people, however, ignore this reality and assert that they can achieve perfection or, conversely, that they should accept their shortcomings as "natural" and therefore beyond their control. Both responses result in disaster. Attempts at perfection can result only in disappointment and, ultimately, lethargy. Passive acceptance of one's imperfections as inevitable, however, guarantees that they will continue and even increase in intensity or frequency.

The trick, then, is to find a path that will diminish our failings even as it concedes that we will invariably disappoint ourselves and others. That path, in

Maintaining any loving relationship requires the honesty to confront our own mistakes and insensitivities, to apologize, and to try to repair the damage we have inflicted on someone we love. *Teshuvah* is the process of recognizing and repairing the inevitable mistakes that come with being human.

Judaism, is known as *teshuvah* (תְּשׁוּבָה , "repentance"). Perhaps the most fundamental teaching of the Jewish religion, *teshuvah* is possible at all times, for all people. All of us have the ability to recognize our own wrongdoing, to resolve not to repeat that transgression, and to rectify the wrong to those who were hurt by the error.

We are not evil, nor are we quite angels. We make mistakes, often serious ones. And those mistakes hurt ourselves and our fellows. But as human beings, we always retain the power to take stock of our own behavior and to change it. All it takes is an act of will, and that act is *teshuvah*.

OVERHAULING OUR PRIORITIES

Teshuvah is more than just a shift in our behavior or even a new assessment of personal strengths and weaknesses. In Hebrew, *teshuvah* means "turning," "answering," or "returning." At its most sweeping, *teshuvah* involves a complete overhaul of priorities–replacing our preoccupation with our own needs, perspectives, and concerns with those of God.

The universe poses these questions to humanity: "What are you?" "What is your worth?" We articulate an answer in the deeds that constitute our lives. Living itself is the response—either a response of smug indifference or one of involvement and compassion.

When we put ourselves at the center of everything, it is impossible not to judge everything else by its usefulness for our own purposes: "What helps me live more comfortably is good; what interferes with my personal interests is bad." Such a stance reduces the universe to the standards applied to choosing among models of vacuum cleaners. *Teshuvah* requires sufficient humility to recognize that we are not the measure of all that is, that we cannot tailor good and bad to fit the dimensions of our own desires and preoccupations. What is good is so by God's standards, and justice is sweet because God establishes it that way.

In a world that mistakes things for goals and status for worth, *teshuvah* corrects our vision and makes us whole.

Stretching back in antiquity to the Torah ("When a person incurs guilt . . . When he realizes his guilt in any of these matters, he shall confess that wherein he has sinned," LEVITICUS 5:1-5), *teshuvah* is at the very center of what Judaism is about. Judaism recognizes the human potential for excellence and goodness and the equally pervasive reality of temptation and weakness. How to reconcile these two warring poles in the context of the human heart and a living society is the mandate of any religion that aspires not only to anticipate a promised tomorrow (עוֹלָם הַבָּא , *olam ha-ba,* literally, "the coming world," traditionally referring to the afterlife) but to transform the here and now (*tikkun olam,* תִּקּוּן עוֹלָם , literally, "repair of the world"). Through *teshuvah,* Judaism integrates the insistence on human goodness with the reality of human shortcoming.

According to several Jewish medieval authorities, *teshuvah* involves a series of concrete steps, which culminate in *teshuvah sh'leimah* (תְּשׁוּבָה שְׁלֵמָה , "complete repentance"). They are:

• *Recognition*—a need to recognize an action as wrong, to regret doing it, and to experience remorse. Recognition also applies to the failure to fulfill ritual mitzvot–the first step to *teshuvah* is recognizing that we did not perform one of God's commandments.

• *Renunciation*—a determination to distance oneself from that deed, to refuse to continue seeing it as a necessary part or consequence of one's personality.

• *Confession*—making something real through the act of speaking. (If you don't believe that speaking makes something real, just ask someone who is sick why he or she won't see a doctor.) Articulating an offense forces a confrontation with its consequences and its seductiveness.

• *Reconciliation*—however commendable regret may be, emotion alone doesn't help someone who has been hurt, deceived, or belittled; it doesn't make things right with God. If *teshuvah* is to be more than simply a way to feel good again, if it is to become a tool for repairing the world and implementing God's *brit* (covenant) more fully, then it must transcend the realm of emotion and conversation, entering the tangible world of action. Reconciliation with the person who was wronged (or with God) begins with an admission of guilt and a sincere apology.

• *Restitution*—rebalancing the scales in precisely the same way that they were set askew. This may be achieved through financial reimbursement, a gift, personal service, or some other means.

• *Resolve*—all the preceding steps are meaningless choreography unless they result in a commitment not to repeat the offense. Having recognized the wrongfulness of the transgression, having apologized and reimbursed the injured party, one must resolve to be better, not to fall into the trap of doing the same thing when the opportunity arises again.

These six steps provide a Jewish ladder for responding to wrongdoing by addressing its causes and eliminating them. The journey of rebuilding ourselves, of molding our souls in the light of our highest visions, begins with a commitment to introspection and unfolds through the process of repentance.

❖ ❖ ❖ ❖ ❖

1 **Take advantage of the beginning of the Jewish year to engage in renewed self-reflection.** The days between Rosh Hashanah (רֹאשׁ הַשָּׁנָה , the New Year) and Yom Kippur (יוֹם כִּפּוּר , the Day of Atonement) are called the Aseret Y'mai Teshuvah (עֲשֶׂרֶת יְמֵי תְשׁוּבָה , Ten Days of Repentance). They are traditionally a period of introspection and resolve as well as an opportunity to apologize to all—even those you don't remember having harmed.

Actually, the theme of repentance starts earlier than the New Year, with the onset of the month of Elul, some thirty days before Rosh Hashanah. For that entire month, the shofar is sounded at the conclusion of the daily Shaharit service, and an additional psalm is read to increase the solemn tone of the month. One week before Rosh Hashanah, on the Saturday night before the New Year, a special service of forgiveness (S'lihot, סְלִיחוֹת) offers a "trial run" through the prayers of Rosh Hashanah and Yom Kippur. And one whole day, Shabbat Shuvah, שַׁבַּת שׁוּבָה —the Shabbat between those two major holy days—is devoted to repentance.

• *Set aside time between the beginning of Elul (the month before Rosh Hashanah begins) and Yom Kippur to re-examine personal ideals and expectations.* Compare your current goals for self-improvement with your past behavior, and consider methods for bridging the gap between the two. I use this season to ask my wife, family, and closest friends to help in the process. A candid talk with these people, sharing what we see as our own and one another's priorities for change and improvement for the coming year, can reinforce the notion that you are cherished, even for your faults.

This is the time the Jewish calendar reserves for the kinds of one-to-one conversations, apologies, and requests for forgiveness that are necessary to keep our relationships healthy and functioning. Make time to meet with those who may feel wronged—relatives, friends, colleagues—and ask them for their forgiveness and ask whether you may bestow yours on them.

This is also a good time to consider your relationship with God, to ask yourself honestly how energetically you have tried to live a Godly life, to observe the commandments, to become a model of decency and holiness. This is the time of year to seek God's forgiveness, too (and maybe to forgive God as well).

• *Use the prayers of the S'lihot service and those in the Mahzor (* מַחְזוֹר *, the High Holy Day prayerbook) as a resource for reflection and analysis.* Through their repetitions of specific transgressions—both improper deeds and callous oversights—these classic lists allow us to evaluate our relationships and interactions of the past year. Use the *Mahzor* as a guide for better self-understanding and a goad for change. That means, of course, reading it outside the synagogue, when services are not in progress, and in an environment conducive to quiet reflection.

• *Taking Yom Kippur seriously doesn't necessarily mean reading every word of every prayer. It does mean using Yom Kippur as a time to think about the kinds of issues already raised, to apologize to those who are still unappeased, and to absorb the sanctity of the gathering and the surroundings.* And if your congregation provides classes or discussions during a midday break, take advantage of this opportunity for a less formal interaction.

2 **Make *teshuvah* a continuous process, not just a once-a-year activity.** Each night before bedtime, take a moment to recall the events of the day, taking particular care to examine interactions that might have given offense. Consider how a conversation might have sounded to the other participants or whether you have a friend, relative, or colleague who would appreciate a friendly call, a note, or a pat on the back.

Nights are, by their nature, rewarding times for soul-searching. As the world grows quiet and the lights dim, the effort to hear and to see what really matters becomes less difficult. Take advantage of every opportunity before sleep to do a little mending of character, a brief *ḥeshbon ha-nefesh* (חֶשְׁבּוֹן הַנֶּפֶשׁ , a personal inventory; literally, a "soul reckoning" of both moral and ritual shortcomings and advances).

3 **Set aside a time at least once a week for an extended, undistracted talk with the person you love.** For my wife, Elana, and me, this involves a weekly Shabbat walk around a nearby lake. The walk takes two hours, which is enough time for us to raise a major issue, come to a resolution, and enjoy just being together. Such weekly time alone, without any distractions, is the only way I know to ensure that two people are still on the same wavelength, still in touch with each other's hopes and values, still sensitive to each other's fears and frustrations.

Of course, there are other contexts for ensuring time together, such as scheduling a weekly lunch or dinner date. Just as with a business meeting, you can write it in your appointment book. The essential requirement is that there be enough time for unhurried talk, so pick a quiet, sparsely attended restaurant where customers are encouraged to enjoy long meals.

4 **Take advantage of Shabbat dinner to raise a family issue or to provide a forum for family members to discuss whatever is bothering them.** Let children talk about something Mommy or Daddy did that they don't like; allow siblings to speak about their feelings toward one another. As long as the discussion is conducted with a view toward resolving problems (rather than assigning blame) and is governed by a subtle but firm and supportive leader, these Shabbat encounters can add depth and purpose to the weekly family dinner. Care must be taken, however, to ensure that these open discussions remain constructive so that the joy of Shabbat remains strong.

5 **When you are wrong, admit it.** Then apologize. When we are challenged for having done something wrong, most of us naturally respond by denying the error or by trying to shift the blame to someone else. Although denying guilt or blaming others may be natural, these reactions render reconciliation less likely and preclude the possibility of our learning from our mistakes. It may never feel natural to say, "I was wrong; I'm sorry," but as a first step toward repairing hurt feelings, there is no substitute for admitting your guilt.

6 **Try transforming an enemy into a friend.** The Mishnah teaches that such an act makes us more powerful. The effort is almost always worthwhile. Sometimes it is as easy as having a few lunches together coupled

We learn the simple truths of life by talking with more experienced people. Taking time to find a wise adult, making time to share your views with a seeking child or teen, is the essential tool for building character and integrity. There is no better investment in our future than a good heart-to-heart talk with a young person.

with frank discussions of the current abysmal state of your relationship and a commitment to get beyond the impasse. At other times, the most prudent method for restoring—or creating—harmony is to agree not to discuss what has already happened and to focus on what you share in common. Occasionally, the reality of competing interests or perspectives may preclude friendship. Still, most people are not evil, and a difference of interest or opinion can translate into competition that is still respectful and within the boundaries of morality, civility, and law.

7 **Set concrete goals for self-improvement.** While this may sound folksy, there is great wisdom in a practical, no-nonsense approach to modifying your behavior. By regularly reviewing your personality defects and actually writing down specific modifications of behavior, it is possible to get a better understanding of your undesirable traits and how you can control them.

8 **Engage in *ta'anit yaḥid*.** There are times when a sense of guilt can feel overwhelming or when the enormity of your own wrongdoing shakes you at your core. For times when the steady, gradual approach of talks and lists isn't enough, Jewish tradition provides for a *ta'anit yaḥid* (תַּעֲנִית יָחִיד, "personal fast"). The use of fasting as a tool for heightened introspection and for demonstrating remorse is ancient and effective. Abstaining from food provides a physical sense of deprivation to match the emotional feeling of sorrow and shame. Fasting also allows you to shift attention away from the physical and to reinforce the centrality (and possibility) of controlling your body and your actions.

9 **Cultivate humility.** Our culture emphasizes pride—in identity, accomplishments, and status. Although pride is an important aspect of a rounded personality, we hear less of the corresponding and equally important virtue of humility. How striking, then, to realize that the rabbis viewed Moses as the most humble of all people and attributed his special intimacy with God to his magnificent humility. The Talmud asserts that Moses' name isn't even mentioned in the Passover Haggadah because Moses was so humble he didn't want any of the credit for the liberation.

Humility is not the same as worthlessness or self-hatred. Humility, quite simply, is a recognition of our own limitations: intellectual, emotional, and moral. It goads us into recognizing that life can be overwhelming and that even when we do the best we can, we often fall short. When taken seriously, humility makes it easier for us to love ourselves and to forgive the flaws of others. Without humility, it is impossible to feel a need to rectify behavior or to judge another person charitably.

A great rabbi of the nineteenth century, Rabbi Israel Salanter, instructed his followers to be concerned with "your fellow's body and your own soul, and not the reverse." What better way to assist others and to improve yourself than to willingly see your own failures as the result of your shortcomings and to understand the disappointing behavior of others as the result of difficult circumstances. As *Pirkei Avot* teaches, "Judge others leniently."

10 **Cultivate a skepticism for the obsessions and standards of society.** Income, status, education, attractiveness—all good to have—are of limited worth in ensuring happiness. Lauded and coveted in films and magazines, achievements and acquisitions are at best supporting actors in life's drama. What makes for lasting happiness is a sense of meaning and a connection to family, friends, and community.

Just as Judaism encourages a healthy skepticism toward our own glory as individuals, it also opposes exaggerating the importance of much that our society esteems. Recategorizing wealth, education, status, popularity, and power from goals to means is one of the tasks that Judaism has struggled to achieve across millennia. The goals remain righteousness, goodness, justice, and caring. Anything less becomes idolatry. *Teshuvah* on a social level presumes a turning away from these overvalued means and restoring the primacy of decency and goodness.

While money can buy many nice things, and when given away through charity can bring even deeper fulfillment, the obsessive pursuit of money wastes precious time and heightens an addiction that can never be fully satisfied. "Who is rich?" the Mishnah wisely asks. "One who is content with his portion."

For Further Reading

Harlan J. Wechsler, *What's So Bad About Guilt?* New York: Simon and Schuster, 1990.

Maḥzor for Rosh Hashanah and Yom Kippur: A Prayer Book for the Days of Awe, ed. Jules Harlow. New York: Rabbinical Assembly, 1972.

17 *Tza'ar Ba'alei Ḥayyim:*

Compassion to Animals

The righteous are concerned for the life of their beasts. —PROVERBS 12:10

Worship without compassion is worse than self-deception; it is an abomination.
—RABBI ABRAHAM JOSHUA HESCHEL

One Ḥanukkah, my wife, Elana, gave me a gift I had wanted for years: a puppy. We drove to the pound and found an adorable and loving two-month-old shepherd-Dobie-Lab. She was all paws and tongue. We fell in love with her the minute the shelter staff allowed us to remove her from her cage. The fact that she would grow up to be a sixty-pound dog didn't dissuade us, and we signed up for her almost immediately. Three days later (her original owner never having reclaimed her), I was allowed to return and pick up our new mutt, whom we named Ḥumie (Hebrew for "brown").

All of our feelings of love and joy have only increased as Ḥumie has grown into maturity. Almost anyone who has brought home a dog, a cat, or some other kind of animal friend knows that sense of love, dependency, and playfulness that animals can bring to our lives. Jewish tradition knows this well. The book of Genesis, for example, records that after Cain

murdered his brother, Abel, God punished him with exile but then agreed to protect him in his wanderings by means of an undefined "mark of Cain." A rabbinic midrash (GENESIS RABBAH 22:12) records that the protective "mark of Cain" was actually the gift of a dog as companion and guard.

Shortly after getting Ḥumie, I began to read books about how animals are raised for breeding and sale in the United States. I read about the cruel "puppy farms," where females are housed in cramped and filthy cages and forced to breed continually. These dogs often suffer from malnutrition and hip dysplasia, and they seldom receive adequate veterinary care—conditions in 25 percent of the breeding kennels are substandard. Puppies as young as one month are

Job reminds us to "ask the beasts, they will teach you." We learn so much from animals: values of love, loyalty, caring, and joy. Our lives are enriched because animals exist, and Judaism gives us a way to repay our debt and to cherish their gifts.

taken from their mothers and packed in crates. Animals not sold before they become adults are killed, often bashed over the head with a board. The same fate awaits the female no longer able to produce pups. And then I read that in many parts of the world, dogs are considered an excellent source of meat!

Reading the morning newspaper, I would get a nudge in the arm, a wet nose forcing itself into the center of my attention, as Ḥumie made it clear that, in her opinion, I had read enough. It was difficult to look back into her moist, round eyes, so trusting, so full of individuality and love, and to think that other people would see her only as a useful tool or a delicious meal.

Yet I, too, ate cows, sheep, lambs, and chickens. We routinely kill these animals, slice them up, roast them, and serve them as meals. Is my lunch really worth their death?

The more I read about the way animals are treated—their horrible and unsanitary living conditions, humanity's reliance on high levels of hormone and antibiotic injections to counter the epidemics that naturally result from their confinement and over-crowding, the brutal methods used to kill them—the less appetizing their flesh became to me. Eating meat was apparently as much a threat to my health as it was an affront to moral sensitivity. Reading about the cruelty to animals and then looking into Ḥumie's eyes caused me to care beyond my species and to extend that compassion to other animals. And once that consciousness emerges, it isn't hard to help animals to suffer far less while still meeting one's own nutritional and medical needs.

That animals can, and do, show affection to people is nothing new. In many parts of the world, ancient stories of drowning sailors rescued by dolphins abound, and tales of dogs giving their lives to save their owners are told not just about Lassie but in the Talmud as well. One midrash tells of a loyal dog who gave up his life by eating poison so that his master wouldn't have to. Another midrash recounts how

I care not for a man's religion whose dog and cat are not the better for it.
—*ABRAHAM LINCOLN*

Abel's dog sat guard over Abel's corpse after the fight with Cain.

What is surprising, when we realize how loving animals can be to humans, is just how enraged some people become at the suggestion that we should reciprocate this compassion. In much of the world, that idea still generates scorn. Take, for example, the annual prairie-dog shoot-out in Nucla, Colorado. Each year, the town holds a festive shooting contest. In 1990, the first day resulted in more than one thousand dead prairie dogs and more than two thousand shots fired. (What happens to all those wounded animals? What happens to all the lead bullets that missed their mark?) One of the hunters, when asked what she would hunt after the prairie dogs were gone, responded, "Protesters."

ACTS OF COMPASSION

While it may be a struggle to persuade humanity to act compassionately toward animals, it isn't hard to find examples of animals extending themselves to help human beings. Several years ago, a man in Australia made international news while surfing off the coral reefs. He was attacked by a shark, which tore off an enormous piece of his surfboard and then proceeded to slash his stomach. Fortunately for this swimmer, a dolphin intervened, driving away the shark and remaining nearby until other human beings could return the man to dry land.

In a less dramatic way, that same kind of interspecies cooperation occurred in my own home. When President Bush launched Operation Desert Shield to force Iraqi soldiers out of Kuwait, I was attending a rabbinical conference in New York. My wife was alone in California when she heard that Israel had been the target of Scud-missile attacks aimed at Tel Aviv, not far from where her brother, sister-in-law, and baby nephew have their apartment. Confirming what anyone who lives with an animal companion already knows, Elana told me on the phone that Humie was especially tender and attentive to her that evening, sensing her mood of sorrow and fear. Normally eager to wrestle and play, Humie spent the evening quietly sitting by Elana's side, licking her hands and her feet, resting her head on Elana's lap.

Often, people who try to extend compassion to animals are branded as freaks. The organizer of that prairie-dog slaughter explained that "we don't subscribe to New Age philosophy," which he characterized as "peace, love, and vegetarian rights." Protesters reported being spat on with tobacco juice or heckled by passing motorists, who screamed at them, "Go eat tofu!"

Imagine being threatened by tofu.

Yet from a religious perspective, there is a reason for not completely trusting the animal rights movements. One of the central claims of Jewish tradition is that human beings alone among the living creatures are made in God's image. People are not simply part of the spectrum of living things that includes other animals. There is something unique and sacred about human life. Yet much of the animal rights movement rejects that primary distinction, with a result that diminishes the worth of human beings.

• As a legislative aide to the speaker of the California state assembly, I had as one of my duties

LEARN COMPASSION

Why is it that some people are so easily angered by a show of compassion for animals? Why is it that advocates of such kindness are written off as a fringe element and crazy? In a world in which so many people suffer from the insensitivity and abuse of other people, it is hard to drum up much passion to minimize animal suffering. Yet the two are linked; callousness is not divisible. As the medieval sage Maimonides writes, "If the Torah provides that such grief should not be caused to animals or to birds, how much more careful must we be that we should not cause grief to our fellows."

Once we desensitize ourselves to the pain of some living things, the torment of human beings also becomes that much easier to bear. The thirteenth-century sage Naḥmanides observes, "The reason for the prohibitions [against cruelty to animals] is to teach us the trait of compassion and that we should not be cruel, for cruelty proliferates in the human soul."

responding to constituents' letters. At the height of the influx of Indochinese refugees (the so-called boat people), we were inundated with letters opposing their admission to California. That same week, the *San Francisco Chronicle* reported the case of a woman whose will stipulated that her pet dog be put to sleep after her death. We received hundreds of letters from people who offered to take the dog into their own homes while simultaneously protesting the rescue of the drowning refugees!

• Students in my tenth-grade Confirmation class found it impossible to decide between saving a drowning dog and a drowning adult if they could rescue only one of them. And when I altered the hypothetical case to a puppy, not a single member of the class was will-

While Judaism affirms our obligation to treat animals with compassion, it also insists on the unique value of human beings. When supporting animal rights groups, one must be cautious to ensure that they do not equate human life with animal life.

ing to save the adult!

The equation of human life with animal life is in opposition to the biblical and rabbinic axiom that human life is uniquely precious. Thus, part of my discomfort with the animal rights movement is a reaction against that demotion of human life which makes the two equal. The primary reason for popular discomfort with kindness to animals, however, is that it is a new issue to consider, and one that takes self-discipline. It is far easier to treat animals exclusively as tools for human use and convenience. Once we begin to worry about where our food comes from and how livestock and poultry are treated—whether our clothing requires the taking of a life and how our affluence affects the health of the planet—then previously simple choices become complex, requiring significant attention, time, and care.

This chapter is an invitation to care, to bring yourself one step closer to the day when "the wolf and the lamb shall graze together. . . and the lion shall eat straw like the ox" (ISAIAH 11:6-9). It makes no sense to love some mammals while filling our closets with the skins and hair of others; to admire the beauty and majesty of some while using the skins of others to cover our car seats.

Rather than allow extremists to preempt a moral and reasonable relationship between humanity and the animal world, we must reclaim the center. There is a middle ground between equating human life with animal life, on the one hand, and disregarding the pain of animals on the other. As responsible stewards charged with caring for Creation and leaving it better than we found it, we can assert the moral defensibility of using animals *when doing so is necessary for human survival.* But killing animals merely to gratify human vanity or to appease our lust for blood and killing is not consistent with heightened sensitivity and appreciation for the marvel of life. And even when we do use animals out of necessity, our claim to act as God's agents imposes an obligation to minimize their pain.

That is precisely the agenda of the mitzvah *tza-'ar ba'alei ḥayyim* (צַעַר בַּעֲלֵי חַיִּים , literally, "the pain of living creatures"). Judaism points us toward an idyllic future, when humanity and animals will live in harmony with themselves and with each other. "In that day, I will make a covenant for them with the beasts of the field, the birds of the air, and the creeping things of the ground" (HOSEA 2:20). What we are willing to kill animals for, and how we treat them up to the point of taking their lives, may well define us as individuals and as a culture.

❖   ❖   ❖   ❖   ❖

Sherirah Gaon, a tenth-century leader of the Jews of Babylonia, instructs us that "animals that do us no harm and are not needed for food or medicine should not be killed." While Judaism recognizes the right of humanity to use animals when necessary for the preservation of human life, cosmetics hardly rise to that level of significance.

KILLING AND TORTURE FOR VANITY

1 Buy products that specifically state that they have not been tested on animals. Most people don't know the extent to which animals permeate the way we clothe, clean, and adorn ourselves every day. Some fourteen million animals are killed each year to produce new forms of facial cream, lipstick, eye shadow, shampoo, and countless other luxuries already swamping the consumer market. In a drive to maintain sales artificially, the clothing and cosmetic industries issue new products when they are not needed or simply "improve" old ones. In the process, these new products are tested in unimaginable ways on immobilized rabbits, cats, dogs, and monkeys.

To test eye products (such as mascara), for example, six to eighteen rabbits are immobilized, and the product is injected inside the lower lid of one eye of each rabbit. Their eyes are clipped open, and the use of anesthesia is rare. (Because rabbits don't shed tears, they can't protect their eyes from harm.) Over the next week, their eyes are examined for ulceration, rupture, and other injuries. Those that survive are often then tested for skin irritation.

As if it weren't bad enough to torture rabbits in order to produce deodorant or aftershave lotion, alternative tests that don't require the use of animals already exist, such as the EYTEX system and the Agarose diffusion method. In addition, the alternative tests are cheaper and more reliable.

Both Revlon and Avon have stopped testing their products on animals. Support those companies. It may take some time to adjust to looking at labels, but a few extra minutes of shopping can alleviate the unnecessary torture and deaths of thousands of animals. (Of course, once you are keeping kosher, reading labels will have become second nature.)

2 Write to the ASPCA for a list of cruelty-free products. Contact the

American Society for the Prevention of
Cruelty to Animals
441 East 92nd Street
New York, NY 10128

Many products contain animal derivatives that are of no measurable benefit to the consumer. Your shampoo may contain animal protein, for example. Two phrases to watch out for are hydrolyzed animal collagen (found in lipsticks, cosmetics, and some shampoos) and lanolin (in lotions). Avoid products with these ingredients.

3 Don't support the fur industry. Fur looks elegant, is comfortable and warm, and lasts a long time. However, the mutilation and death of many animals are required to make a single fur coat. One forty-inch coat requires the death of sixteen coyotes, sixty minks, twenty otters, forty-two foxes, forty raccoons, or fifteen beavers.

These animals are trapped in spring-loaded steel leg-hold traps, which cause an average of fifteen hours of pain before an animal is finally clubbed to death by a trapper. These traps are so painful to the animal that it often chews off its own leg in terror, limping off to die of infection, loss of blood, and starvation. Of course, the animals that die of their injuries are never recovered for "use." And for every animal intended to be trapped, two others are trapped as well, including dogs, cats, deer, and birds of prey. Trappers refer to these undesired victims as trash animals.

In addition to the trapping of wild animals, there are several "fur farms" in the United States. Animals raised on these farms live in such hideous conditions that in 1987, mink farmers reported that 450,000 animals died of heat stress on their farms. These farm animals are killed in the cheapest way possible, often by

The Talmud reminds us that "the sign of a *tzaddik* is concern for the welfare of animals." Surely there are more compassionate ways to stay warm than by wearing the hair of dead mink and foxes.

suffocation, poisoning, or the insertion of an electrode into the animal's anus. What a shameful contrast to the traditional Jewish insistence, in Maimonides' terms, that "the law enjoins us that the death of the animal should be as easy and painless as possible."

It is time for us to take responsibility for this needless disgrace. No one buys a fur coat out of necessity. Luxury purchased at the cost of such tremendous pain and terror is shameful and degrading. The fact is that fur looks elegant only on its original owners; on human beings, it is a sign of callous barbarity. Consider these steps:

• *Don't wear fur.* Even if you have had a fur for years, your wearing it only makes fur look desirable and acceptable for others.

• *Support legislation to ban the leg-hold traps.* Write to the ASPCA for information on the current status of this legislation and what you can do to help.

4 **Refuse to buy and to accept ivory products.** Extinction is a natural part of the evolutionary process. As species become unable to adapt to a changing environment, new species emerge to take their place. But humanity has now become a factor in accelerating the process in a way that no longer enhances the ability of life to thrive. This high-speed and artificial extinction diminishes the variety of life forms, thereby also damaging Creation's responsiveness to environmental challenges ("God desires that the species be perpetuated," according to *Sefer ha-Ḥinnukh* 545).

Only by altering our sense of what is elegant and what we are willing to buy can we hope to slow down the extinction of some of the most beautiful forms of life on this planet. We must remove humanity as a factor in the question of which species will live and which will die.

The African elephant is prized for its ivory tusks. At the current rate of poaching, the elephant will be extinct within a few years after

There is a majesty and a beauty that can inspire religious awe if we allow ourselves to see animals as God's handiwork rather than simply a source for sport and profit. As Rabbi Abraham Isaac Kook notes, "The hidden yearning to act justly toward animals will emerge at the proper time. What prepares us for this condition is the mitzvot, particularly those of *tza'ar ba'alei ḥayyim*."

the year 2000. As the supply of elephant ivory drops, poachers are turning to walrus, killing up to twelve thousand each year. The only way to stop this slaughter is to refuse to buy or accept as gifts ivory products. If consumer demand dissolves, then so will the incentive to poach.

Urge your local zoo to set up a display of ivory products near the elephant habitat to point out the danger that results from the purchase and use of ivory products. Help the zoo establish a program through which people in the community can donate their ivory goods to the zoo for this worthy cause. At the same time, donors can sign a pledge not to purchase or to accept as gifts any more ivory.

5 **Reduce the number of leather products you use.** The same gradual approach that allows for spiritual growth and reasonableness in other areas of mitzvot applies to *tza'ar ba'alei hayyim* as well. It isn't necessary to forswear all animal products in order to make a difference in the way animals are treated. Rather than confronting an all-or-nothing choice that almost guarantees doing nothing, follow a path of simple restraint and balance. This will allow you to lessen dramatically the number of animals tortured and killed in the interests of fashion.

It is difficult to dispense with all leather products. Formal shoes, formal belts, and other accessories are virtually impossible to find except in leather. So rather than going for complete abstinence, try to decrease the number of leather belts, purses, and shoes in your wardrobe. With leather products, cutting back is often enough to make a difference. And many products are not really necessary at all. Leather sneakers wear out just as fast as cloth or canvas ones, and they get just as dirty and beat-up. Leather jackets, notepad cases, pants, car seats, and coats simply encourage a bloated industry to continue abusing and slaughtering cattle without

need. (Desire is not the same as need.) No one has ever died or grown ill from cloth car seats or from nonleather running shoes and sneakers. If we don't need a leather item in order to maintain our health, then it isn't worth the cruelty. We can give it up. Perhaps this is one lesson we can derive from the popular practice on Yom Kippur, the Day of Atonement, of refraining from wearing leather shoes: Adorning ourselves by killing is incompatible with seeking God's mercy and forgiveness.

KILLING AND TORTURE FOR LOVE

6 **When choosing a pet, go to a nearby pound.** I've already mentioned the puppy farms, those overcrowded, often filthy kennels dedicated to mass-producing puppies to generate profits. Such places continue their practices because of our insistence on pedigreed dogs. Even though we already know that inbreeding and inhumane conditions often create dogs that are nervous, hyperactive, and often aggressive, we continue to prefer these blue bloods to their more mellow and balanced motley cousins.

When choosing a pet, go to a nearby pound. Millions of wonderful dogs and cats, often purebred, are waiting for the right home. These animals come in all shapes and ages and make lovely pets. And if not taken, they will often wind up as high school dissection projects or will simply be killed to make room for newcomers. It is a mitzvah to give these animals a home, and if you were planning to buy a pedigreed animal, this choice will save you hundreds of dollars at the same time.

7 **Neuter your pets.** A fertile dog and its pups can give birth to 4,372 dogs in just seven years. In the United States alone, nearly twenty-one million dogs and cats are born each year, with fifteen million winding up in pounds. Some eight to ten million are put to death, unable

While leather goods are highly prized by many people, we often forget that they are made of the skins of an animal that was killed. A midrash states, "God has compassion for anyone who has compassion for fellow creatures." Isn't the value of compassion worth minimizing our use of leather?

to find a human home to care for them. With so much suffering on the part of animals, a responsible way to show love for a pet is to get it "fixed." By neutering a dog or cat, often an inexpensive procedure, you can ensure that fewer puppies and kittens will suffer unnecessary deaths or will be abandoned and unloved because of human irresponsibility. For information on low-cost neutering, call Friends of Animals toll-free at 1-800-321-7387.

8 **Do not alter an animal's appearance because you think it makes the animal look better.** No one wants his or her ears lopped off or a finger removed, so why chop off a piece of a pooch? The mystical book *Sefer Ḥasidim* explains that we are prohibited from altering the general appearance of animals because every part was "created to match their needs. . . . God created the tail in a place where there are no horns to be able to brush away flies." Unnecessary surgery, in animals or humans, is simply another form of vanity and cruelty. Don't take off the dog's tail–it's there to help the animal communicate and to maintain balance and speed. The ears are necessary to collect sound and facilitate hearing. Avoid plastic surgery for pets. "We refrain from committing such acts because we do not wish to behave cruelly toward animals." These words are from a prominent medieval code of Jewish law; the message is as contemporary as the pets of today.

KILLING AND TORTURE IN THE NAME OF SCIENCE

9 **Limit the number of animals used in scientific experiments and research.** Perhaps the most controversial topic on the agenda of animal compassion versus human need is the use of animals in scientific research. There is no shortage of extremists on either side. Some animal rights activists insist that all living things have an equal right to live, so that causing pain or death to animals, even when doing so might save human lives, should be prohibited in the name of immoral exploitation. At the other extreme, there are those who argue that any human benefit, however trivial, justifies using animal subjects, no matter how many animals are killed in the process or how extreme the agony involved.

There is, however, a growing consensus (reflecting the traditional Jewish blend of compassion for animals and emphasis on the primacy of human health) that would permit the use of animals only in experiments that are essential for medical purposes (provided there is no equally reliable method of testing that does not involve animal subjects). The Office of Technology Assessment estimates that between seventeen and twenty-two million animals are used in experiments each year, at a cost to taxpayers of some four billion dollars. Although animal research is indeed sometimes necessary, many scientific discoveries have been the result of clinical research, observation of patients, and human autopsies. For example, X rays, penicillin, and the vaccine against yellow fever were all developed without the use of animal subjects.

Not only are animal subjects often unnecessary, but the results of experiments on animals are often downright misleading as well. The Medical Research Modernization Committee revealed that prior to 1963, every study on human subjects showed a strong link between cigarette smoking and the development of cancer. But every effort to establish a similar link using animals failed. This divergence postponed health warnings against smoking for years, causing the deaths of thousands of uninformed people. A similar difference in results between animals and humans resulted in a misunderstanding of polio, delaying the development of its vaccine.

There already exist many effective alter-natives to animal experimentation, and more are in the works. The National Cancer Institute has already decreased its use of laboratory animals from six million to less than three hundred thousand each year. During its six-day conference, the Society for Neuroscience holds two day-long sessions devoted to exploring the ethical treatment of animals in research. Science and scientists are not the enemy—ignorance, habit, and indifference are. Scientists and concerned laypeople need to work together and speak to one another in order to keep necessary research funded while elevating the level of attention paid to limiting the pain of animals.

• *Donate your organs to scientific research.* Human subjects will allow the pursuit of scientific and medical research without requiring the death of animals. The Rabbinical Assembly Committee on Jewish Law and Standards has ruled that "where there is help to other people, and where the general public consider it *pikkuah nefesh* (saving a life), this use of the body (willing it for medicine) is . . . not only permitted, it is a mitzvah."

• *Don't fill unnecessary prescriptions or buy unnecessary over-the-counter drugs.* As more kinds of drugs are purchased, more animal experimentation is generated. There are more than enough kinds of decongestants and headache tablets already, and using fewer drugs is better for your health and for the environment.

• *Write to the college or university that you attended or graduated from, urging it to establish peer and lay review panels to draw up strict guidelines on the use of animals in scientific research and experiments by faculty members and students.* If you give money to the institution, send your letter with your contribution. Money talks.

• *If you are involved in a school program that requires dissection, check with the school's administration about state guidelines providing alternatives for those who conscientiously object to participating in animal dissection.* Almost everyone who has graduated from high school has witnessed the bloody ritual of animal dissection. Each year, some 6.7 million dogs, cats, rabbits, chipmunks, pigs, frogs, mice, rats, pigs, and sharks are killed in classrooms. The dogs and cats are often supplied by puppy farms, were stolen, or are rejects from pounds and shelters.

Having endured high school dissections, how many of us actually remember enough later in life to justify having taken a life? Wasn't the lasting lesson of dissection that animals don't really matter, that life is expendable for mere curiosity? Alternative methods of teaching anatomy already exist, including models, films, videotapes, and computer programs that allow the simulated dissection of a wide range of animals. At the high school level and generally at the undergraduate level, it simply isn't necessary to kill animals to learn about internal organs. Several states already grant students the right to refuse to participate in dissections or experiments that are harmful to animals. The ASPCA can help you take this moral stand.

If you are interested in psychotherapy as a career but don't want to torture rats to help humans, investigate programs that specialize in clinical psychology. These programs tend not to require animal experimentation, because it's tangential to human psychodynamics. Of course, familiarity with drugs and the chemical bases of illness is crucial for all therapists. But it is possible to study the results of research without having to participate in it directly.

KILLING AND TORTURE FOR FUN

10   **Prevent hunting for sport.** Every year, more than 175 million animals are killed by hunters in the United States. For every animal actually killed, two are simply injured and left to die. In addition, hunters accidentally kill an average of four hundred people and injure an additional fifteen hundred each year. While only 10 percent of the American population hunts, we all pay for their "fun" through taxes that support the state and federal wildlife agencies (primarily the Fish and Wildlife Service).

The primary argument hunters will offer in defense of their cruelty is the prevention of overpopulation. Yet our government spends about five hundred million dollars annually to inflate artificially the numbers of wild animals so hunters can then kill them. In addition, the lead shot from shotguns is fatal to the wild birds that mistake them for pebbles; these shots fatally poison three million waterfowl every year. Finally, hunters add about thirty billion pellets to our wetlands each year, poisoning birds for decades to come.

The second argument hunters often make in their own defense is that they enjoy the closeness to nature experienced during hunting and the challenge of their activity. A hunter armed only with a knife might encounter a challenge, but one who kills a deer with the sophisticated weapons of war employed in contemporary hunting is hardly engaged in a contest. In addition, one could argue that hunters would find nature much more pleasurable if they encountered it as appreciative visitors rather than purveyors of death.

For Jews, hunting has always been a sign of barbarity. The Talmud understands the verse in Psalms, "Happy is the man who has not walked in the ways of the wicked," as referring to the "wicked" who hunt beasts with their hounds. Several medieval sages prohibit hunting on the grounds that it causes unnecessary pain to animals, is a form of wanton destruction of God's Creation, and results in the reckless spilling of blood. Animals killed in a hunt are automatically rendered *treif*, impermissible as food. Maimonides sums up the Jewish position by insisting, "We must not kill out of cruelty or for sport."

- *Don't hunt.* It is unnecessary, unnatural, cruel, and destructive of the natural balance.
- *Contact the ASPCA.* Find out how you can best oppose hunting.
- *Before contributing to a wildlife or conservation group, ask for a copy—in writing—of its position on hunting.* Among the groups surprisingly refusing to take a stand against hunting are the National Audubon Society, the National Wildlife Federation, and the Sierra Club. Only pressure from actual and potential members will force these groups to begin protecting wildlife by opposing hunting.

- *Contribute to the Nature Conservancy.* This wonderful organization takes the money it raises and purchases natural lands that are privately owned, thereby ensuring their status as havens for wildlife. Their address is 1815 North Lynn Street, Arlington, Virginia 22209.

11 **Don't attend circuses or rodeos that abuse animals.** I retain happy childhood memories of circuses and rodeos. Fortunately, as a child, I didn't know that the cir-

> We use animals to amuse ourselves and our children, with the no-so-hidden message that artificial behavior and bizarre antics is what makes life fun. Perhaps a deeper look would remind us that life without tinsel or glitz is a precious gift. We diminish the beauty of Creation by recourse to "tricks" and "gimmicks," just as our own worth emerges from reflecting God's image as we are.

cus and rodeo workers often abused, injured, and maimed the performing animals to get them to act so unnaturally. I also didn't know the Jewish position that "a person who causes needless pain to cattle is worthy of punishment, . . . as is one who wounds a horse with spurs" (*Sefer Ḥasidim* 138).

Circus animals are taken out of their natural habitats and confined to small cages. Their "training" often involves tight collars and muzzles, whipping, prodding, and drugging to render them more obedient. Often, their teeth and claws are removed.

Rodeos are part of the heritage of the American West. But so were rampant prostitution, vigilantes, posses, and gunfights. They were all part of a brutal and lawless past, and all are well worth discarding. Rodeo performers wrap tight straps around a horse's groin in order to cause such intense pain that the horse will kick, squirm, and leap to try to remove the strap. Electric prods and painful ointments also help stir up an otherwise docile animal. In calf roping, baby cows run at about thirty miles per hour, until ropes around their necks bring them to an instant halt. This "thrill" causes severe bruising, neck and back injuries, internal bleeding, and broken bones. Steer busting does the same, and many rodeos don't even offer veterinary care to treat the injuries, all inflicted in the name of fun.

There are wonderful circus troupes that don't torture animals to please children. Two of them are the Cirque du Soleil and the Pickle Family Circus. Let the bigger circuses know why they will be losing a previous customer and what they can do to make amends.

Instead of teaching yourself and your children that it's fun to cause pain to living things, why not drive to a wildlife preserve or a dude ranch and enjoy the fact that animals are beautiful, curious, and often friendly?

KILLING AND TORTURE FOR FOOD

12 **By far the greatest single way in which we cause the pain and death of animals is in the thoughtless consumption of them.** Few of us consider where our meat comes from, how it is raised, killed, and packaged. Instead, we buy conveniently wrapped containers of red meat that serve to sever any connection between dead flesh and the meat we are about to consume. Caring for animals may not require that everyone become a vegetarian, but it does require that we begin to think about our food and set some limits to our appetites and our desires.

A stirring story in the Talmud relates that a calf was being taken to the slaughter when it broke away and hid its head under Rabbi Judah's robes and cried. "Go," he said, "for this were you created." Thereupon they said [in heaven], "Because he has no pity, let us bring suffering upon him."

Rabbi Judah's pains did not depart until one

> "In the killing of animals there is cruelty, rage, and accustomizing oneself to the bad habit of shedding innocent blood." So wrote the medieval Rabbi Joseph Albo.

day his maidservant attempted to sweep away some weasels she had discovered while cleaning. Rabbi Judah rose to the animals' defense. "Let them be," he said to her, "for it is written in Scripture, 'And God's mercy is over all God's works.'" Said they [in heaven], "Because he is compassionate, let us be compassionate to him."

Rabbi Judah was simply asserting the consensus of his and our times when he pushed the calf away. Meat, after all, is one reason people raise cows in the first place. Rabbi Judah was so accustomed to habit that he was blind to the pain and terror that slaughter imposes on its victims. Hence the Talmud's condemnation of his callousness.

Not only is meat consumption a moral issue, but it is also a threat to human health. Animals are raised in dark, cramped confinement, and as a result they are almost constantly ill. To counter those illnesses, regular injections with hormones and antibiotics are administered to them. In fact, between 40 and 50 percent of all antibiotics in America are used, without medical supervision, on factory-farmed animals. And their food is laced with chemicals, pesticides, arsenic, fungicides, and other additives. One out of three chickens sold in supermarkets is infected with salmonella bacteria, and meat is the leading source of pesticide residue (55 percent) in our diet; chicken liver contains a concentrate of nearly twenty synthetic, biologically active steroid hormones. Reducing the consumption of meat, dairy products, and eggs by 50 percent can reduce the risk of heart attack by at least 45 percent.

Finally, the way we raise animals for food endangers the environment. Some 85 percent of the topsoil lost in the United States is related to livestock production. Over 50 percent of the water consumed each year is used for factory farming, as is 95 percent of the oats and 80 percent of the corn. The Department of the Interior notes that "the value of raw materials consumed to produce food from livestock is greater than the value of all oil, gas, and coal consumed in this country." And these animals produce 250,000 pounds of excrement each second! Much of that waste winds up in our streams, lakes, and groundwater, without having been treated at all.

The way we produce meat is cruel, violating the mitzvah of *tza'ar ba'alei ḥayyim*. Its danger to human health violates the mitzvah of *rappo yirappei* (רַפֹּא יְרַפֵּא, preserving health), and its destruction of the environment violates the mitzvah of *bal tash'ḥit*. In light of this, consider taking the following steps.

• *Don't eat veal.* Veal is the code word for a baby cow. Taken from its mother less than a day after birth, the calf is raised in a crate so small that the animal cannot turn, lie down, or stretch. It is never given water to drink, nor any solids to eat. Instead, it is kept anemic, with a diet exclusively of milk replacers, which is deliberately deficient in iron. This diet causes chronic diarrhea. The animal lives in darkness twenty-three hours a day, in barns storing up to four hundred other crated calves. Fed a steady stream of antibiotics, one in every thirty calves has been found to contain illegal residues of tetracycline, neomycin, and gentamicin. Most are slaughtered after only sixteen weeks. Regardless of what else you may choose to consume, surely the cruelty to the animal and the threat to human health compel you to proscribe the eating of veal.

• *Buy only "dolphin-safe" tuna.* Unfortunately, these beautiful mammals swim above schools of tuna fish, attracting fishing expeditions by their presence. The purse seine often used to catch tuna also drowns the dolphins in the process. In the past thirty years, 6.5 million dolphins have drowned. The good news is that 70 percent of the tuna market now sells only "dolphin-safe" tuna. These brands include Chicken of the Sea, Bumble Bee, and Star-Kist.

• *Eat less meat.* A good way to begin eating less meat is to start on the path toward kashrut. (See Chapter 8.) Rabbi Abraham Isaac Kook, the first chief Ashkenazi rabbi of Israel, observed, "So will the hidden yearning to act justly toward animals emerge at the proper time. What prepares the ground for this state is the mitzvot, those intended specifically for this area of concern." If you begin by giving up pork and shellfish and then progress to eating only meat that has been slaughtered according to the dietary laws, the amount of meat you consume may greatly diminish.

• *Become a vegetarian.* This need not be an all-or-nothing affair. You can give up just red meat (becoming a pollo vegetarian) or red meat and poultry (becoming a pesco vegetarian). You can give up red meat, poultry, and fish (becoming a lacto-ovo vegetarian), or you can eventually give up all animal products entirely (becoming a vegan). Why not consider keeping a vegetarian home (that is, nothing fleischig in the house). Even if you ate turkey only once a year (on Thanksgiving) and used fish as your only source of animal protein (I think the Jewish term should be a milchig parevetarian), the number of animals' lives that would be spared and the vast improvement in your health would make a staggering difference. Try it on a provisional basis, and see how it feels.

❖ ❖ ❖ ❖ ❖

Abraham Lincoln once said, "I care not for a man's religion whose dog and cat are not the better for it." The Jewish religion has insisted on humanity's responsibility for minimizing the pain of animals. In our own age, that millennial concern has expanded to include responsibility for the earth's ecosystem and our own health.

At its core, however, *tza'ar ba'alei ḥayyim* remains a moral charge, an insistence that the way we treat the living things around us shapes the contours of our souls and the measure of our compassion. By restoring our traditional sense of priorities so that once again compassion, morality, and responsibility direct our course, we may again become a "light to the nations" and a symbol of God's loving providence for the work of Creation.

God has compassion on all who have compassion on their fellow creatures.
—SIFREI DEVARIM 96

For Further Reading

The Animal Rights Handbook. Los Angeles: Living Planet Press, 1990.

Elijah Judah Schochet, *Animal Life in Jewish Tradition: Attitudes and Relationships.* New York: Ktav, 1984.

Richard H. Schwartz, *Judaism and Vegetarianism.* Marblehead, MA: Micah Press,1988.

Anna Sequoia, *67 Ways to Save the Animals.* New York: Harper Perennial, 1990.

III. Conclusion

18 Judaism as a Living System

To be is to stand for.

—RABBI ABRAHAM JOSHUA HESCHEL

At the very outset of this book, I promised that its perspective would be that of the individual, and that it would respect the integrity and needs of each seeking soul. Now, having concluded a survey of several mitzvot, let's look at Judaism not as a smorgasbord of goodies, any combination of which can be combined to fill a plate. Instead of considering only what discrete mitzvot can do for us, let's consider Judaism as an entity in its own right, with a history, an integrity, and a connectedness that lends additional value to its individual parts.

The heritage of Judaism can remain a vital and humanizing force only if it is seen as a living, integrated system. Rather than selecting only those parts of Judaism that feel meaningful, and thereby detaching them from the network of a living Jewish worldview, we will serve ourselves better by incorporating the wholeness of the Jewish way; and we will serve ourselves better if we are convinced that only as a living organism—complex and interdependent—can Judaism attain its fullest coherence,

> Long before we articulate a theology, we absorb the feelings of love, acceptance and belonging that Judaism offers. A parent, grandparent, or friend can open us up to experiencing the wonder of mitzvot.

vitality, and meaning.

In this regard, Judaism is not unique. Every civilization, every language, survives because its practitioners utilize interlocking symbols to signify objects and to communicate meaning. Each society develops a network of stories, prohibitions, festivals, and institutions to distinguish its adherents and to propagate its own values and vision. As we treasure Jewish values, identity, and practices, so we must work to maintain the fullest organic complexity of Judaism as an entity.

In Jewish terms this means that our worldview emerges from the revelation of Sinai and that we consider ourselves to be the latest extension in time of that earliest encounter with the sacred. Such a view is not rigidly bound by the past because the past still lives in the present. In connecting past and present, however, we cannot abandon the needs or the tensions of this generation; we cannot ignore the gap— of knowledge, practice, and meaning—between *am Yisrael* (the Jewish people) and *masoret Yisrael* (Jewish tradition). While our mode of learning and renewal will necessarily involve selecting new mitzvot as they become meaningful to us individually, our aim must ever remain to achieve the fullest extent of Jewish wisdom and practice.

❖   ❖   ❖   ❖   ❖

Neither Jews nor Jewish law is engraved in stone. Where we currently stand, mentally and spiritually, is but one point on a trajectory that began with our birth and will continue beyond our death. Seen in this light, the piecemeal implementation of Jewish practices reflects a growing wealth of Judaism in our lives and values. Too few of us are encouraged simply to take the next step, however small or partial that step may be. This reticence is particularly hard to understand in light of the fact that our tradition does not operate well on the level of lofty imperatives or sweeping theoretical constructions. Rather, Jewish civilization—indeed the very essence of *brit* ("covenant")—emerges from a collection of small and concrete actions. Our philosophy emerges from our deeds.

Our calling across the millennia hasn't changed. Nor have our needs. The mitzvot are still our path of return, our way toward wholeness and belonging. It has always been in our hands to heal the world. It is still in our power to love one another and to care. We can still build families and communities together. Not through some grand philosophy, not with a new world vision, but with the simple courage of the single holy deed.

Glossary

GLOSSARY

Ahavat Tziyon:
Literally, "love of Zion," the mitzvah of caring for and identifying with the land, State, and citizens of Israel.

Aleinu:
The last prayer of most Jewish services, celebrating the privilege of serving God and anticipating an age of universal harmony under God.

Aliyah:
(1) being called up to say a blessing for the reading of the Torah, and (2) moving to Israel.

Arba Knafot:
Also tallit katan, a four-cornered undershirt worn in order to fulfill the mitzvah of wearing tzitzit.

Arvit:
The evening prayer service.

Aseret Ha-Dibrot:
The Ten Commandments (Exodus 20 and Deuteronomy 5).

Aseret Y'mai Teshuvah:
The Ten Days of Repentance from Rosh Hashanah to Yom Kippur.

Bal Tash'hit:
Literally, "Do not waste or destroy," the prohibition against waste; a general term for the commandment to conserve natural resources.

Bar/Bat Mitzvah:
Literally, "The child responsible for fulfilling the commandments." The term used to describe the thirteen-year-old boy or girl who celebrates this occasion by reading from the Torah and Haftarah during the Saturday morning service.

Bentsch:
To recite Grace After Meals (Yiddish).

Berakhah/Berakhot:
Blessing/blessings.

Beta Yisrael:
The Jews of northern Ethiopia. Many are now living in Israel.

Bikkur Holim:
The mitzvah of visiting the sick.

Bimah:
Literally, "high place." The platform in the synagogue where the Torah is read and sermons are delivered.

Birkat Ha-Hammah:
Blessing of the sun.

Birkat Ha-Mazon:
Grace After Meals.

Birkhot Ha-Nehenin:
Blessings of benefit, recited over natural wonders.

Brit:
Covenant.

B'tzelem Elohim:
"In God's image." Based on Genesis 1:26.

Davar Hadash:
A halakhic category signifying an object that has been altered so much that it is no longer considered in the same category as its component parts.

Daven:
To pray (Yiddish).

Deuteronomy:
The fifth book of the Torah; includes Moses' farewell address recounting the experiences of his lifetime from a religious perspective.

Diaspora:
The Jewish communities outside of the Land of Israel. From the Greek for "exile."

Elul:
The Hebrew month preceding Rosh Hashanah.

Eretz Yisrael:
Hebrew for the Land of Israel.

Exodus:
The second book of the Torah, relating the birth of Moses, the liberation of the Israelite slaves from Egypt, basic biblical laws, and the building of the Tabernacle.

Falashas:
A demeaning term for the Beta Yisrael, the Jews from Ethiopia.

Fleischig:
Meat or food containing meat products. A category of kashrut.

Hakhnasat Orḥim:
The mitzvah of hospitality to guests.

Halakhah:
Jewish law.

Ha-Motzi:
The blessing over bread, generally recited at the beginning of any meal.

Havdalah:
Literally, "distinction." The ceremony marking the end of Shabbat and the beginning of the weekdays.

Ḥaver:
A colleague or friend.

Ḥavruta:
A fellowship, generally for study of sacred literature.

Ḥeder:
Traditional Jewish elementary school.

Ḥeshbon Nefesh:
Literally, "a soul reckoning," moral inventory.

Ḥevrah Mikra:
Bible Fellowship.

Israel:
Name for the third patriarch of the Bible (Jacob), his descendants (the Jewish people), their land (also known as Canaan, or Palestine), and the modern Jewish state.

Ivrit:
Hebrew, the biblical and modern language of the Jewish people.

Kashrut:
The Jewish dietary laws.

Kavanah:
Literally, "intention or devotion." Also refers to short meditations often printed before formal prayers.

Kedushah:
Holiness.

Kibbud:
Honor.

Kibbud Av Va-Em:
The fifth commandment in the Ten Commandments: to honor one's father and mother.

Kibbutz/Kibbutzim:
A collective, usually agricultural settlements in Israel.

Kiddush:
Blessing over wine for meals, Shabbat, festivals, and holy days.

Kiddush L'vanah:
Blessing over the new moon praising God's role in creation and the cycles of nature.

Kippah:
Headcovering, also called "yarmulke."

Kohen Gadol:
The High Priest of the biblical period who ran the services in the Temple in Jerusalem.

Kosher:
Meat that was slaughtered according to Jewish ritual requirements. The word is often used to refer to the entire body of Jewish dietary laws, and the ways in which one eats when following the laws.

K'riat Sh'ma:
Reciting the Sh'ma.

Leviticus:
The third book of the Torah, the priestly code which relates the rules of biblical sacrifice and contains the Holiness Code (Leviticus 17-19).

L'shon Ha-Ra:
Literally, "evil speech." Gossip, slander, and repeating private information publicly.

Ma'akhil R'evim:
The mitzvah of feeding the hungry.

Maḥzor:
The prayerbook for the High Holy Days.

Mazal Tov:
Literally, "a good star," congratulations.

Melakhah:
Work, a halakhic category prohibited on Shabbat.

Menuḥah:
Rest, a halakhic category mandated on Shabbat.

Mezuzah / Mezuzot:
The kosher scroll with quotations from the Torah which is affixed to the doorposts of the home and each room inside the home. Colloquially, "mezuzah" is used to mean the container for the scroll.

Midrash / Midrashim:
Rabbinic interpretations, stories, and laws based on biblical verses.

Milchig:
Food made from, or containing, dairy products.

Minḥah:
The afternoon prayer service.

Minyan:
The quorum—ten adult Jews (among the Orthodox, and some Conservative, ten adult Jewish males)—necessary to recite all Jewish prayers. The minyan represents the Jewish people as a community.

Mip'nei Darkhei Shalom:
"For the sake of peace," a rabbinic principle that allows the alteration or abrogation of other Jewish legal rulings.

Mi Sheh-Berakh:
"The One who blessed..." The opening words of a petitionary prayer for healing the sick or blessing an individual.

Mishnah:
The earliest compilation of rabbinic law, maxims, and guidelines; dated around 200 C.E., produced by the school of Rabbi Judah ha-Nasi.

Mishneh Torah:
The magisterial digest of Jewish law by Rabbi Moses ben Maimon, also known as Maimonides; written in a simple and beautiful Hebrew in 1180.

Mitzvah or Mitzvot:
Commandment/commandments. There are 613 biblical commandments upon which the rabbis of the Mishnah and Talmud based their own expansions.

Mizraḥ:
Literally, "east." Also the name of a plaque placed on the eastern wall of a home or institution in memory of the Temple and to focus attention to Jerusalem.

Muk'tzeh:
Objects that cannot be touched or moved on Shabbat as a protective measure to prevent using them (e.g., a pen).

Naḥat Ru'aḥ:
Peace of mind or soul.

Netillat Yadayim:
The blessing for washing the hands before blessing bread at a meal.

Numbers:
The fourth book of the Torah, containing priestly legislation and the narrative of the wandering in the wilderness to the border of the Land of Israel.

Parashat Ha-Shavuah:
The weekly Torah portion read in synagogues around the world.

Pareve:
Food that is categorized neither as meat nor as dairy, such as grain, fruit, and fish.

Parvetarian:
A vegetarian who keeps kosher.

Pidyon Sh'vuyim:
The mitzvah of rescuing the captive.

Pirkei Avot:
A book of the Mishnah that contains pithy maxims by the founding figures of rabbinic Judaism.

Pushke:
A box where coins and bills are put for *tzedakah*; found in most synagogue chapels for the weekday minyan, as well as in the home.

Rappo Yirappei:
Literally, "you must heal," the biblical mitzvah to heal the sick.

Rashi:
Eleventh-century French rabbi. Masterful commentator to the entire Hebrew Bible, the Mishnah, and the Talmud. His comments are essential study aids to this day.

Refusenik:
A Jew who has applied for—and has been refused—the right to emigrate from the Soviet Union.

Rodef Shalom:
A pursuer of peace.

Rosh Hashanah:
The Jewish New Year, which occurs in the early fall.

Rosh Ḥodesh:
The holy days of the new month in the Hebrew calendar.

Sefer Ha-Ḥinnukh:
Thirteenth-century Spanish compilation of Jewish law organized by the weekly Torah readings, written by Rabbi Aaron ha-Levi of Barcelona.

Sefer Ḥasidim:
Pious work of Rabbi Yehudah he-Ḥasid of Germany, twelfth century.

Sefer Tehillim:
The biblical book of Psalms.

S'liḥot:
Literally, "forgiveness," the prayers that introduce the penitential season before Rosh Hashanah.

Se'udah Sh'lishit:
The third meal held on the afternoon of Shabbat.

Shabbat:

The Sabbath, from seventeen minutes before sundown on Friday evening to Saturday night, one hour past the time candles were lit the previous evening.

Shabbat Shuvah:

"The Sabbath of Repentance," which falls between Rosh Hashanah and Yom Kippur.

Shaharit:

The morning worship service.

Shalom:

"Peace," "Hello," "Good-bye."

Shalom Aleikhem:

The traditional greeting of welcome and farewell. It means "Peace to you."

Shehitah:

The method of ritual slaughter used to produce kosher meat.

Sh'liah Tzibbur:

The one who leads communal prayer, generally a hazzan (cantor) or the rabbi.

Sh'lom Bayit:

Peace in the home, a prime Jewish value.

Sh'mirat Ha-Lashon:

The observance of the laws of responsible speech.

Sh'mirat Kashrut:

The observance of the dietary laws.

Shoah:

The Holocaust (1936-1945), during which the Nazis and others murdered approximately six million Jews.

Shofar:

The ram's horn used to produce stirring blasts during the month of Elul, on Rosh Hashanah and Yom Kippur.

Shomer Adamah:

A guardian of the earth, also a Jewish environmental organization (Shomrei Adamah).

Shulhan Arukh:

The code of Jewish law of Rabbi Yosef Karo, published in 1564. It is arguably the most well-known and popular of the codes.

Siddur:

Prayerbook.

Simhat Mitzvah:

The joy of observing a commandment.

Sofer:

A trained scribe for the calligraphy of Torah scrolls, tefillin, and mezuzot.

Ta'anit Yahid:

A private fast, used to commemorate a private tragedy or its anniversary.

Tallit/Tallitot:

The ritual prayer shawl used for the morning service and by the *sh'liah tzibbur* at most services. At its four corners are the tzitzit.

Talmud Torah:

The mitzvah of Jewish learning.

Tefillah:

Prayer.

Tefillat Ha-Derekh:

The traveler's prayer.

Tefillin:

Known in English as "phylacteries," these leather boxes and straps contain the four biblical passages of the Shema and are wrapped around the arm and on the forehead in accordance with Deuteronomy 6:4-9 and 11:13-21.

Teshuvah/Teshuvot:

(1) Repentance; (2) a legal finding by a duly authorized sage. One who returns to Jewish observance from a secular life is called a *ba'al teshuvah*, a master of repentance.

Teshuvah Sh'leimah:

Literally, "complete repentance." One who is in the same situation that led to a transgression in the past but who this time is able to resist.

Tikkun Olam:

Literally, "the repair of the world," now used to mean social justice.

Tisha B'Av:

The fast day commemorating the destruction of the First Temple in 586 B.C.E. and the Second Temple in 70 C.E. as well as subsequent tragedies in Jewish history.

Torah:

Literally, "instruction" or "teaching." The first five books of the Bible: Genesis, Exodus, Leviticus, Numbers, and Deuteronomy. In the larger sense, Torah is all Jewish learning.

Tov M'od:

Literally, "very good"; God's assessment of creation.

Treif:

Literally, "torn meat." Has come to mean any food not kosher.

Tsfat:
Also spelled "Safed," a city in the hills of northern Israel that is one of the four talmudically designated holy cities of Israel. Achieved particular prominence as the center of Jewish mysticism in the sixteenth century.

Tza'ar Ba'alei Ḥayyim:
Compassion to animals.

Tzedakah:
Righteousness, justice, charity. Has come specifically to mean financial contributions.

Tzitzit:
The ritual threads and knots (often called fringes) on the four corners of the tallit.

Tziyon:
Zion. The name of the mountain in Jerusalem on which was built King Solomon's Temple. Because of its importance, it lent its name to all of the Land of Israel.

Ulpan:
From the word for "learning," used to designate intensive Hebrew language courses.

Va-Ḥai Bahem:
"And you shall live by them," what God tells us in the Torah is the underlying goal of the mitzvot.

Yarmulke:
Also known as *kippah/kippot*. Headcovering for Jewish men, and increasingly for Jewish women as well. Must be worn during prayer, study, and eating. The more pious often wear it all the time.

Yerushalayim:
Hebrew for "Jerusalem," the capital of Israel, established as such by King David about 1000 B.C.E.

Yeshivah/Yeshivot:
Academies of talmudic learning.

Yirah:
Hebrew for "awe." A devotion owed to God and to parents.

Yom Kippur:
Literally, "the Day of Atonement," one of the holiest fast days of the Jewish calendar.

Zayde:
Yiddish for "grandfather."

Zemirot:
Traditional Hebrew songs for Shabbat, holy days, and festivals.

Zionist:
One who affirms the right of the Jewish people to a national homeland and state in the Land of Israel. The modern movement of political liberation of the Jewish people worldwide.

Appendix

Jewish Law: Its Roots and Development

Jewish law is a dynamic process, rooted in the love between God and the Jewish people. The earliest expression of that love and commitment is the Torah, the first five books of the Hebrew Bible. Embodied in the Torah—in the second part of She'mot (Exodus), all of Vayikra (Leviticus), and parts of Bemidbar (Numbers)—are the extensive legal codes. The legal codes' focus on behavior receives confirmation and development in the fifth biblical book, Devarim (Deuteronomy). All later Jewish traditions grow out of this first encounter with the ineffable.

Emerging from the roots of Jewish law is a body of literature called the Mishnah (the first systematic compilation of rabbinic law) and the Gemara (a discussion commenting on issues raised in the Mishnah). These rabbinic works, completed between 200 and 600 C.E., form a lengthy elaboration of the legal codes contained in the Bible. The Talmud (the combination of the Mishnah and Gemara) addresses all aspects of Jewish life: business, agriculture, criminal and civil law, philosophy, and language. Most important, the Talmud establishes a precedent that values equally the *process* of settling a dispute and the answer that is reached. Thus, for example, the Talmud records a dispute about how to observe Ḥanukkah, a post-biblical holiday. From a seemingly petty argument (resolved some two thousand years ago)—about whether to light one more candle each day or one fewer—emerged the expression of divergent under-standings of the nature of a holiday and of what it means to celebrate it. While the principal rabbinical schools differed in their conclusions,

> Just as we praise God for having commanded us to light the Ḥanukkah candles (even though there is no such explicit command in the Torah), so we continue to elevate and sanctify new aspects of Jewish living.

they continued talking with each other, insisting on taking each other's viewpoint seriously. The rabbis' example demonstrated that one can relish a good dispute while respecting one's ideological opponent. The rabbis also maintained a remarkable sensitivity to subtle nuances in the Torah, a great loyalty and love for the Jewish people, and an unwavering commitment to the God of Israel.

The many arguments contained in the Talmud testify to the dynamic nature of Judaism and Jewish law. If, as some contemporary Jews insist, the practice of Judaism were immutable, what need would there be for living interpreters? Were Judaism to continue without change to the end of time, one authoritative book would be enough. Every question would be answered there; we could resolve all cases by referring to the appropriate page. We could consult a thorough index; we certainly wouldn't require rabbis or study to find answers to our questions. Such a static system might be simpler—and would certainly provoke fewer disputes—but it could not respond to the complexity of life, society, new insights, and technology. Also, it would not be traditional Judaism. Judaism was never threatened by divergent opinion. Rather, the Torah and the Talmud reflect a recognition that controversy, properly motivated and respectfully conducted, can be an essential sign of health and vitality. What matters is not that Jews all think and pray alike but that we cultivate our disagreements within the context of love and commitment and covenant. Not uniformity but unity is the continuing need for Jewish survival.

At the other extreme, some confuse Judaism's love of discussion and challenge, its openness to new insights and sources of knowledge, with a lack of any boundaries whatsoever. Some congregants have told me that what they love about Judaism is that they can believe and do anything they want. While it is certainly true that traditional halakhah contained a range of different opinions (and still does), it is important to remember that there are limits as well. Recall that Judaism is the ongoing interpretation and expression of the Torah and that the Torah speaks in the language of divine commands rooted in the revelation at Mount Sinai. Some may understand that revelation more literally and some more metaphorically, but there is little room within a traditional Judaism for the idea that anything goes. Starving the poor and feeding them are not equal options; and the observance of Shabbat is a mitzvah, but its desecration is not. There are arguments about how best to make Shabbat holy and how best to visit the sick, but there is no dispute that the mitzvot are the commanded deeds through which Jews demonstrate the sovereignty of God. Between the extreme group that hears only one voice within Judaism and the extreme group that hears any note one wishes to play, the tradition steers a careful middle path of moderation, respect for reasoned discourse, and religious humility on the part of its practitioners. Throughout the centuries, Jews have related to a Judaism that was evolving and conserving at the same time. That relationship still unfolds.

Great scholars have contributed their own distinct voices—and the perspectives of their own communities—to the symphony of halakhah. Each presented his own understanding of the written sources and his own perception of the needs of the hour: commentaries such as Rashi's; systematic codifications of Jewish law, such as Maimonides' *Mishneh Torah* and Rabbi Yosef Karo's *Shulḥan Arukh*; and lengthy *teshuvot* ("responses"; singular, *teshuvah*) on particularly interesting or complicated cases. Each added a new branch to a tree already massive and hoary. And each insisted on the right of the others to do the same (without necessarily conceding that he accepted their conclusions).

The foliage continues to bloom to this day. At rabbinical seminaries, synagogues, and universities, wherever Jews study our sacred writings—Judaism still thrives. In each generation, each individual adds a distinct personal touch to the living, growing tradition. Each time a Jew discovers some new meaning, he or she reaps a new harvest of Torah, adding that much more to the storehouse of our ancestral tradition. Each time a Jew practices what he or she learns, Judaism becomes that much more vital and compelling.

Like any living organism, halakhah and Jewish practice demonstrate an ability to change and a will to survive. To some degree, these two traits are contradictory, one emphasizing difference and the other, continuity. Yet both are the necessary characteristics of any living creation. Halakhah accepts new insights, new needs, and new possibilities while retaining its ancient integrity. An example: About nineteen hundred years ago, the rabbis faced a terrible dilemma. Much of public worship during the biblical period involved the holy Temple in Jerusalem and its prescribed animal sacrifices. Yet the Roman army destroyed the Temple in the year 70 C.E. If the central symbol of the Passover festival was the pascal sacrifice performed in the Temple, how were Jews to celebrate their freedom from Egypt now that the Temple had been destroyed? Rather than abandon the festival entirely or simply ignore the new reality, the rabbis of antiquity used the precedents found in the Torah to develop a new mode for observing Passover. That balance between continuity and innovation resulted in the Passover seder, which is today the quintessential Jewish practice.

That balance can be found in our own age—for example, in the requirement that women rabbinical students make the same halakhic commitments as their male counterparts. Because the option of full participation by women was not available to previous generations, today's rabbis had to exercise yet again that ancient balance between innovation and continuity. Rather than abandoning the traditional emblems of Jewish piety or simply following the existing forms, many Jewish women now accept the same standard of Jewish responsibility that pertains to Jewish men.

It is important to remember, however, that while many aspects of Jewish law making may change, certain general guidelines remain throughout the ages:

1. *Jewish law requires an understanding of what has come before.* The Bible itself and certainly later midrashim—rabbinic commentary and explanation of the Bible (singular, midrash)—as well as codes and *teshuvot,* show a reverence for and an attentiveness to the relevant traditions of earlier ages. Related to this understanding is the requirement that only those who make themselves knowledgeable in, and obedient to, Jewish law are authorized to issue rulings. In this way, the authority of those "living magistrates" strengthens Judaism rather than automatically conceding or rejecting all perspectives of the modern world.

2. *Jewish law is communal.* While individuals have influence over particular decisions, ultimately those decisions are ratified by the Jewish people in their communities. Scholarly decisions to renounce or amend specific practices are not left to the individual (although they are generally initiated by an individual sage). While each congregation's rabbi is the *Mara d'Atra* (the authority in Jewish law for that particular synagogue), ritual committees serve as the rabbi's "eyes and ears," offering counsel on how to implement the rabbi's understanding of Jewish law in their community. But there are times when a rabbinic decision is simply rejected or ignored by the Jewish people as a whole. In this way, the Jewish people exercises a veto power over the rabbinic role in halakhah.

3. *Jewish law exhibits a healthy self-respect.* This respect translates into an unwillingness to change too drastically or too quickly. In the words of Rabbi Louis Finkelstein, of blessed memory, "Change as little as possible, as late as possible." As the primary vehicle for maintaining communal identity, for developing character, and for expressing our love of God, Jewish law is precious. Because halakhah is a repository of millennial insight and profundity, changes in Jewish law are undertaken with gravity and deliberation and only after a consensus is developed. Changes in specific rulings on Jewish law are introduced only when their adoption would strengthen Judaism and Jewish identity, thereby adding to the greatness of the Torah, the sensitivity and engagement of Jews, and the glory of God.

BOOKS OF THE TANAKH

FIVE BOOKS OF MOSES / HUMASH (חוּמָשׁ)

ENGLISH TITLE	HEBREW TITLE
Genesis	בְּרֵאשִׁית
Exodus	שְׁמוֹת
Leviticus	וַיִּקְרָא
Numbers	בְּמִדְבַּר
Deuteronomy	דְּבָרִים

PROPHETS / NEVI'IM (נְבִיאִים)

ENGLISH TITLE	HEBREW TITLE
Joshua	יְהוֹשֻׁעַ
Judges	שׁוֹפְטִים
I Samuel	שְׁמוּאֵל א
II Samuel	שְׁמוּאֵל ב
I Kings	מְלָכִים א
II Kings	מְלָכִים ב
Isaiah	יְשַׁעְיָה
Jeremiah	יִרְמְיָה
Ezekiel	יְחֶזְקֵאל
Hosea	הוֹשֵׁעַ
Joel	יוֹאֵל
Amos	עָמוֹס
Obadiah	עוֹבַדְיָה
Jonah	יוֹנָה
Micah	מִיכָה
Naḥum	נַחוּם
Habakkuk	חֲבַקּוּק
Zephaniah	צְפַנְיָה
Ḥaggai	חַגַּי
Zechariah	זְכַרְיָה
Malachi	מַלְאָכִי

WRITINGS / KETUVIM (כְּתוּבִים)

ENGLISH TITLE	HEBREW TITLE
Psalms	תְּהִלִּים
Proverbs	מִשְׁלֵי
Job	אִיּוֹב
Song of Songs	שִׁיר הַשִּׁירִים
Ruth	רוּת
Lamentations	אֵיכָה
Ecclesiastes	קֹהֶלֶת
Esther	אֶסְתֵּר
Daniel	דָּנִיֵּאל
Ezra	עֶזְרָא
Nehemiah	נְחֶמְיָה
I Chronicles	דִּבְרֵי הַיָּמִים א
II Chronicles	דִּבְרֵי הַיָּמִים ב

MAJOR HALAKHIC AUTHORITIES

THE RIF: The *Hilkhot Rav Alfas*, commonly called the Rif, an acronym for the author's name, **R**abbi **I**saac al-**F**asi (1013-1103). The Rif is the preeminent authority in Spain and North Africa. It came to be known as the **Talmud Katan** (תַּלְמוּד קָטָן), or "abbreviated Talmud." The Rif follows the order of the Talmud and decides outstanding questions of law between the close of the Talmudic period and the eleventh century.

THE RAMBAM: Maimonides (1135-1204) is usually known as **Rambam**, an acronym based on the name **R**abbi **M**oshe **b**en **M**aimon. Rambam was one of the greatest scholars in Jewish history. Although he wrote works of philosophy and science, as well as commentaries on Bible and Mishnah, he is most famous for his law code, the **Mishneh Torah** (מִשְׁנֵה תּוֹרָה). The code, which covers fourteen volumes, is sometimes called the **Yad HaHazakah**, which literally means "the mighty hand"; the name arose because in Hebrew יָד is made of י and ד, which together add up to fourteen. The Mishneh Torah does not follow the order of the Talmud but instead organizes the laws and principles of Judaism according to the internal logic of the halakhah.

THE TUR: The four Turim, or "rows," by Rabbi Jacob ben Rabbenu Asher (1270?-1340), form the basis for the Shulḥan Arukh. Written in Germany, about 150 years after the Mishneh Torah and 200 years before the Shulḥan Arukh, the Tur describes Jewish practice from morning to night, from weekdays to holidays. Unlike Rambam's code, which covers all of Judaism, the Tur presents only laws relevant to daily Jewish living.

THE SHULḤAN ARUKH: The Shulḥan Arukh, which means "Prepared Table," is based directly on the Tur and was written by Rabbi Joseph Karo (1488-1575) in the sixteenth century in Eretz Yisrael. Karo had a brilliant mind, and his code remains today the most authoritative source of all Jewish law. The code has four divisions:

1. Oraḥ Hayyim ("The Way of Life"): Considering the Torah as the source of everyday living, this division describes Jewish conduct in daily life, Shabbat, and festivals.

2. Yoreh De'ah ("Teaching Knowledge"): This section teaches traditions and laws that require rulings by authorities, such as kashrut, mikveh, brit milah, and mourning. Rabbis today must know this volume and its sources in order to qualify as authorities.

3. Even HaEzer ("The Rock of Help"): This division, whose title is based on the Bible's use of the term "helpmate" to describe woman, deals with male-female relations and with families. It covers the laws of marriage and divorce.

4. Ḥoshen Mishpat ("The Breastplate of Judgment"): The laws of Judaism cover not only religious practices but also civil and criminal disputes. Ḥoshen Mishpat—named for the breastplate which the ancient High Priest, or **kohen** (כֹּהֵן), wore and consulted regarding political affairs affecting the entire nation—covers laws of evidence, judges, personal injury cases, and other legal matters.

THE REMA: Moses Isserles (1525?-1572), a Polish rabbi known as the Rema, is famous chiefly for his additions, or "glosses," to the Shulḥan Arukh. His additions are called the **Mapah** ("Tablecloth") to Karo's "Prepared Table." While Karo wrote mainly for Sephardic Jewry—the Jewish communities of North Africa and the Middle East—the Rema wrote his glosses for the Ashkenazic communities of Germany and Eastern Europe.

LATER CODES: The following works apply the laws of the Shulḥan Arukh to problems of their own times and include customs introduced in a variety of lands.

1. Shulḥan Arukh HaRav, by the founder of Ḥabad Lubavitch Ḥasidism, Rabbi Shneur Zalman of Lyady (1747-1813).

2. Ḥayyei Adam, by Rabbi Abraham Danzig (1748-1820).

3. Kitzur Shulḥan Arukh, a condensation of the original work by Rabbi Solomon Ganzfried (1804-1866). Written in a simple—but sometimes oversimplified—style, this text is found in many Jewish households.

4. Arukh HaShulḥan, written by Rabbi Yeḥiel Michael Epstein (1829-1908) of Novogrudok, covers all four books of the original Shulḥan Arukh. A comprehensive work renowned among rabbinic scholars, Arukh HaShulḥan includes all halakhic decisions down to Epstein's own day.

5. Mishnah Berurah, by the saintly Ḥafetz Ḥayyim, Rabbi Israel Meir HaKohen Kagan (1838-1933) of Radin, Poland. This work, a detailed commentary on the Oraḥ Ḥayyim section of the Shulḥan Arukh, is a scholarly, authoritative work of contemporary Jewish law. It is one of the most important sources of guidance for observant Jews.

A PAGE OF TALMUD

1 MISHNAH, the first great codification of the Oral Law, or Torah sheb'al peh, compiled by Rabbi Judah HaNasi in Eretz Yisrael around the year 200 C.E. The rabbinic authorities quoted in the Mishnah are called **Tanna'im** (תַּנָּאִים).

2 GEMARA, written record of the discussions of Jewish law, along with philosophy and ethics, by the rabbinic authorities who lived between 200 and 500 C.E. These authorities are called **Amora'im** (אֲמוֹרָאִים).

3 RASHI, the great biblical commentator.
His explanations of the Talmud are likewise indispensable.

4 TOSAFOT (תּוֹסָפוֹת), literally, "additions"; collections of comments, generally based on Rashi, by French and German rabbis between the twelfth and fourteenth centuries. Notable among the **tosafists** was Rashi's grandson, Rabbi Jacob ben Meir Tam (c. 1100-1171), who is known as Rabbenu Tam.

5 GILYON HASHAS, by Rabbi Akiva Eger (1761-1837), a German scholar of extraordinary learning and piety.

6 EIN MISHPAT, NER MITZVAH, by a 16th-century Italian scholar and printer, Rabbi Joshua Boaz ben Simon Baruch. His legal notes list where the halakhot of the Talmud may be found in the major early codes, including the Mishneh Torah and the Tur.

7 MESORET HASHAS, cross-references that indicate other places in the Talmud where the same issue is discussed.

8 HAGAHOT HABAH, textual emendations by Rabbi Joel ben Samuel Sirkes (1561-1640), a Polish scholar who was the father-in-law of the Taz.

6

3

מאימתי

קורין את שמע בערבין. "משעה שהכהנים
נכנסים לאכול בתרומתן עד סוף האשמורה
הראשונה דברי ר' אליעזר. וחכמים אומרים
עד חצות. רבן גמליאל אומר "עד שיעלה
עמוד השחר. מעשה ובאו בניו מבית
המשתה אמרו לו לא קרינו את שמע אמר
להם אם לא עלה עמוד השחר חייבין אתם
לקרות ולא זו בלבד אמרו אלא "כל מה
שאמרו חכמים עד חצות מצותן עד שיעלה
עמוד השחר "הקטר חלבים ואברים מצותן
עד שיעלה עמוד השחר "וכל הנאכלים ליום
אחד מצותן עד שיעלה עמוד השחר א"כ
למה אמרו חכמים עד חצות "כדי להרחיק
אדם מן העבירה: **גמ'** תנא היכא קאי דקתני

1

4

2

רב נסים גאון

7

8

5

237 *Appendix*

Index

Greenhouse effect, 52
Guarding your tongue (Sh'mirat
  ha-Lashon), 148-57
Guests, treatment of, 79-82

H

Haftarah, 26-27
Haggadah, 36
Hakhnasat orḥim (hospitality),
  74-83, 223
Halakhah, 24-25, 27-28, 30-31,
  223, 231
Halakhic authorities, major,
  234-35
Ḥallot, 135, 136, 137
Ha-Motzi, 136, 137, 143, 223
Ḥanukkah, 228
  candles in celebrating, 101
  reasons for celebrating, 160
Hartman, David, 40
Havdalah, 141, 223
  ceremony observing, 139-40
Ḥaver, 163, 223
Ḥavruta, 163, 223
Hebrew
  beginnning study of, 163-64
  classes in modern, 40
  learning, 45
Hebrew school, choosing
  whether to continue in, 4
Hebrew Union College—Jewish
  Institute of Religion, 166, 168
Ḥeder, 161, 223
Herzl, Theodor, 39
Heschel, Rabbi Abraham Joshua,
  22, 34, 99, 174, 218
Ḥevrah Mikra, 223
Homelessness, 81-83
  attacking on global level,
  82-83
Homeless shelter, volunteering at,
  82
Hospitality (Hakhnasat orḥim),
  74-83
  and feeding the hungry, 74-83
Hungry
  feeding, and hospitality, 74-83
  and homelessness, 81-83
Hunting, preventing, for sport,
  210-11

I

Immigrant Jews, welcoming of,
  108-17
Isaiah, 36

Israel, 34-49, 223
  as center of Jewish cultural
  life, 40
  diversity of, 38
  enrolling children in summer
  programs in, 48
  as focus and symbol of Jewish
  unity, 37-39
  as haven for Jewish refugees,
  40-41
  historical attachment of Jewish
  people to, 36-37
  living in, 49
  making donations to charities
  in, 48-49
  planting trees in, 44
  reading about, 42
  and restoration of pride and
  creativity to Jewish people,
  39-40
  studying about, 42-45
  studying at university in, 47
  visiting, 44-45
Israel Day celebration, 35
Israel festivals, attending annual,
  42-43
Israeli advocacy organizations,
  becoming active in, 46-47
Israeli art, displaying, 44
Israeli banks, open savings and
  checking accounts in, 47
Israeli English-language newspaper or magazine, subscribing
  to, 47
Israeli fiction, reading, 44
Israeli folk dancing, participation
  in, 43
Israeli music, collecting, 43
Israeli musicians, 180
Israeli products, using, 43
Israel Museum, 37
Israel Programs, Department of,
  48
Ivory products, refusing to buy or
  accept, 205, 207
Ivrit, 45, 223

J

Jerusalem, 36
Jerusalem Post, International
  Edition, 47
Jerusalem Report, 47
Jewish calendar, using, 56
Jewish Community Federation,
  116-17
Jewish Community Relations
  Council, 125-26, 126

Jewish cultural life, Israel as
  center of, 40
Jewish Dietary Laws (Dresner
  and Siegel), 91
Jewish Family Service Agency, 114
Jewish Federation, 48
Jewish festival, inviting guests to,
  79
Jewish immigrants
  assisting, 116-17
  welcoming, 108-17
Jewish law, 7, 22-31
  roots and development of,
  228-32
Jewish Library, building, 164,
  171-73
Jewish music, collecting, 43
Jewish musicians and composers,
  180
Jewish National Fund, 44
Jewish people
  achievements of, 36
  continuing vitality of, 17-18
  continuity of, as people, 36
  historical attachment to Israel,
  36-37
  identity of, 17-18
  pride and creativity in, 39-40
Jewish refugees
  Israel as haven for, 40-41
  welcoming, 108-17
Jewish rituals, practicing traditional, 56-57
Jewish Spectator, 165
Jewish Theological Seminary of
  America, 7, 165, 168
Jewish traditions, centrality of
  peace in, 121
Jewish unity, Israel as focus and
  symbol of, 37-39
Jews-by-choice, honoring parents
  personal preferences by, 106
Judaic Studies, Seminary of, 168
Judaism, 165
  demands of, 10
  language of, 12
  as lifelong journey of, 3
  as living system, 218-20
  as path for spiritual growth, 22
  survival of, 159
Judaism, University of, 165, 168
Junk mail, 59-60

K

Kashering utensils, 94
Kashrut (dietary laws), 56, 84-95,
  223